Just Because

LOVE LOSS RENEWAL

Just Because

LOVE LOSS RENEWAL

PEPPER PRESS

First published in 2023 by Pepper Press, an imprint of Fair Play Publishing
PO Box 4101, Balgowlah Heights, NSW 2093, Australia
www.pepperpress.com.au
ISBN: 978-1-925914-47-4
ISBN: 978-1-925914-48-1 (ePub)

This is a memoir. The names of some individuals, or identifying characteristics of individuals, may have been changed to respect their privacy.

An early version of this book was self-published by the author in 2018 under the title *Hitting My Reset*.

Edited by Christine LePorte
Cover design by Lisa Rafferty
Typsetting by Ana Secivanović
Printed by SOS Media, Sydney

All inquiries should be made to the Publisher via sales@fairplaypublishing.com.au

A catalogue record of this book is available from the National Library of Australia.

"*Just Because* hits you like a tonne of bricks! This is a brave, brave book by Lisa Gallate and one that will live long in the memory. Lisa has courageously charted her experience through love, loss and grief and not only in a vulnerable way, but in a manner that gives back generously to the community. I highly recommend this book to everyone, especially if you have lost a loved one and are in need of honest, beautiful encouragement."

Geoff Olds, Executive Counsellor and author of *Death of an Entrepreneur* and *Break Up, Break Down, Break Through*

"*Just Because* is an incredible story of the author's journey through life changing losses, grief and renewal that is raw, real and topical with a backdrop of the global impact from the Covid pandemic. It is a riveting and inspiring chronicle of resilience through life's toughest challenges filled with equal measures of humour, joy, love and of course sadness. Lisa Gallate writes without any pretension but with the precise intent to share stories of resilience and hope and inspire others to think beyond limits. It is an uplifting book that calls to the strength of the human spirit in all of us to be the best versions of ourselves and to live our best lives."

Sam Buckingham, TV Presenter, Voice Coach and Yogi

"*Just Because* is a poignant, yet insightful read about the messy, inexplicable and often misunderstood journey called grief. Lisa exposes her deepest vulnerability as she thoughtfully explores the complexities and heart wrenching depths of death and loss, yet also the ironic beauty and joy of living. At times I felt I was sitting right next to Lisa in her mourning; inviting me to reflect on my own personal experiences of death and deep loss. Her touching words and sense of humour not only made me cry but also laugh out aloud. From a psychological perspective, *Just Because* provides pragmatic and evidence-based strategies to cope with the many stages of grief, cutting out unnecessary psychobabble - a welcomed relief for anyone in a time of mourning."

Georgia Ray, Registered Psychologist

ABOUT THIS BOOK

Having been asked many times about my own coping skills and strategies, I decided to put pen to paper as a means of finding the real answers that might help me and others who are interested in those answers.

Part One (Love) of the book gives a brief account of my early childhood with my parents and siblings. Part Two (Loss) concerns the loss of those closest to me in life. Part Three (Renewal) examines strategies for healing and renewal.

My hopes are that this book:

- shares enough of my experiences to provide you with comfort in relation to your own loss and grief;
- invites you to openly share your loss and grief with others; and
- provides some key themes and strategies that may resonate with you in the context of your own journey.

CONTENTS

INTRODUCTION

We all know something about love. We feel it for others and ourselves, and we are willing and happy to speak of our experiences of love, joy, happiness and peace.

But what of our losses and grief? In our modern society, why are *loss* and *grief* still considered taboo words? Why do we not speak of them and about them? Because they are complex, difficult and painful? Instead, we seem to demand of ourselves and each other that our losses and grief be avoided or managed or endured, and sometimes suffered, in silence.

It is an extraordinary feature of human behaviour that transcends cultures and continents, and must surely now demand our attention, given the COVID-19 pandemic, in which over 6.4 million confirmed deaths[1] have been directly attributed to the pandemic globally, many thousands of jobs, businesses, industries and livelihoods have been lost or destroyed, and millions of people have been separated and isolated from their loved ones for extended periods.

We can readily say that almost all of us will come to know the pain of loss and the burden of grief, and this has been exacerbated by the COVID-19 pandemic. If we can teach ourselves and our young that our emotional wellbeing is something to be actively protected and nurtured, we can begin the conversations with ourselves and each other that create the opportunity for shared experiences and emotions in healthy, loving ways. In this shared human experience of loss and grief, we might just better understand, heal and rebuild ourselves on our own grief journeys.

This will allow us to create new relationships and experiences that acknowledge our losses, honour our loved ones, and continue to provide our lives with meaning, joy and purpose.

But if we don't do that, and instead seek to avoid or inhibit our grief, then we may find ourselves experiencing 'incomplete grief'[2] or 'complex grief' in which we experience prolonged preoccupation with our loss and painful emotions in ways that are debilitating to the bereaved. Our grief may then manifest itself in some physical way, such as in sleep disorders (I have had mine!), sickness, fatigue, headaches (I have had my share!), obesity or loss of appetite (ditto!), anxiety and depression. It can also cause us to become isolated from family and friends, colleagues and others, from the very people who might be available to provide us with care, kindness, support and a listening ear.

Whilst we might find it hard to vocalise our thoughts, feelings and emotions, we can gradually develop our confidence to share them in safe and loving ways. In doing so, and by practice, we will teach our brains to find the words that give voice to our difficult and complex feelings and emotions. You may just find that by sharing your grief, you will learn of the grief experiences of others, taking on board their insights and reflections, and know that in the realms of loss and grief, you are not alone.

From my own experiences, I have come to appreciate that one of the hardest losses in life to endure is the death of a loved one. I had never been truly aware of my own mortality until my sister, Zoie, and her partner, James, died. They were only young adults, with their whole lives ahead of them, and it made me realise how brutally short life could be. In my anger, fear, sadness, grief and loneliness, I questioned why I was still alive when they were not. Why had they died? Just because? Did it mean something? And yet, how could there be any meaning to such a tragedy?

The loss of loved ones adds layers to 'living a full life'

In his insightful book *When Bad Things Happen to Good People,*[3] Harold Kushner explains that whilst we can't explain the loss of a loved one, we must live in the knowledge that just as we inherit their prized possessions, we also inherit their unlived years, and must live them along with our own. However, this is much easier said than done.

In my own life, I have tried to find some meaning to explain and help me accept the tragic death of loved ones. I have wanted to tempt fate in as many ways as I could, but I have also tried to live as full a life as possible, in the knowledge that those closest to me cannot. It is the loss of loved ones that for me has added another layer of meaning to 'living a full life', a layer in which you also try to live your life for them.

And so, I have lived my life for myself as much as for others. At Whakapapa, on Mt Ruapehu in the North Island of New Zealand, I skied with no regard for my own safety, hurtling down the slopes, totally out of control. My sister had always been a fast skier. After she died, whenever I was on the snow, I always felt her just ahead of me, and I seemingly chased after the image of her. On one occasion, I fell badly and split my ski suit right up the middle. It was very embarrassing. On another, I cracked my shin bone and had to be taken off the mountain by the medical team. The joys of skiing.

Bungy jumping was made famous by AJ Hackett and Henry van Asch at

Kawarau Bridge in Queenstown, New Zealand. As a day trip, my brother Justin and I, with one of my girlfriends, drove out from Christchurch to Hanmer Springs. On impulse, my girlfriend and I decided to double bungy jump off the Waiau River Bridge at Thrillseekers Canyon. Our feet were tied together by the bungy, and we had to dive off the bridge together. We didn't give any thought to the possibility that either of us might 'flunk' or fail to jump at the last second. Instead, we half jumped, half fell off the bridge. Our screams echoed through the canyon. The first few seconds were terrifying and then it was exhilarating. Afterwards, we felt like warriors—nothing could defeat us. We wined and dined on our bravery that day, and for many lunches afterwards.

Have you ever driven at reckless speeds on country roads or on beaches? I have watched the speedometer dial climb and felt like I was indestructible. It has only been for brief moments, and then my fear and my conscience take over, and I slow down. After my sister died, I made a solemn promise to my mum that I would be careful when driving, and I have tried hard to keep my promise (most of the time).

And what about paragliding? This is not for the fainthearted, the squeamish or those afraid of heights—and I was all three. On a beautiful day in the stunning city of Queenstown, an instructor pilot known to one of my friends, called Mike, took me paragliding from the skyline gondola above Queenstown. The vantage point was amazing as it meant we would fly over Queenstown and Lake Wakatipu.

I took the gondola up the hill, enjoying the scenery but quietly wondering what on earth I was doing. Mike met me at the top. After some preliminary platitudes, he said:

"Are you ready for the best time of your life?"

How do you answer that?

"Yes, I think so." So lame.

"Okay, then, that's GREAT! Let's go over to our take-off point and I will give you a briefing."

"Sure." My throat constricted around this solitary word; I was so nervous. I wandered along behind Mike, agonising about what I had agreed to do.

We walked for about ten minutes to our take-off point. Mike strapped me into my harness and safety equipment. So far, so good. He then gave me a briefing on what to expect and what I had to do. In an instant, Mike was running behind me, pushing me along. I had to run as well, or I would fall over. We ran fast down a grassy bank to the edge and then simply ran off what I saw as a very safe, very stable cliff. The wind grabbed us and lifted us up, and we climbed through the air until we levelled out. I was breathless and speechless. Immediately struck by how quiet it was, we glided along like birds. After making sure—with some prodding—that I was okay, Mike found his camera to take photos of me, strapped in, looking terrified!

After about ten minutes flying over Queenstown, with views out to Lake Wakatipu and the Remarkables, we came in for our landing. We descended at a regular speed for some time, and then, without warning, Mike tilted the paraglider towards the Earth, and we descended rapidly, the Earth rushing up to meet us as we landed in a field. We landed on our feet and then I lost my balance and we both fell over, rolling through the grass.

“Well done, you did it!” Mike shouted.

“Thanks, I think!” Another lame response. It felt like my whole being had just been pushed up into my mouth as we landed.

“So, how do you feel?”

“Well, that was incredible. It was petrifying and amazing, at the same time. Thanks a lot for the experience, Mike, but I don’t think I will do it again.”

“Haha, no worries,” said Mike, no doubt having heard that a hundred times before.

My whole paragliding experience had been so fast and frantic that I was immensely glad that I had the photos to prove it.

The irony of something so certain as death being so unknown

Since those adventure-seeking experiences, I have lost many more loved ones. From both my adventures and grief experiences, I have realised that although we might think we are each responsible for, and in control of, our own destiny, we in fact have very little control over how, or when, we will die. Although each of our own deaths will always be certain—it cannot be avoided—what death will look like to each of us remains the great unknown. It is ironic that something so certain in our lives can be so ill-defined and so out of our control.

The loss of my loved ones has affected me greatly, and I have found it very hard to understand why death can be so cruel, so unforgiving and so relentless. When I lost my sister and her partner, I was a young woman studying at university, and I had never lost a member of my family. I had never known how mean death could be, snatching my sister from us in an instant.

After Zoie and James' funerals, I searched for books that might help me with my grief, to explain why this tragedy had happened, and give comfort to deal with the pain and anguish I felt. But at that time, I only found academic literature about death and grief. From my searches, there seemed to be very few books written by authors about their own grief experiences. I desperately wanted to read and understand the grief experiences of others, so that I could better understand my own, and know that in what I was feeling, I was not alone.

Mitch Albom's book *Tuesdays with Morrie*[4] is a wonderful chronicle of the time that Mitch spent with his professor Morrie Schwartz, who was dying from amyotrophic lateral sclerosis. It was a very sad and yet uplifting book. However, reading it didn't provide me with any comfort as Professor Schwartz had been reaching the end of seventy-eight years of a wonderful life, and my sister's adult life had only just started.

Death and loss change your landscape

The pain of the death of loved ones in my life has, at times, been excruciating. I have felt incredible loneliness and wondered, why am I still here, living my life without them? I have had so many people through the years ask: How do you cope? How do you manage? What have you done to make it through so well? How are you able to keep going? Where do you find your strength from? How can you be so brave?

I have worked hard to understand and manage my own grief, and to find my own way through it, so that I can continue to appreciate and live my life with meaning and purpose, and so that I might live those 'unlived years' of my loved ones. I continued my studies after Zoie and James died, completing my Bachelor of Law and Commerce degrees, and a Master of Laws from one of the world's most respected universities. I have lived overseas in the UK and Australia, and I have now made Sydney my home. As a lawyer, I have been involved in acting for external administrators of some of the largest corporate collapses in Australia. I have run half marathons and marathons. I have competed in ocean swim races. But most importantly, I am a mother to three beautiful young children, a wife, a daughter, a sister and sister-in-law, a niece, a cousin and a friend. I would like to think that I have lived my life in a landscape that has been irrevocably changed by death, loss and grief with humility and grace.

Grief grabs us in moments unaware

Even now, my grief seems to sit on my shoulder and goes where I do. At any time of the day or night, my grief can make itself known to me. It is easily triggered—by something someone says, by a song on the radio, by a change in my environment, or perhaps by the signs of a change in season. At times, it is simply a poignant moment that I can acknowledge and even appreciate, but at other times, I feel the urge to burst into tears, or I feel knotted and sick in my stomach.

Now, I have learned to manage that moment, to block everything else out and to focus on passing through it, breathing deeply and pausing long enough to let it pass. I can choose not to listen to my own thoughts, and I can choose not to act on them. I am in control of me, my thoughts, my emotions, my body, my actions and my words.

I also believe that I am in control of how I live my life, even though my grief and my healing will always be part of that journey.

PART ONE: LOVE

CHAPTER ONE: THE EARLY YEARS

"Look, no hands!" shouted Mark as he waved his long, spindly jazz hands in the air, the steering wheel held between his legs. The car screeched and swerved along the Wellington motorway to Miramar, as four little heads bobbed in the back seat, letting out a mix of screams and giggles and a few "whoas" and "go faster, Mark, go faster". Mark delighted in waving with both hands to oncoming traffic, as the passing drivers looked at us with horrified faces.

We were out for a drive, a chance to get out of the house and go for an 'outing'. A little light relief for our babysitter Mark, who was looking after me and my three siblings, all of us aged under ten years old, whilst Mum and Dad were away on holiday.

We turned into a parking bay off the motorway so we could watch the planes come into land at Wellington International Airport. The airport has a short runway bordered by the sea at each end, the Wellington Harbour at one end and Cook Strait at the other. The sea borders create gusty wind pockets, causing turbulent, choppy landings and the occasional swerving plane on the runway, much like Mark's driving! For us kids, it was great entertainment. After watching a few landings and take-offs, we left the parking bay and drove past the airport. A plane took off and soared right above our heads. It seemed so close to the car's roof that we all ducked in the back seat. The noise of the jet engines was deafening. Mark chuckled at our silliness.

"Can we stop for an ice cream, Mark?" screamed my sister, Zoie, from the back seat, followed by a chorus of "Pleeeease, pleeeease, can we?"

"Okay, but single scoops only. Let's stop at the next dairy" (Kiwi slang for corner store).

Zoie and I knew this dairy well. We often stopped here on our afternoon walks from school to our dance academy. Not only did it stock the best flavours of Tip Top ice cream, but the old man behind the counter was always very generous with his serves. A single scoop here was a double scoop anywhere else.

Of course, it's hard to choose when you're limited to one flavour. My all-time favourite was hokey pokey, followed closely by boysenberry, which was Zoie's favourite. My sister and I often shared licks of our ice creams, especially when the coins in our pockets didn't extend to double scoops.

We entered the shop with Mark, falling over each other with excitement to get to the ice cream cabinet, contemplate our choices and place our orders.

"Me first!" said Zoie.

"No, I'm the oldest, it's me first," said George.

The bickering had started.

"Okay, okay, you can all look at the same time and decide what you want," sighed Mark.

Since the store had run out of hokey pokey, it was an easy choice for

Zoie and me, but my brothers dithered, peering into the ice cream cabinet, calling out one flavour and then changing it to another, a deliciously hard decision to make.

My mum, Iris, was born in Castlefin, Donegal, Eire. She was one of thirteen children and had a difficult childhood living on a farm with her parents and many siblings in rural Ireland. Determined to seek a better life for herself, she trained as a registered nurse at Leeds Infirmary and as a maternity nurse in Portsmouth. As a young Irish woman, she made the courageous decision to immigrate to Wellington, New Zealand, in a scheme sponsored by the New Zealand Government to recruit trained nurses to the far away land of Aotearoa, the 'Land of the Long White Cloud'. It meant a free passage by ship, a secure job and a new life in a new country. After she arrived, Mum worked at Wellington Public Hospital as a staff nurse in the fracture clinic and on the orthopaedic ward.

Not long after she arrived in Wellington, Iris was invited by her Irish nursing friend Norah to a Saturday night dance at a dance hall in Wellington City. Unbeknownst to my mum, Norah and her partner, George, had set Iris up on a blind date.

During the dance, George tapped Iris on the shoulder, and over the music of the band, George leaned into her shoulder and half whispered to her, "Iris, please meet my cousin Nick."

Iris spun around, her beautiful green silk cocktail dress floating around her long legs, and her big brown eyes framed with golden hair. She looked stunning.

"Good evening, I'm Nicholas, but you can call me Nick."

"Hello, I am Iris," said Mum in her lilting Irish accent.

"Very nice to meet you, Iris. Would you like a cigarette?"

"Yes, thanks."

Dad only had one cigarette left, but he gave it to Iris, and lit it for her.

They spent the evening dancing and from that night on they were inseparable, attending many dances with friends at the various dance halls in the city, or dinner parties at the homes of friends and colleagues. They married twelve months later.

My father was a solicitor and barrister, a sole practitioner who worked from an office in Lambton Quay, what is now an illustrious shopping district in Wellington City, adjacent to New Zealand's Beehive Parliament.

Dad was also an immigrant, having travelled as a young child with his parents and his young brother, Stathi, from Ithaca, Greece, to live in Wellington. They moved to Napier in Hawke's Bay, a rural horticultural area which takes its name from Hawke's Bay, the harbour 'bite' on the east coast of the North Island. Dad would return to Wellington as a young adult to study law at Victoria University and his brother, Stathi, trained as a doctor at Otago University in the South Island (affectionately known as 'the Mainland' to many Southern Kiwis). Stathi then worked at Wellington Public Hospital, where he was a respected, gifted and quick-witted junior doctor who was kind and friendly to both patient and colleague alike.

Mum and Dad settled in Wellington and started their own family. The firstborn was George, followed by Zoie, then me, and finally the baby in our family, Justin. When Justie arrived, Mum and Dad had four kids under five years of age.

Our lives as young children were typical of other families in Wellington. Most months of the year were spent battling the bitter winds of 'Windy Wellington', traipsing to school in our gumboots and raincoats on wet weather days, playing sports and dancing at the weekends. My brothers played rugby union, while my sister and I played netball and went to dance academy. I was a better ballerina than my sister, but Zoie was a talented jazz and contemporary dancer.

Mum was determined that we learn to swim, so her Friday night routine involved taking us to swimming lessons at the Freyberg Pool in Oriental Bay. I am sure she would have preferred relaxing at home in front of the fire, watching the TV. Mum sat at the top of the stadium in a large, draughty indoor pool complex, diligently scanning the pool for her children. Being of different ages and swimming abilities, we were in different classes, but it didn't stop us chatting to each other across the lane ropes, or trying to dunk each other when we could, away from the prying eyes of our teacher.

After each lesson, Mum helped us have 'rinse-off' showers and get dressed. Mum then elaborately wrapped up Zoie's and my hair in our towels, creating exotic turbans. We left the pool complex through the front glass doors, braving the wind and rain, with shouts of "run for your lives" as we raced to the carpark. We would stop for four orders at our local fish 'n' chip shop, each wrapped as individual parcels in butcher's paper. In the back seat of Mum's car, we tore the top off our parcels and carefully pulled out and nibbled on our hot chips in the dark. At home, Mum sat us in front of the fire and towel dried and then brushed our hair, as we ate dinner from our parcels.

We lived in a four-bedroom but modest home in the hilly suburb of Hataitai. Zoie and I shared a bedroom. Mum decorated our room in yellow and brown hues, complete with matching duvets that she had made on her Singer sewing machine, and bright yellow round bedside cabinets.

Zoie was a terrific storyteller, relating tranquil, captivating stories of princesses and ballerinas, magicians and mystical figures in faraway lands of paradise.

"Tonight, I'm going to tell you the story of the great Empress of Zion."

I was cuddled up in my bed, lying on my side in the dark, but able to make out the shape of Zoie in her bed beside me. I listened to her magical words as they sent me drifting off to sleep each night.

Zoie also loved to tell scary stories about the council rubbish collectors who used to climb our driveway to collect our rubbish from our outside bin before heading up the hill to the next house. I was scared of them in the daylight, and terrified of them when they appeared in my dreams at night.

Our Saturdays were invariably spent being driven around Wellington to attend sports and dance classes. For years, my sister and I attended the same dance academy. We spent hours there, either studying for dance exams or learning new dances that we performed at various fairs and fetes and nursing homes in the community. When we weren't in a class, we would hang out at the dance academy, stretching, reading, nibbling on snack foods Mum had packed for our lunch, chatting to our dance pals, feeling bored waiting for our next class.

Zoie was my best friend and I loved every moment with her. I secretly wanted to be just like her.

Zoie was two years older, two years wiser, and she had a whole lot of sass. She had rich brown hair, with blonde streaks like sun kisses, that stretched down her back and ended with a blunt cut. Her fringe framed her oval face, her dark brown eyes peered through the fringe whispers, and her apple cheeks were matched by a wide smile with straight white teeth. She was gorgeous. When we were young girls, she was taller than me, and looked so much more grown-up in her leotards and tutus. I loved dancing with her, and I also loved to watch her dance. Zoie had great rhythm for a young dancer and moved so easily and fluently through her pique and chaine turns as she flew across the dance floor. Her battement kicks seemed to reach the ceiling, and she loved to pirouette. I felt that I was a more robotic, technical dancer without much 'spunk'.

When I was ten years old, I found out that Zoie was changing dance schools; I was devastated. I took it personally and thought that I had done something wrong. But Zoie was just growing up and wanted to focus on her jazz and contemporary dancing at a specialist dance academy. It was the first time I realised that although we were sisters, we were not always going to be a team.

It was a great loss, as my sister started immersing herself in her own interests without me. I found it hard to keep going to dance classes by myself and I missed her terribly. I no longer had my buddy with me to help me get ready or to sit around with, killing time until our next class. I missed seeing her dance and missed being able to practise our dance moves together at home. Over time, I lost interest and gave up on my dance classes. My passion for dance had been inextricably tied to the time spent with my big sister.

I don't know if Mum ever really understood how I felt as I struggled to understand my own feelings, and I didn't know how to vocalise them. I didn't want to take anything away from Zoie starting at a new dance academy, but I also didn't want her to go. Zoie was steadily developing her dancing talent and, luckily for her, was enjoying every minute.

Mum and Dad seemingly managed to be in many places at once every Saturday. Having four young children to take to sports and dance classes must have been a logistical nightmare. By Saturday afternoon, they were exhausted. But somehow, they would find the energy to either have a family over for dinner, or they would take us to dinner at another family's house.

Sometimes, our babysitter Mark would be asked to spend the evening with us when my parents went out to dinner parties. He was a wonderful man with a terrific sense of humour, and we relished his company. Mum and Dad also hosted dinner parties for their friends, and we were relegated to my older brother's room to watch an old TV. Instead, we often sat at the top of the stairs, eavesdropping on the adult laughter and conversation that travelled up the stairwell. We knew the dinner party was ending when Dad brought out his collection of liqueurs, a kaleidoscope of colours in fancy bottles that were stored in a secret cupboard. As Dad placed them on the table, asking his guests which exotic potion they would like as a nightcap, we rushed to our beds.

On Sunday mornings, we would often lie in our beds, with the wind howling outside and rain pelting against the windows, listening to the children's stories told on Wellington's weekend radio programs. The characters of those stories came alive with the wonderful rich voices of the actors who played them. Sometimes Zoie and I would bake muffins in the morning for a late lunch. We rather fancied ourselves as mini Betty Crockers, even though the flour and sugar would be strewn from one end of the kitchen to the other (and the sieve may have been used to spray each other with flour!). Whilst Mum took the mounds of flour and sugar and splats of butter in her stride, she would still make us clean up the kitchen while the muffins were cooking.

"A good cook is a clean cook, so you should always clean up as you go, or when the food is cooking in the oven. Here, let me give you a hand."

Mum washed the baking dishes so Zoie and I would race each other to see who could get the wiping down done before our muffins were cooked.

"Wow, come see, I think they are ready."

"Watch out, Lise, let me get them out, I ammmm the oldest, you know."

"What's age got to do with getting muffins out of the oven?"

"Well, for starters, my hands are bigger for the oven mitts, and I can tell if they are cooked or not just by looking at them!"

"Really?! Well, I don't need to look at them. They smell cooked to me!"

We would pull our hot muffins from their trays onto Mum's cooling racks and set them by the kitchen windows. Both Zoie and I were desperate to eat them hot, cut in half with some blobs of creamy New Zealand butter spread on them, so the butter would melt along the top and drip down the sides. There was nothing quite like it.

But instead of devouring our hot home baking, we were rushed to get dressed for church. My mum was an Irish Protestant but never really spoke to us about her faith. Instead, she attended a Sunday service at the local Presbyterian Church and made us attend Sunday school next door. Our religious immersion was a smorgasbord. We had been baptised in the Greek Orthodox Church, attended a Presbyterian Sunday school, and were educated at Catholic schools. From my early experiences, I came to appreciate, as an adult, the many different approaches to Christianity.

After church, our big treat on the way home was to stop at the local bakery for some fresh crusty bread. Mum would cut it into thick slices and lather them with butter and cheddar cheese, which we would delve into, followed by a generous serve of muffins and a glass of milk. We were typical young Kiwis, fuelled on a diet of dairy, red meat, a mix of muffins, scones and pikelets, and green veggies grown in our back garden.

Mum was very loving, but like any parent, could also lose her cool. One day, I almost destroyed our back lawn, a long, narrow strip of grass that ran the length of the house. At the far end, away from the house, sat a large, round tin container which my parents used to incinerate garden waste. It was a cloudy but very windy day and Mum was busy feeding the fire in the incinerator. I was charged with watering the garden with the hose as she worked.

"Quick, Lisa, give me the hose, I think it's getting too high."

My back was turned away from Mum as I pottered in the garden, spraying the bushes, plants and weeds with the hose. Big puddles were forming in the garden beds as I overwatered anything in reach. I watched as the puddles turned into creeks that ran through the garden bed and pushed the soil around with my feet to create little dams.

As I spun around to calls of "Lisa, Lisa, quick, the hose," I saw the huge flames dancing out of the top of the incinerator. Mum's fire was out of control. It was being fanned by the wind and looked like it was about to jump onto the surrounding bushes and lawn.

As I turned, I paid no attention to the direction of the hose. I totally soaked Mum, head to toe. The water was running down her hair and face and dripping off her nose. Her T-shirt was stuck hard to her body, and her mouth was open in horror. It would have been quite funny had I not been devastated that I had upset my mum.

Mum started shouting at me in Gaelic. I couldn't understand a word, but very quickly had the sense of what she was saying.

"Oh, Mum, Mum, I'm so sorry."

I ran to her as she grabbed the hose and fully wet down the incinerator, extinguishing the fire. Mum was wet through, but as she let out a big sigh, I could see her relief that the fire hadn't got out of control. Both we and her lawn were safe and sound, but it was a while before I was allowed to be on water duties again.

When we weren't playing in the garden or making a racket in the house, and perhaps to save my parents' hearing, we would often go for a Sunday afternoon drive. These were unplanned, chaotic and risky trips in Dad's prized possession, an old mustard-coloured Daimler with leather seats and double exhausts—not really the ideal family car—which he would spend most weekends cleaning and polishing, and which he drove at speed.

"Nick, slow down."

"Nick, slow doooown."

"Nick, slow down or you can pull over and we will get out of the car and then you can drive as fast as you like."

These were common catchcries as Mum held the armrest on the passenger door for dear life, her body twisted with anxiety and fear. She would continue shouting at Dad, pleading for him to slow down.

"But I'm not speeding."

"Of course you are. You're driving far too fast, and our children are in the car. Nick, pleeeease. Slow down or stop the car NOW."

Reluctantly, Dad would slow the car, but it wouldn't be long before his lead foot started pumping the accelerator pedal again, the speed dial started to climb and Mum resumed her pleading.

One Sunday, I decided Mum needed reinforcements in getting her point across to Dad. I layered myself with my roller-skating knee pads, my elbow pads and my helmet, just as we were being called to come to the car. I went downstairs, walked past the bemused faces of my siblings and headed outside.

"Lisa, what on earth are you wearing?" It was Dad.

"Just some extra gear for our Sunday drive." My siblings had followed me outside and were cackling with laughter. Even Mum was giggling.

"But why?"

"Just so I can protect myself in case you have an accident."

"We won't have an accident. Now take that gear off and get in the car," Dad scolded, with a smirk on his face.

My point was made, and it served to slow our speedster for a while, but not for long.

Dad's driving style also included tailgating other cars, moving out erratically to check for oncoming traffic so he could overtake on the other side of the road, speeding short distances between cars "so we can get there faster" and providing a running commentary on just about everything outside the car. Or he would stretch his left arm across Mum's body to point at some random object at the side of the road, or in the distance on the horizon. It might be one of the millions of sheep that inhabit New Zealand, or a cow, bull, horse, goat, deer, chicken shed, disused bridge, farmhouse or shed—the list of random objects that attracted Dad's attention was endless.

Dad liked to drive towards a destination with no concept of directions and we would often spend our Sunday drives lost, doing U-turns, listening to Mum and Dad argue about where they were going, how we were going to get there and where we were. Dad was always adamant that he knew where he was going, and didn't need a map. Long before Google maps, Dad's road maps were gigantic paper maps that folded into A5 squares but were totally impractical to read from in a car that was screaming down the road with the driver looking in every direction for the next road sign, and five passengers sitting terrified in their seats.

"Will you stop at the next town and ask for some directions?"

"No, we don't need to, I know where we are going."

"You might know where we want to go, but you have no idea how to get there."

"I do."

"No, you don't. I feel like we have been driving around in circles for hours."

"We haven't."

"Yes, we have."

"Okay, okay, let's just wait and see what the next road sign says. If the next town has a service station, I will stop there."

Despite the debates, many Sunday afternoon drives were fun. A favourite destination was north of Wellington to find 'pick your own' (PYO or u-pick) corn farms and fruit orchards. My siblings and I loved being outside running through the corn fields, the sun on our backs, the smell of soil beneath our feet.

We often played hide and seek or tag, running and chasing each other down the aisles between the corn bushes. Because we were young kids, the height of the corn bushes made for great camouflage from our brothers and sister. Mum and Dad were pleased to see us distracted, running and playing through the fields, and busied themselves picking cobs of corn and stacking them in buckets for weighing and payment at the exit.

Our favourite fruits to pick were boysenberries and strawberries. The boysenberries were the easiest to pick, as they are usually grown as high bushes so don't require bending (unlike the back-breaking strawberry patches) to pick the fruit. We loaded our ice cream containers and then sneakily sat cross-legged in an aisle and sampled our pickings. The berries tasted of summer, the outside flesh soft and warm from the sun, the inside juicy and tart. We emerged with tell-tale berry smiles and bulging bellies. Mum and Dad admonished us for eating the produce and made us confess to the owners at the exit. Usually, the owners were very understanding and appreciated our honesty, especially with Dad's extra dollars as compensation. Containers overflowing and our bellies bursting, we headed home so Mum could make delectable jams and berry pies.

Mum was a terrific cook and made the most delicious meals for her tribe. On Sundays, she often cooked a lamb or beef roast for dinner. Justin and I loved our roast dinners, Mum's fresh mint sauce from her home-grown mint, or brown onion gravy, crunchy roasted potatoes and vegetables from her garden, topped off with her little Yorkshire puddings. We would sit at the kitchen table, watching Mum as she flew around the kitchen preparing the food.

"Mum, can we help you?" We had no idea what we were doing but wanted to be involved.

"Of course you can. Here, I will get you some vegetable peelers and you can peel the carrots and then I will chop them and add them to the roast veggie tray."

She passed us the peelers and giant bag of carrots, and away we went. It was hard to get started but we soon developed the knack of using the vegetable peeler, creating lovely long swirls of peeled carrots stacked in lovely big piles before us. Mum was busy in the kitchen at the oven with her back to us.

"Mum, look," I shouted with excitement. "We've peeled them."

Mum turned around, her face showing at once surprise, and disappointment. Then she let out a laugh.

"That's terrific, kids, thank you. But we just needed the skins peeled so I can chop them. But no matter, we will have a carrot salad with dinner tonight, it will be delicious!"

In the few months that counted as our school summer holidays, we spent the weekends climbing trees in our garden, making up plays in our tree fort, using the water hose to create a makeshift plastic waterslide on the back lawn and jumping for hours on the trampoline. Sometimes we just lay on the trampoline and gazed up at the clouds, creating animal shapes with our fingers pointing to the sky.

We also chased the butterflies that were attracted to milk plants that grew in Mum's garden. As milkweed leaves are the only food the caterpillars eat, the butterflies rest on the leaves and lay their eggs. When the eggs turn into caterpillars, they feed on the plants. The butterflies made for very colourful visitors in the garden, and we enjoyed chasing them, trying to catch them in our bare hands. Occasionally we were kind enough to just tiptoe up to the garden beds and watch them quietly, studying their beautiful wings as they sat on the leaves in the sun.

Mum had a green thumb and loved to spend time in her gardens, planting and weeding her vegetables and flowering plants, and planting bulbs in the hope that they might produce some happy colours in the spring. She encouraged us to play in the gardens with her, and we loved making mud pies and snail sandwiches.

On the exceptionally few days that counted as 'hot' weather, we would endure the traffic on the drive to the beach. The sea was always close to freezing, and we didn't spend much time swimming in it, but we would run in and out of the water and play on the beach, building sandcastles and throwing sand at our siblings. The relentless Wellington winds blew in all directions, joining the fun by spraying us with sand.

As my siblings and I grew, developing our own interests, hobbies and friendships, we started spending less time together. My older brother and sister started high school, leaving Justin and me to defend the family name at our local primary school. We walked together to school, which wasn't much fun as it was all uphill. But while we walked, we occupied ourselves playing 'Don't step on the crack or you're a dirty rat', 'I Spy' or running races between lampposts. Sometimes we held hands and would swing our arms as high as we could to see which of us might fall over, or we would play some modified game of hopscotch as we walked. Amazingly, we always got to school on time.

After school, Justin and I would run down the hill to home, charged with speed from the gravity of the hill and our empty bellies, hungry for afternoon tea.

Justin and I were in different classes at school, but Justin always had my back in the playground. Although he was my younger brother, he was my protector from an early age. He wasn't an aggressive boy; instead, he was happy and funny and always had a smile on his face. But Justin was fiercely loyal to his siblings and his friends, often playing the peacekeeper in the playground or in our tree fort at home.

Whilst Justin and I were still at primary school, Mum and Dad made the decision to move the family to Sydney. It was an enormous undertaking but made sense as Mum and Dad already had family living in Australia. Dad interviewed for and secured a job in Sydney and Mum received Australian recognition of her nursing qualifications.

But logic doesn't always sell arguments, and my siblings and I didn't want to go to Sydney. We had our own individual lives, activities and friends, and didn't want to leave the sanctity and security of our home. My older brother and sister had settled well at secondary colleges in

Wellington and didn't want another new start. But Mum and Dad couldn't be persuaded, and we packed up our lives and moved to Sydney. It was awful saying goodbye to my school friends and my dance buddies and even sadder saying goodbye to our babysitter Mark. I loved my bedroom with my sister, and I didn't want to leave it. It was a crazy attachment, but my bedroom meant that I always had more time with my sister than anyone else and I knew Zoie like no one else did. Would that change? Would we still share a bedroom in Sydney? I felt I was losing everything in my life that was important to me, and I didn't know how I would manage in a new city and a new country where everyone said "G'day, mate" and "Howz it going?" I felt like I was losing who I was, all those little things that make up your identity, in the move across The Ditch. I was filled with equal amounts of anxiety and excitement.

I wondered what our new school would be like. Would we make friends? Where would we live? Would we live close to the beach? My cousins were keen surfers who lived near Manly, with a beach lifestyle that I could only imagine whilst sitting on my bed listening to the rain and howling wind in Windy Wellington.

Eventually the day arrived for us to fly to Sydney. My first overseas flight. We were young kids who loved every minute on the plane. Initially, we stayed with my grandmother but then moved into an apartment. Our first days, weeks and months in Sydney were busy. There was a lot to organise—unpacking and setting up our home in the tiny apartment, settling into the community, school enrolments, uniforms and books, and creating new daily routines for ourselves. I felt unsettled and unsure about what we were doing and why we were there. Granted, the weather was much nicer, but our lives had been upended, and I wasn't sure I wanted to be in Sydney.

It would take us all months to settle into our new lives, build up our activities and sports, and create new friends. Over time, I settled into Sydney and came to enjoy my new life as an 'Auswi'. I made many wonderful friends who embraced my Kiwi accent and my fascination with everything Aussie. But it was to be short-lived as my parents didn't settle well in Sydney and decided that we should return to New Zealand. After just three years, we were again torn by the prospect of another move, but as adolescents, we ultimately didn't have much choice, and we weren't thrilled by the prospect of another upheaval. Only my brother George was able to stay and studied in Australia to qualify as a commercial pilot.

Zoie, Justin and I were charged with embracing yet another change in our young teenage lives, saying goodbye once more to the close friends we had made, and the beach lifestyle we had come to love. It was very disruptive, as it was a loss of everything that was familiar to us in our lives. I felt unsettled and anxious as we weren't returning to our hometown of Wellington, but to a much smaller city in regional New Zealand.

Although an upheaval for my siblings and me, it was in many ways a homecoming for Dad as we settled in Napier, Hawke's Bay, where Dad had lived as a young boy with his family. My mum was offered a role at Napier Public Hospital in the orthopaedic ward. Dad joined a law partnership in Hastings and my sister, brother and I attended local high schools. When my sister and I completed high school, she studied nursing at the Hawke's Bay Polytechnic, and I left Napier to study law and commerce at university. Justin completed high school and applied for

Police College with the New Zealand Police Force. We were all growing up as young adults and starting to build our own independent lives.

However, within a few years, our lives and our worlds would be irrevocably changed in one single autumn day.

PART TWO: LOSS

CHAPTER TWO: YOUNG LOVE NEVER DIES

There is a sacredness in tears. They are not the mark of weakness, but of power. They speak more eloquently than ten thousand tongues. They are messengers of overwhelming grief, of deep contrition, and of unspeakable love.

—Washington Irving

"Lise, you have to come home now."

It was my brother Justin.

"Why?" I asked.

"I can't say, you just have to come home."

"But I don't have a car."

"Then you will have to fly. Dad will reimburse you for your fare when you get home."

The reality would be much worse than I could ever have imagined.

At the time, I was nineteen years old, studying at Victoria University in Wellington. My parents lived in Napier, Hawke's Bay. I had missed the last train that day and had to catch the first flight home the next morning.

It was a sleepless night worrying about my parents and whether something had happened to them. I caught a taxi to Wellington Airport and raced to the desk to buy a ticket for the first flight home. I waited an hour before the flight was called for boarding. With little opportunity for people watching, as the terminal was empty, and not feeling hungry enough to entertain myself with food, I wandered around the terminal, walking in long circles to pass the time.

The plane boarded for the short flight to Napier. I felt less anxious after we had taken off and were on our way, although I worried about what lay ahead.

My brothers met me at Hawke's Bay Airport. They were both great talkers, and like typical brothers, would usually have asked a thousand questions about my university life, what my grades were like, who I was dating, was he a nice guy, and when would they meet him. Instead, they were unusually quiet, and I wondered what they were hiding as we left the airport in Dad's car.

"Can you tell me what has happened? Why I've had to come home so quickly? Are Mum and Dad okay? Is Zoie at home as well?"

"We can't say much, Lise, you'll just have to wait until we get home."

It was a long ride home in silence.

We arrived at my parents' home, and I went upstairs to say hello to Mum and Dad. Their home was built with the bedrooms downstairs with the living rooms, dining room and kitchen upstairs so that the homeowner could enjoy the vast views out across the paddocks to Te Mata Peak in the south and the Kaweka Ranges in the west.

"Hi, honey, come and sit down." My parents looked distraught.

"Come sit on the couch."

"What's wrong, Mum? Dad?"

"Lise, there has been a terrible car accident. Your sister has died. Zoie and James were driving up in his car to Te Kuiti to see his cousin."

"Oh my God, really? Really, what? What about James?"

"I'm sorry, honey, he died as well."

I didn't feel as though I heard their words properly. The words didn't sink in. They kept talking, but I couldn't hear them. Their words floated on the air around me, and I didn't want them to land.

I was stuck somewhere else, away from the reality, but I instinctively knew that my world and my life had changed forever in that moment.

Zoie had been travelling with her partner, James, to Otorohanga near Te Kuiti and Hamilton. Otorohanga is a service town for the surrounding dairy farming district and is recognised as the gateway to the Waitomo Caves. The Waitomo Caves are a major tourist attraction as they are formed from Oligocene limestone. The main caves are the Glowworm Caves, which have stalactite and stalagmite displays and contain glowworms that light the caves and their roofs in an amazing spectacle of twinkling lights. My family had visited the caves when Zoie and I were very young, and we had loved the twinkling roofs. It was another world, like something out of a fairy tale.

James had decided to go up to Otorohanga to visit family and say goodbye before he left to go overseas to Europe. Zoie was a nursing student in her final year of studies at the Hawke's Bay Polytechnic Institute and was to meet up with James in Europe at the end of the year.

THE REALITY OF LOSS CAN OVERWHELM AND SHOCK US TO OUR CORE

It was too much to take in. I remember feeling like I wanted to be sick; I was dizzy and hot. I fainted. When I came to, I was lying on the couch. I felt a cold cloth on my forehead and Mum sitting on the couch next to me. It took some time for me to be able to sit up and longer to ask Mum and Dad to tell me again exactly what had happened. I was scared to ask. I didn't want to know, but at the same time, I needed to know more to help me believe that this was real.

Dad told me that the car had missed a corner on the open road, an area with a speed limit of 100 km per hour, that the car had gone off the road, and then flown across a river. It had hit the bank on the other side and landed upside down in the river.

Zoie and James died instantly.

The reality was too much for me to bear. I broke down and wailed inconsolably as the truth took hold. Zoie was just twenty-one years old, and James was only twenty-six years old. It was the worst day of my life and one that I would never forget. It changed my life, and my parents' lives forever. The day before the accident was my parents' wedding anniversary, and my mum's birthday was in four days' time.

Mum and Dad never celebrated their wedding anniversary again after Zoie's death, and it was many years before Mum would allow us to make a fuss on her birthday.

The rest of that first day passed in a blur. I would lie down and try to take deep breaths to stop crying, but the tears kept filling my eyes, and I would stand up again. My body shook with sadness. My parents were concerned about me and called a doctor to the house, but I didn't want or need medication. In my heart, I knew that there was simply no cure for the terrible shock that was travelling through my body, or for the inconsolable grief and heartache.

A RACE TO BEAT THE PRESS

Mum and Dad had been at pains to get me home, to tell me in person as soon as they could. They also knew they had to tell me before the news hit the press. The day after Zoie and James' deaths, the local newspaper reported that their workmates and fellow students:

'*. . . were in shock today following the deaths of a popular couple, Mr. James Cook and Miss Maria Zoie Gallate, in a car accident yesterday. They died when their car crashed off the road and into a river southeast of Te Awamutu yesterday at 2 pm. They were both dead when emergency services arrived at the scene.*

'*James was one in a million and was well liked,*' and '*Zoie was well liked by her peers and was a sparkling student*'.

It was all true. I had always looked up to James as a wonderful, loving and caring partner to my sister. And my sister sparkled. She had an amazing presence wherever she went. Zoie was a loving, caring, gregarious lady with a high energy, high spunk personality. I had spent my life, to that point, in adoration of her. I thought that she was the most beautiful, amazing, spirited, creative lady with a larger-than-life personality, and I wanted to be just like her. I couldn't bear the thought of living my life without her. I was devastated.

My parents had many arrangements to make. One of those was to ask someone known to Zoie to travel north and formally identify her. It was a hideous request to ask of anyone but my godfather, Arthur, agreed to go. He was my father's best friend and they had grown up together as young children. They now lived next door to each other in Napier, separated by a creek that harboured ducks in the winter. Arthur's paddocks were a dangerous flight path. If the ducks flew over his paddocks, it was likely that Arthur and Dad were out there trying to shoot them for dinner.

Arthur had known my brothers, my sister and me all our lives. He later told me that after identifying Zoie, he spent months being woken at night by dreams about her. I felt terrible guilt that he couldn't escape the memory of seeing Zoie's body after the accident, as I wished I could have had the strength and fortitude to be the one to identify her. I think those last memories of Zoie stayed with Arthur until he died. But I know too that he never regretted going to identify her, and he tried hard to focus instead on his memories of Zoie's beautiful, smiling, happy face.

Over the next few days, the family shared the terrible news with extended family and friends in New Zealand and overseas. It is news that no parent should ever have to share. I had no idea how my parents would survive this tragedy.

Talking to people was unbearable and I avoided answering the phone, which rang incessantly. The constant deliveries of beautiful bouquets were appreciated but we knew that the house would soon be overflowing with flowers.

THE LASTING LEGACY OF A CHARITABLE DONATION OR AWARD

We decided to include an invitation in the funeral notice for mourners to make a donation (in lieu of flowers) to the Children's Ward at Hastings Hospital. It was a useful way of sharing people's generosity so that there might be some small benefit to others, and it was also very appropriate. Zoie had always loved children and had often spoken about specialising in paediatric nursing. We also sponsored an award for 'best and fairest' netballer at Zoie's netball club in her memory. They were wonderful legacies of Zoie.

There were so many telegraphs and cards being sent to our post box at the post office that the postman made regular visits to deliver them personally to the letterbox at the end of the driveway. Mum and Dad had lived in Hawke's Bay for many years and were well known in the community. We received many sincere wishes of sympathy and understanding from the medical, nursing and legal communities, from other legal practitioners, and from judges of the various courts in Hawke's Bay in which Dad practised law. It seemed that the wider community were also trying to come to terms with their own shock and sadness, wrapping Mum and Dad up in their outpouring of love and messages of sympathy and concern, and their tributes to Zoie and James.

Before Zoie's funeral, Mum asked me to go to James and Zoie's house and collect some of her clothes for Zoie to wear in the coffin. It was difficult to be in their home without them, knowing that they would never return.

KEEPSAKES CAN INCLUDE CATS (OR DOGS OR OTHER PETS)

Zoie had a little cat called Max that we gave to one of her closest friends; he was a living keepsake. I would have loved to have taken Max back to university with me, but I couldn't offer him a home. I was living with student friends in a pet-free apartment, and in any case, I wasn't sure that our varsity lifestyle suited a cat.

As I entered James and Zoie's house, I was sure that I could smell Zoie's perfume. It was as if it rushed to meet me at the door and followed me around the house as I looked for her things. It felt surreal, and I wanted to believe that my sister was with me, helping me, as my body heaved with emotion while I wandered through her house.

It was an easy choice of clothes for Zoie to wear for her funeral. Mum had sewn a beautiful emerald-green silk dress for Zoie, and Zoie was very proud of it. She also loved wearing bright, colourful, vibrant scarves, and I chose one that would match her dress. Later, after the funeral director had dressed her, I realised that he hadn't placed the scarf properly around her in the same way that my sister wore it. I was too shy to ask the funeral director to fix it, but I have always wished that I had. It would have annoyed Zoie as she had a great sense of style, and things had to be worn in a particular way. Whilst at the house, I collected some of my sister's treasured jewellery and trinkets that could be placed in with her.

The irony was that it was so hard to be in their home without Zoie and James, and just as hard to leave it. I felt a strange sense of closeness to them both by being in their home, surrounded by their furniture and personal items, but it also felt so foreign to be there without them. And so silent. I wished that the walls would talk so I could again hear their voices, their conversations and their laughter. Closing their front door and stepping away reinforced the awful reality that they would not be coming home.

SYMBOLS IN NATURE

In the days waiting for Zoie's funeral, a fantail entered my parents' house. As its name suggests, the fantail is a small, sparrow-like bird with a tail that fans out as it flies. They make a beautiful chirping noise, and will follow you in the park or forest; they are considered the friends of the forest. According to Maori mythology, when a fantail flies inside a house, it means that death is either present, or that a death is imminent. Maori people see the fantail as the messenger of death, that someone has passed or will pass from this world. Although the fantails loved Mum's garden, we had never seen one enter the house before. It was an ominous but equally nice distraction for us, at that moment, to have to help this little bird back out into the garden.

I spent time walking through Mum's vast garden, looking at her flowers, watching the fluttering butterflies as they danced in and out of the garden beds, and listening to the birds chirping in the trees. Mum's driveway was lined with Canadian maples that changed into beautiful reds and oranges in autumn, their large teardrop-shaped leaves scattered by the wind across the lawn and down the driveway. For just a moment, as my feet sank into Mum's lawn, it seemed as if Mother Nature was also leaning in, offering beautiful, peaceful surroundings in which to mourn my sister and her partner James.

The night before Zoie's funeral, my parents' home was filled with family and friends, many of whom had travelled great distances within New Zealand and from overseas to be with us, including my Uncle Stathi and Aunty Beth (who would become my 'Sydney Parents'), and my mum's two sisters who were close in age, the babies in a family of thirteen siblings. They shared their childhoods and much of their adult lives together and were known as the 'Three Musketeers'.

The house overflowed with platters and dishes of food for the wake, which was to be held at home the next day. I wandered around in a daze, finding it hard to speak and engage with all these people, who were genuinely concerned for us. I knew that they meant well but it was confronting and claustrophobic. I couldn't bear to be alone with just my thoughts and the awful reality of what had happened. I decided to stay and quietly appreciate their company from a distance.

GRIEF IS THE PRICE OF LOVE[5]

I spent some time sitting with my godmother, Ersi. She had also immigrated to New Zealand from Crete, and she and her husband, Arthur, were best of friends with my parents. She shared with me the rituals of rural Greece.

"You know, Lizaki, when there is a death in the family, we all wear black, black, black, black, us women, for at least forty days." My godmother's rich Greek accent spun through her words, her arms spread widely, her hands dancing as she spoke.

"Why do you wear black for so long?"

"Aaah, it's not so long. It's important that we do it to honour the dead, as they pass from this life to the Afterlife. In the Greek Church, we believe that the soul wanders the Earth for forty days and then passes into the Afterlife."

She then pointed to me and said:

"But you know, Lizaki, if Arthur died, then I would wear black for the rest of my life. The rest of my life."

My godmother shook her head a few times.

"Can you believe that? The rest of my life. Well, maybe until I remarry." And with that, she chuckled loudly, her ample bosom beneath her clothes shifting as she laughed.

"But not so bad, hey? As you know, I LOVE black"—my godmother was almost always dressed in black—"it just needs a few colourful beads and some bright lipstick. You must add a bit of colour. That's life, isn't it though, Lizaki? There is often much darkness, but you can always find some colour."

Although I was a New Zealander, I decided to respect my Greek heritage and wear black for the next forty days. Trying to think about what I would wear made me tearful.

"Oh, my poor daahling, you loved your sister so much, didn't you?" said Ersi with concern.

"Yes, Aunty, and I still do, and I don't know how I will be able to live the rest of my life without her."

"Oooh, my daahling, you will be okay, Lizaki, we all love you. The thing is, you may grieve the rest of your life for her, but that is because you love her."

That night was another sleepless, tear-filled night. I dodged the tear-soaked patches on my pillow. I must have eventually fallen asleep because before I knew it, the morning of my sister's funeral had arrived. I didn't want to get up, I wanted time to stand still, so that we would never have to say the final goodbye, and we would never have to bury her. I couldn't move. My legs felt frozen. I stayed in bed for the longest time, until there was a knock at the door. Before I could answer, before I could scream "Go away and leave me alone," it opened.

"Hi, honey." Mum peered in from the hallway. "You have to get up."

"But I don't want to, Mum. And … I really don't think I can." I burst into tears.

"I know, honey, I feel the same. But you know, today is your sister's day. It's important that we say goodbye, that we show our love to Zoie up in Heaven, that we honour her today. We won't get this day again to farewell her. We must do our best."

At that moment, I felt like I would spend the rest of my life saying goodbye to my sister. And I had no idea what my best was.

"Okay, Mum, I know, but I wish none of this was happening. I want Zoie and James back; I don't want to have to do this. I want to stay here in bed and not get up, and then it won't be real."

"I know, honey, but don't you think I feel the same way? Come on now, you must get up."

BLACK WAS MY SHIELD

I reluctantly got out of bed, showered and then dressed in a black-and-white-spotted blouse, a black linen skirt and black heels.

The funeral was held at Waiapu Cathedral of St John the Baptist in Napier. My father was a longstanding parishioner so it was a special church to him. My sister and I used to love going out for drinks together with our friends on the night of Christmas Eve, before we would meet up with Dad at the cathedral to sing Christmas carols. We might both be a little tipsy, but Dad relished our company, and my sister and I enjoyed singing our hearts out.

This day was to be a very different occasion in the very same space, within the very same four walls. It was so hard to fathom.

WHAT DO LIFE'S CHALLENGES HAVE TO DO WITH GOD?

As we prepared for Zoie's funeral, I kept asking myself if there really is a God, then why hadn't God stopped the accident from happening? Why would God take such young, beautiful adults who had their whole lives ahead of them? Until the accident, I had always believed in God, but now I struggled to believe that a loving God existed, to allow Zoie and James to be taken from us in such cruel, sudden and violent circumstances.

It was very difficult to reconcile my faith and the devastating loss of Zoie and James. They were young, good people who deserved to live full, healthy and happy adult lives. How could we now attend a farewell for

Zoie in God's House? Why was God now allowed to watch us mourn and apparently 'be with us in our hour of need'? Where was God just before the accident? Why did God's angels not protect Zoie and James in their hour of need?

But I knew that no one, not even God, promises us a long life. We only get the years that we do. Even so, it didn't offer me any solace, and I felt very awkward going to church to now bid Zoie farewell 'before God' when I felt He had abandoned her when she most needed Him.

As George drove us to the cathedral, Justin sat in the front passenger seat, and I sat between Mum and Dad in the back seat. They cried quietly, with collapsed shoulders and bowed heads, all the life sucked out of them. When we arrived at the cathedral, the minister met us at the side door. I could hear tender organ music in the background.

Not having attended a funeral for anyone in my family before, there were many firsts. In hindsight, I would have liked to have known what lay ahead. My parents were too devastated to be able to offer me any tips, but I wished I had asked one of our family or friends so that I was prepared for what was to come.

Stepping into the cathedral with Mum and Dad, I saw hundreds of faces. I didn't know whether I was supposed to acknowledge the other mourners as we walked or keep my head down. Deciding to get my parents and myself up to the front of the cathedral without tripping over seemed enough. I didn't look around, cry, smile or speak. Instead, we just walked slowly to the front of the cathedral and took our seats.

Since losing Zoie and James, I have been to many funerals for elderly family and friends. Their funerals have been wonderful celebrations of their long lives, of many fond memories, of achievements and successes, of love and marriage, of children and grandchildren. My sister's funeral was very different.

We had lost my dearest Zo Zo just as she was preparing to take on the world as a young adult woman with her great zest for life. She had been denied the time and joy of building her career, getting married, buying her first home, managing the big M (mortgage) and welcoming children into the world. Whilst we were blessed with Zoie for twenty-one years, and had wonderful memories of her, she had been cheated, and so had we. There wasn't anything to celebrate.

My father was instrumental in arranging Zoie's funeral service with the minister. I don't know how he found the strength to do it, as he must never have thought that he would ever be in that situation.

A 'VILOMAH' IS A PARENT WHO IS PRE-DECEASED BY THEIR CHILD

Parents shouldn't have to bury their children. It is simply not in the natural order of things. The English language provides us with the word 'widow' or 'widower' for the loss of a spouse, and the word 'orphans' when children lose their parents. But there is no English word to describe a parent who loses a child. Karla Holloway, a James B. Duke professor of English at Duke University, found the word 'Vilomah', a Sanskrit word that means 'against a natural order', to describe a parent who has lost his or her child through death. They are 'vilomahed'. 'Vilomah is a name for the grief they represent.'[6]

And what of the sister who loses her sister and best friend? There seems to be no English word to describe a sibling who loses their sister or brother. Perhaps we too are 'vilomahed'.

Zoie's farewell service was beautiful. I had asked Dad to arrange for the song 'Lean on Me'[7] to be played during the service as Zoie and Justin had danced to the cover version at Zoie's twenty-first birthday party, ten months beforehand. Her twenty-first was a terrific party at the Zanzibar Bar and Nightclub in Hastings, where James and Zoie had both worked at the weekends and made many special friends with staff. I often still hear this song being played on the radio and it always stops me in my tracks.

A good friend of Zoie's also read the following poem to the congregation:

Safely Home

I am home in Heaven, dear ones; Oh, so happy and so bright!

There is perfect joy and beauty

In this everlasting light.

All the pain and grief are over, Every restless tossing passed;

I am now at peace forever, Safely home in Heaven at last. Did you wonder how I so calmly Trod the valley of the shade?

Oh! but Jesus' arm to lean on, Could I have one doubt or dread? Then you must not grieve so sorely, For I love you dearly still;

Try to look beyond earth's shadows, Pray to trust our Fathers will.

There is work still waiting for you, So you must not idly stand;

Do it now, while life remaineth, You shall rest in Jesus' land. When that work is all completed, He will gently call you Home; Oh, the rapture of that meeting, Oh, the joy to see you come!

All the pain and grief are over, Every restless tossing passed, Now at peace forever,

Safely Home In Heaven At Last!

-Anon

Before we knew it, we were at the end of the service, and Zoie was carried from the cathedral and into the hearse. My parents and I followed behind her coffin, surely the hardest walk of my parents' lives.

We were escorted into the car that would follow the hearse to the cemetery. I felt hot and claustrophobic sitting between my parents. The drive was small respite before our arrival at the cemetery.

THE SOLIDARITY OF THE PROCESSION

As we left the cathedral, we turned into Taradale Road, a long, straight stretch of road that runs some distance towards the cemetery. I turned around and saw a very long procession of cars, their headlights on, following us slowly. It was an amazing sight to see these cars tailgating each other to keep the procession together. Other cars on the road would move in or change lanes so the procession could slowly advance towards the cemetery, uninterrupted by other traffic.

Dad said, "Turn around, honey."

But I couldn't help it. I wanted to watch and capture that moment in my memory. I was so proud that so many people had come to mourn, and farewell, my sister.

I felt such a strong sense of camaraderie and solidarity as we travelled together to take Zoie to her final resting place. Zoie would have loved the spectacle.

We arrived at the cemetery, and I now had to navigate burying my sister. I helped my parents out of the car.

We stood silently by the car for a long time, looking at the beautiful mature trees swaying in the sunlight with a cool breeze. It was a change in seasons, from summer to autumn, and it felt surreal. I have never forgotten that feeling, and I am always reminded by the change in seasons when the anniversary of my sister's death is approaching.

The cemetery stretched out in long sections of well-cut grass, with row upon row of tombstones. It was so sad to look across the vast expanse and know that so many people had died before her. It was eerily quiet, the silence only broken by the birds singing in the trees. And now we were there to lay my sister to rest.

We walked down across the lawn to Zoie's designated final resting place. She would lie below some beautiful trees, facing the northern sun.

COMMITAL TO THE FINAL RESTING PLACE

The minister arrived at the gravesite and said some committal prayers, as we stood silently, in shock that we had reached the end of my sister's service. I didn't want the service to finish, as that would mean we would never see my sister again. As the coffin was lowered, everyone cried deeply, the tragedy and finality simply too much to bear. None of us wanted to leave Zoie. It seemed so wrong to have to step away from her graveside, leaving her alone, surrounded only by the graves of strangers. I wanted to stay with her. I didn't want to have to return to my parents' home and resume my own life without her. We stayed for the longest time, until someone took my arm, guiding me back to the car. We now had to return to my parents' house for the wake.

THERE ARE MULTIPLE OPTIONS FOR A WAKE

In different countries, cultures and religions, a wake can mean different things. With reference to death, the original meaning of the word 'wake' was a 'watch' or 'vigil', to refer to a prayer vigil, and to mourners keeping watch over the dead until they were buried or cremated. In the USA, a wake can be the viewing of the deceased person prior to the final service, often at a funeral home or sometimes at the home of the deceased or an immediate member of the family. In the UK, a wake often refers to the social gathering after the funeral, whereas Irish wakes usually take place before the funeral. There are also many nuances to a wake within the practice of different religions. In Australia and New Zealand, it is usual for a reception to be held after the funeral and burial or cremation.

Mum and Dad had always been very hospitable and held the wake at home. It was well meaning but the house quickly filled with mourners, downstairs and upstairs, in the kitchen, out on the deck and even in the garden. There was nowhere to hide. In hindsight, a better venue might have been the cathedral hall, a sports club or even the local pub, so Mum and Dad could leave when they wanted to, and the sanctity of their home was not disturbed. However, thankfully, many wonderful friends managed the catering, drinks and cups of tea. The wake couldn't have happened without them.

My mum was taken upstairs to the lounge, and she sat out on the balcony. She looked so defeated; she had nothing left to offer. I felt her pain. I also felt my own pain, and just like her, I wanted to shut myself down and hide for the longest time. Instead, many people approached me to share their own memories and love of Zoie and James, their own sadness and pain, and to ask about Mum. I didn't know what to say. I wanted so much to hear, and to listen, but ultimately, I fumbled through the afternoon.

By the end of that day, we were exhausted. That night, my mum went to bed early, and after tidying the kitchen with the help of some fabulous friends, the rest of us drifted off to bed as the exhaustion became overwhelming. We knew the next day would be just as demanding.

A FINAL FAREWELL TO JAMES

The next day, a requiem mass was held for James at St Joseph's Church in Waipukurau, a ninety-minute drive from Napier. My parents, brothers and I travelled together to Waipukurau, to farewell James. It was also Mum's birthday.

We were greeted at the church steps. James' family and friends were very gracious and offered us seats together at the front of the church.

We sat quietly, in shock that we should now also be saying goodbye to James. It was a beautiful service. Our family spent most of it in tears, crying for James, and of course, crying for Zoie. I don't think any of us could really comprehend the magnitude of our losses, or the depth of our sadness. Another family had lost their precious son, brother, grandson, nephew, cousin and dear friend. Our collective lives would never be the same again without the joy and privilege of being able to share them with James and Zoie.

After the service, we drove home in silence. It was a long drive. Depleted of all energy, we couldn't talk. We were defeated by the events of the last several days.

Over the next several weeks, I tried to come to terms with what had happened. I stayed at my parents' home as I wasn't ready to return to university. I thought I could catch up on my studies the following term. It would be a challenge, but I simply couldn't contemplate returning to my varsity life so soon after Zoie and James had died.

My dad returned to work, but I still don't know how he managed to do so. He seemed to summon up the courage from somewhere—maybe it was from his belief in God, or his sense of purpose, or just to keep him distracted. He showered and dressed for work and left the house each morning without saying very much. Every day, Dad had to attend his office, presenting himself outwardly as a man in control, able to return to work, able to engage with staff and clients, able to apply his mind to the complicated civil and criminal legal issues of his clients, and able to appear in court on behalf of his clients. I'm sure that he, too, just wanted to hide from the outside world.

MUSIC AS THERAPY FOR THE BEREAVED

Mum didn't return to nursing for some time. Instead, I spent many hours sitting quietly with her, taking her for walks in her beautiful garden, or visiting different parks in Hawke's Bay when we could both summon enough energy to leave the house.

At night, we would sit in the lounge 'into the small hours', watching DVDs of Luciano Pavarotti. Luciano was her favourite tenor and she enjoyed listening to his voice reverberate throughout the lounge. Together, we watched many operas, but she would always come back to Giacomo Puccini's opera *Turandot*. Maybe it was because she loved how brilliantly Pavarotti performed the aria 'Nessun Dorma' (None Shall Sleep).[8] Mum also loved listening to Pavarotti's predecessors, Mario Lanza and his idol, Enrico Caruso. She also loved the angelic voice of the American Greek soprano Maria Callas. It was in these dark hours that I came to develop an appreciation for opera music. They would also come to hold many memories for me of time spent with Mum when she was at her most vulnerable.

It was bittersweet to spend time with Mum and Dad, as I wasn't processing my own grief. It felt like my own grief was subsumed by my concern for my parents. They didn't talk very much to me and didn't talk to each other very much at all. The house became very quiet.

MY SISTER'S NAME BECAME A REVERED WORD

I often tried to talk about Zoie to them, but they didn't seem to want to, and wouldn't engage with me.

"Dad, how are you feeling?"

"I'm okay, honey."

"Do you want to talk about Zoie? About Zoie and James?"

"Not right now, honey, maybe in a while."

"Okay, but I can't seem to get Mum to talk about them with me either. She just stares out the window at the hills; sometimes I am not even sure if she hears me."

"I know, honey, she just needs some time."

Oddly enough, Mum and Dad and I had time in abundance. It just wasn't more time with Zoie and James. What any of us would give for another minute with them.

I often checked in with Dad, but his responses were the same. It seemed that my parents couldn't bear to hear or speak Zoie's name, as if to do so would cause reality to come crashing into the house and engulf them, taking them back in time to the moment that they were told that Zoie and James had died.

After many nights at home, I joined my brothers for a drink at one of the local bars in Napier where a band was playing. The bar was busy, the other patrons having fun spending time with their friends, drinking and dancing to the music. Struggling to talk or engage, I was miserable and wanted to be anywhere but there. A rising wave of anxiety took hold of me, my chest tightened, and I felt sweaty, dizzy and claustrophobic.

"I don't know why God took Zoie and James; I can't understand it. I would swap places with her if it brought her back."

My brother replied, "Lisa, I know how you feel, but you can't talk like that. And Zoie is with you, she always will be."

It seemed nearly impossible for me to share with my family how I felt, without judgement. I didn't know how I was supposed to deal with my own grief, or who I could talk to about it, so I didn't. Instead, I dug a deep hole in my heart and planted it.

DISCONNECTING CAN BE PROTECTIVE BUT ALSO ISOLATING FOR THE BEREAVED

I had to return to university, or I would fail the year. I flew back to my apartment in Wellington, back into university life. My flatmates were kind to me, but I struggled to communicate how I felt. Instead, I spent many hours in my room, away from the world. Sometimes, I wouldn't eat and didn't sleep well. I developed a sleep disorder that caused interrupted slumber. Most mornings, I would go for a run before starting my day. I left my running gear out the night before so there were no excuses. Often still half asleep, I would fall into my gear and be out the door before I was fully awake. The first part of my run was a very steep hill that was a half walk, half run until I found my running legs. I knew that some of my daily runs should be skipped for the lack of sleep, but I was desperately trying to hold on to some routine, and I felt I needed it for my own sanity.

COMPARTMENTALISING GRIEF TO FUNCTION IN OUR DAILY LIVES

Inevitably though, the lack of sleep and food created health issues. I wasn't functioning well. I was falling asleep in my lectures, my hair had started falling out, I was isolating myself from my friends and flatmates, and I looked and felt fatigued. I ended up seeing a doctor, who recognised that I was struggling with my grief and was referred to a counsellor. The counsellor was very empathetic and encouraged me to compartmentalise my grief, so that I could function in my everyday student life. I would allow myself some time every day to cry, and to think only of my sister.

Usually, it was in the shower in the mornings after my runs, or it was at night when I went to bed, and I could cry silently into my pillow. If I had these dedicated times to grieve, then hopefully, I could manage the rest of each day. As it turned out, it worked well on most days, but not always, and I accepted that there really was no magical wand for grief. Instead, it required many different tools, including patience, distraction, active reflection and attention, some mental discipline, understanding, self-love, tenderness and compassion.

At the end of the year, I sat my final exams in a dedicated room for those with 'special needs', so that I had extra personal space if I got upset and made noise that might disturb others. It wasn't particularly helpful. Some of the other students spent the exam time walking around the room, moving around in their chairs, pulling at their hair (or splitting the ends of their hair which was a regular pastime of mine) or daydreaming. They were a terrible distraction. Thankfully, I passed my exams!

PLANTING A TREE AS A LIVING MEMORIAL

Shortly after Zoie and James' funerals, Mum and Dad received the most beautiful but heartbreaking letter from the couple who owned the farm next to the river where Zoie and James had died. They were the only witnesses to the accident and had rushed to the scene. They stayed with Zoie and James until the emergency services arrived, and wrote that they had been very impressed at the dignified, caring way in which the emergency services personnel had treated Zoie and James at the accident site. It was wonderful for them to reach out to my parents. They invited Mum and Dad to make contact when they were ready.

Some months later, after I had returned to university, my parents arranged for us to travel north to meet this very kind and brave couple. My parents thought it would help me to meet them and to see the accident site, and I thought it would help my parents and this brave couple to meet each other. Dad, Mum and I met in Napier and travelled up to Te Awamutu to meet them at their home.

It was the first time that I had seen the accident site. It was a warm day and the sun glistened on the shiny green of the paddocks. The road itself had a sharp bend that led into the Owairaka Stream Bridge. There was still evidence of an earlier bridge further down the river, with old concrete pillars jutting out on either side of the riverbanks. The first police officer to arrive at the accident scene later informed the coroner that he had spoken to this farming couple, who reported that the car had turned sharply as it came around the corner, skidded across the grass verge, and then flew across the river, before hitting the bridge abutment on the other side of the river. The car had then flipped and fallen upside down into the river.

It was overwhelming to see the place where Zoie and James had lost their lives. I could only imagine how much harder it must have been for this couple. The farmer told us that he had been standing in one of his paddocks at the time, and he had seen the entire accident unfold. I couldn't imagine how he would ever escape that image.

My parents, with the permission of this beautiful couple, arranged to plant a tree where the farmer had been standing on his farm at the time of the accident. It would be a living memorial to Zoie and James.

HEADSTONE MEMORIAL SERVICE TO RECONNECT AND REMEMBER

Exactly a year to the day after my sister's death, we held an unveiling of Zoie's headstone at the cemetery. Many family and close friends attended the ceremony. It was a wonderful opportunity to connect with each other, to share our experiences of the last twelve months, and to share our memories of Zoie. The minister presided and shared some beautiful prayers for my sister as the headstone was unveiled. My dad had chosen the Greek Orthodox sign of the Cross, with the words:

In this sign I shall prevail.

Also, too, the words:

Safely home, In perfect joy and beauty, In the Everlasting Light.

There was a spectacular colour photo of my sister on the headstone that had been made in the United States. It was a very fitting tribute to my beautiful sister, who had had the world at her young feet just as she was about to make her mark in life.

The memorial was brief, but it was long enough to have meaning, and for all of us to be in tears. It took me back to when Zoie and James had died and to her committal a year earlier. It felt truly awful that a year had passed since their deaths, and that our lives had moved on without them. The Earth had kept spinning on its axis—how many times??!!—and many more people had died and been buried near Zoie. It was a dreadful reminder of how much we had lost. My grief seemed to rise through my body, constricting my throat. I found it hard to swallow, and hard to stop the flood of tears. As if it were just yesterday.

Instead of watching her enjoy her adult life, succeed in her chosen career and have a family, I have spent all my adult life without her. At times, I would like to think that she is nearby, and I miss her desperately every day. But I am so grateful for one small mercy: my youngest daughter is her mirror image. She has the same wonderful, gregarious personality and all the fire in her belly that was my sister. I can't wait to see my daughter become a young adult woman, and how much more she will resemble my sister.

It is a travesty that my children will never get to meet her. I often daydream how much fun we would have had if Zoie and James were still with us, and they had had children. They would have made the most wonderful parents, aunt and uncle. We could have enjoyed holidays together, going skiing, planning getaways at the most exotic tropical beachside resorts, or just kicking around in each other's company. My sister was 'a natural' with children, and I know she would have been such a great teacher to me as I embarked on motherhood. It was not to be. Instead, it has become my changed landscape.

While it has been many years since my sister's death, I still feel immensely sad in my heart. I watch other siblings together, the special relationships they share, and I feel alone. My sister was my best friend, and my 'partner in crime'. I often feel lost without her. However, I am now blessed with my own family, a loving husband and three beautiful young children to parent and love, to care and provide for. There are a million more moments ahead of me when I will miss my sister desperately, but I must try to manage them with dignity and grace. I still want Zoie to be proud of her younger sister.

INSIGHTS

- Sudden, unexpected and violent deaths by accident (or other causes) can be extremely traumatic and distressing experiences for the bereaved. Even more so where the deceased are young people, since their unexpected deaths are an affront to our perceived natural order that we should each expect to live long lives.
- The grieving process may involve a myriad of emotions, including shock, numbness, sadness, anger, loneliness, feelings of isolation and aloneness, guilt and regret. It may also affect our cognitive ability, causing us to be in denial or disbelief of our loss, cause confusion and an inability to concentrate, and affect our ability to make decisions. Grief may also be reflected in our behaviours, the most obvious being crying and wailing, and other positive behaviours such as talking about our loss, reaching out for support from others, exercising, taking rest and other self-care behaviours, as well as negative behaviours such

as isolating ourselves socially (such as when my mother withdrew herself from the wake, and I isolated myself at university from my flatmates and friends), high risk-taking behaviours (such as my paragliding and bungy jumping!) and excessive behaviours (such as compulsive shopping, gambling, drinking).

- Multiple losses can cause compounded loss which inhibits our ability to feel and process our grief separately in respect of each loss.
- In addition to the 'primary loss' of loved ones, there are numerous associated 'secondary losses' to be acknowledged and addressed in our grieving. They may include changes in identity or family role (I no longer have an older sister and am no longer the younger sister of Zoie), changes within the family (the initial inability to talk about Zoie within and outside the family, my parents' understandably obsessive concern for my safety), loss of our dreams for the future (that my sister and I would be wonderful aunts to each other's children and grow old together), changes in financial or social position, and changes in our support networks (such as when I felt that my supporters did not/would not understand my grief).
- The loss of a loved one may reinforce your own spiritual beliefs, or it may challenge them (just as my own religious beliefs in the existence of God were challenged by the deaths of Zoie and James).
- Within families, each family member may grieve differently. It is important that family members, especially children and young adults, do not feel neglected, isolated or overwhelmed by the grief of others. We need to make space for, and embrace, the grief of each family member.

CHAPTER THREE: ON THE EDGE OF TIME

And we wept that one so lovely should have a life so brief.

—William Cullen Bryant

We met on my first day at work in a national law firm in Auckland (known as the 'City of Sails'). The firm's offices were located at Viaduct Harbour at the end of Queen Street, a precinct made famous by the 2000 America's Cup, which was hosted by the Royal New Zealand Yacht Squadron. The offices had uninterrupted views of Auckland Harbour out to Waiheke Island and the other Hauraki Islands. The view was stunning, and rather distracting on my first day.

"Hi, I'm Mark."

"Hi, Mark, I'm Lisa."

"Hi, Lisa. So, you're the new junior. Welcome. I hope you have a great first day."

"Thanks."

"Have you come from another law firm?"

"No, I've been working in-house."

"Oh, that's great. Well, maybe I can give you some advice."

"Great, yes, please."

"Make sure you know these rules inside out." Mark had the loose-leaf High Court Rules in his hand. They were quite unwieldly, contained in a hardback cover but with a multiple ring binder in the middle so that the pages could be easily substituted as the rules of Court changed.

"If you know these rules, you can be one step ahead of the other side."

"Okay, that's great advice, thanks. I'll be sure to study them."

Mark was taller than me, slender build, light brown hair and blue eyes, as vivid as the blue sea behind him. He also wore what I thought were very funky rimless glasses and seemed to 'lean in' as he spoke.

I was immediately impressed by Mark's willingness to help me as a junior lawyer in the group. He was a senior commercial litigator, who for his young age and experience had incredible commercial acumen. He also understood the importance of being intimately familiar with Court rules and procedure, as this might provide you with a tactical advantage over the opponent, assisting you with your advocacy before the Courts. Over time I was to discover that he had a calm, gentle soul, with a terrific intellect and a warm sense of humour—not the usual traits of a high-flying commercial litigator!—and I liked him even more for it. We became good friends during his tenure at the firm and started dating after he moved to another firm.

Our relationship developed very quickly, and within a matter of months, Mark proposed to me, and I said yes. He first asked me at his parents' house, but as he was a sentimental romantic, I suspected he might have another plan.

"Hey, let's go out to Piha. We should go for a walk along the beach."

It was a cold, wintry day and Piha was on the west coast of Auckland.

"Really, are you sure? Maybe we could pick a better day."

"No, don't worry, it will be fine. The weather will have improved by the time we get out there."

Ever the optimist, Mark was able to persuade me with his cheerful 'let's do this' attitude. I knew that Piha was one of Mark's favourite beaches with its black sand, rough surf and rugged hillsides that seem to fall into the beach. We drove out to more wind and rain at the beach. But Mark's mind was set, and we climbed Lion Rock, a hill that sits on the black sand and has the natural profile of a lion lying down in the sand. We reached the top and looked out at the vast Tasman Sea, in drizzling rain and wind that swept around our legs.

"Come over here," he said as he climbed over the walking path ropes.

"No, it's okay, thanks, I will just stay on this side. That looks way too steep, and you shouldn't either. If you fall, it's a long way down."

"Lise, it will be fine, come on, just step over the rope and come down here a little." I wasn't sure why it was so important to Mark to find a special spot off the path, but I had an inkling of what he was up to.

"Okay, okay, I'm coming, but only this far." I swung my leg over the rope and stood just a foot away from it. I was so 'chicken', worried I would go crashing down the hillside and be covered in scratches and prickles.

It was too steep to get down on one knee, so Mark shuffled down the hill more so he could look up at me and propose.

"I know this seems really weird, but I wanted you to have a very special memory of my proposal. Will you marry me?"

"Mark, you have already given me a very special memory, but you're right, this is awesome!! And yes, of course I will marry you. Now, please, can you come back up the cliff?" We were both laughing as the rain became heavier and we ran down the hill to seek sanctuary in the car, our clothes soaked and water dripping down our faces. We were bedraggled but pleased to be out of the rain.

Not long after we became engaged, Mark and I moved into a flat together in Mission Bay, a popular seaside bay alongside Tamaki Drive, in Auckland City. From there, we walked to dinner, went for runs along the water and beach in the mornings, and stopped in for coffees on our way home to get ready for work. We also drove into the city together for work, as quality 'catch-up' time to work out the week's plans, social plans, weekend commitments and our next trip to Napier to 'plan the wedding'.

MY WEDDING WAS OF SPECIAL IMPORTANCE TO MY PARENTS

My parents immediately liked Mark from the first time they met him and were excited about the prospect of a wedding in the family. As Mum and Dad now only had one daughter whom they would see get married, Mark graciously agreed that we should let them be actively involved in the preparations, and that the wedding be held in Napier.

During our visits to Napier, we both enjoyed exploring the wineries, dining in their restaurants, tasting wines at the cellar door and contemplating wines for our wedding. Mark was knowledgeable about New Zealand wines and enjoyed learning more about the Hawke's Bay winemakers. We also enjoyed walks on Te Mata Peak, runs down at the beach, and catching up with friends at the various pubs and nightclubs.

On one visit, the aborist had lopped back the shelterbelt trees around my parents' home and we stacked them in the centre of the paddock for a bonfire that night. After dinner, we sat around the fire in a circle, the light illuminating our faces and the heat keeping us warm in the winter night. Mark and I sat together, looking up at the vast night sky and all the stars that sparkled without the pollution of city lights. We could see the Milky Way and the four stars of the Southern Cross.

SHOOTING STARS ARE NOT RARE BUT THEY ARE ROMANTIC

"Wow, did you see that, Mark?"

"What was it?"

"I just saw a shooting star. It was over there." I pointed to the black sky with all its twinkling lights. "I think I just saw it out of my periphery. Did you see it?"

"No, I didn't, but I'm glad you did. It's a great omen. It's supposed to mean good luck."

"Oh, that's awesome, what a shame you didn't see it too."

"Doesn't matter, I have all the luck I need right here," and as he said it, he pulled me in and squeezed me tight. I felt safe, warm and content.

We spent the night sharing stories, telling jokes and singing songs that are the purview of campfires and weekends away in the forest. When we eventually went into the house, our hair and clothes full of smoke, we showered and climbed into bed, muscles aching and arms tired from our hard work. We were exhausted but happy.

After we returned to Auckland, Mark's demeanour gradually changed and he became quiet, vague and withdrawn. He wouldn't talk to me or tell me what was wrong. I also started noticing that he would go to bed early, often not long after we came home from work. He was extremely fatigued and wasn't interested in our usual runs, coffee walks or dinners at our favourite local restaurants. He was also struggling to concentrate on his final paper for his Master's.

We talked at length one night and Mark admitted to me that he was feeling depressed. I assumed and hoped that his depression was just an isolated experience, perhaps brought on by the major stressors or changes in his life. What I didn't know was that Mark would continue to experience multiple depressive episodes, known as major depression.

MAJOR DEPRESSION CAN PRESENT AS A SINGLE EPISODE OR RECUR THROUGHOUT ONE'S LIFE

At the time, Mark appeared to be on a downwards spiral and I felt out of my depth, not knowing what to do or say. I urged him to see a doctor, and he agreed he would. He wouldn't let me come with him but promised me he would go. Mark did see a doctor and was prescribed antidepressants, which he took regularly. For the first few weeks, he was even more lethargic and said he found it hard to concentrate. He also found it very hard to engage in conversation; we shared hours of silence together. After some weeks, and with regular sleep, runs around the bays in Auckland, taking medication, and concentrating on a nutritious and alcohol-free diet, Mark seemed to bounce back to his relaxed, engaging and animated self.

PROTECTING MY HUSBAND AND BEING IN DENIAL EXACERBATED THE ISSUES

I didn't speak to my parents or my friends about Mark's depression. Instead, I stayed silent to protect Mark, because I was in love with him, and I was really excited about our future. I didn't want anything to change that. Subconsciously I was in denial that it was a major health issue for Mark, and for us as a couple, who were about to embark on married life and overseas travel.

What I didn't appreciate was that Mark was at risk of further depressive episodes that would last longer and become more severe if he didn't receive the proper treatment. What was to later unfold would turn out to be much worse than I could have imagined.

Our wedding was a spectacular day, celebrated at the Waiapu Cathedral of St John the Baptist where we had held Zoie's funeral. It was apt that we should marry there as a lasting tie to my sister. Afterwards, we wined and dined our guests at Ormlie Lodge, a beautiful character homestead that was built in 1899 by wealthy Hawke's Bay farmer William Nelson, as a wedding gift to his daughter Gertrude. It was a great night, with many wonderful speeches and dancing, including some Greek dancing led by my father to gather our guests as the Syrtaki dance snaked through the dining room.

THE BIG 'OE'

After our wedding, we had a short honeymoon in Fiji to unwind, rest and have some fun in the sun. Our 'OE', (or overseas experience that young New Zealanders often take as a 'gap year') would be our extended honeymoon.

As I also wanted to further my studies, I applied to study a Master of Laws at Cambridge University in the UK and was thrilled to be accepted. I was stunned by the opportunity to study at a globally prestigious university. Mark planned to apply for a legal role in London once we arrived.

The exhilaration of my planned post-graduate study and our OE was soon tempered by Mark becoming depressed. He saw his doctor and went back onto his medication, and after some time, he relaxed and settled. We were ready for our extended honeymoon trip en route to London. We were excited to be taking off to see the world.

Our OE took us to Singapore to check out the sights and sounds of Singapore's nightlife, shopping districts and its local cuisine, and then to Hong Kong where we had a few days of sightseeing and appreciating the amazing skyline of Hong Kong Island, the open-air street stalls, the noodle soups and Peking Duck, and shopping at the street markets.

Greece awaited us next. I was excited to explore the homeland of my ancestors and wanted to share the experience with my husband.

TRAVEL ADVENTURES AS A GREAT DISTRACTION

After a few crazy days sightseeing in Athens, we caught the train to Piraeus and bought ferry tickets to go island hopping around the Aegean. Our first stop, the Cycladic Islands of Paros, Naxos and Santorini are all popular with tourists for their whitewashed houses with colourful trims, rocky coastlines and idyllic beaches. We enjoyed relaxing on the beaches under the hot sun, swimming in the warm and clear water of the Aegean, drinking iced coffees and chilled beers, watching local fishermen bring their catches into harbour, and indulging in fresh seafood, especially octopi and crumbed sardines, at the many seaside tavernas.

On Naxos, we went inland to explore some of the villages, hidden chapels, olive groves and more mountainous areas. We travelled on a local bus, walked and hitchhiked our way around the island. Our backpacks were heavy, but bearable, for the joy of exploring off the beaten track.

Mark loved this carefree time spent exploring the island, walking along dusty roads, being greeted by locals and taking rests at different tavernas. It seemed to awaken his adventurous spirit and he loved the sense of freedom and spontaneity.

When we returned to port, we boarded the ferry for Santorini. Santorini is by far one of the most picturesque islands in Greece. The main town of Fira is perched atop giant cliffs that literally fall sharply into the sea, the result of massive volcanic activity many hundreds of years ago. We relished all the beauty and grandeur of the island; the beaches and the local cuisine at tavernas and hotels. We gorged on the most gigantic but sweet tomatoes with crusty bread bought from local stores and tried (but didn't enjoy!) the local wines bought at market. We also walked up to the town of Ia to contemplate a truly splendid sunset across the Aegean.

LISTENING TO INSTINCTS AS A MEASURE OF ORDER OR CHAOS

In Santorini, Mark became more reflective and less talkative. He withdrew from me into the pages of his novel that he read for hours on the beach. Despite my prodding, he assured me that he was "fine". I felt nervous and anxious about Mark's wellness.

We returned by ferry to Piraeus and onto Meteora, a very surreal and spiritual landscape of amazing rock formations that sit high above the town of Kalambaka. At the top of the rock formations are monasteries, built by monks in the fourteenth to sixteenth centuries. The resident nuns explained to us that the monks had used ropes and ladders, nets and baskets to transport the construction materials to the top of the rocks to build the monasteries. They are a tribute to the efforts, courage and determination of the monks, and their aspirations to construct these buildings high in the sky, almost as if by doing so, they were seeking to reach God. We were astounded by the feats of these men living hundreds of years before our time. Before we left, Mark spent some time sitting perched on the rocks, enjoying the vast landscape, commenting to me on the incredible feats of these men, and marvelling at their brilliance and tenacity.

From Kalambaka, we headed to Patras and ferried to Ithaca, one of several Ionian islands surrounded by the Ionian Sea, which lies between the boot of Italy and the Peloponnese. Ithaca is the homeland of my father, and his parents and grandparents. Dad and his parents left Ithaca when he was just two years old for a better life in New Zealand, but he has always had a strong connection to his birthplace.

A PILGRIMAGE TO THE VILLAGE OF MY ANCESTORS

My extended paternal family lived in Vathi, the capital of Ithaca, and we were welcomed into their home as family. We spoke little Greek, and they spoke little English, but luckily, some other extended family were able to act as translators. They told us that we must travel to Anogi in central Ithaca, where my great-grandfather and great-uncle had lived, as my great-grandfather was the village priest at the church of Agia Panagia (the Church of the Annunciation of the Virgin Mary).[9] Sadly, the catastrophic earthquake of 1953 destroyed most of the houses on Ithaca, including their house. Only ruins remained. But as Mark and I were fascinated by my ancestry, we decided to hire scooters and take a trip up to Anogi. I first had to learn how to ride a scooter!

"It's easy," shouted Mark as he took off at speed up the hill.

"Wait for me," I called, trying to manage the scooter, and steering as I revved the engine. I wobbled (and swerved!) along the road before I managed to get up some speed to navigate the steep and windy roads.

Anogi is a small town in the hills of Ithaca, the highest built settlement on the island. The views from the top are magnificent, wide vistas of the island and its edges, embraced by the Ionian Sea. The church, small and old, dates to the fourteenth century and has the most magnificent

Byzantine frescoes adorning the walls. Many locals travel from mainland Greece to see these frescoes. Mark and I admired these amazing frescoes that added beauty, rich colours and depth to the old walls of the church.

We also met the owner of the village square store, who spoke some English. She had New Zealand relatives who knew my father. She was friendly and excited, asking many questions in half-English, half-Greek. We did our best to understand and reply, to share our stories from our travels, what life was like back home in New Zealand and how my parents were now coping after the death of my sister, Zoie. I was surprised that news of my sister had reached the island.

She offered us a cold drink and told us:

"Hurry. Hurry. Everyone wants to see you and say hello, *nai, nai.*" Yes, yes.

"*Nai, nai, efcharistó.*" Thank you.

Word had spread amongst the village that a descendant of my great-grandfather was visiting Anogi. Turning from our table in the cafe to look out at the square, I was overwhelmed to see many locals waiting to meet us. It was an honour to be there in that moment, almost as if my own ancestors were calling to me. We went outside to be met with greetings, handshakes and hugs from these wonderful, friendly strangers. We did our best to introduce ourselves and exchange words.

We explored the rest of the island by scooter and returned to Vathi, then went onto Corfu by ferry. From Corfu, we travelled by ferry to Bari, and then caught the train to Rome. We only had a few days in Rome but loved every minute exploring this incredible bustling and romantic city. We enjoyed the gelato and large pizza slices from street vendors as we walked between the various iconic landmarks, statues, fountains, steps and museums—the list was endless. Mark seemed to have picked up and was relaxed and happy to be enjoying our carefree adventures in Europe.

After weeks of travel, we flew to London and caught a train to Cambridge. The English countryside that rushed past our windows was a stark contrast to the hustle and bustle of Rome. We were grateful for the rest on the train.

A CITY STEEPED IN ACADEMIC HISTORY, WONDER AND MAGIC

Arriving at Cambridge Station, we walked into the town centre to find my college, Sidney Sussex.

It was like stepping into a different time. Cambridge is full of historical buildings displaying marvellous architecture, incredible college buildings, cobbled streets, gorgeous parks and bridges along the River Cam. Universally known for its prestigious university, it is a student town, with plenty of lively pubs and restaurants.

Over the next twelve months, my daily routine involved walking to lectures through the majestic grounds of the other colleges, attending lectures and tutorials, studying in the library and building friendships with other international students. Mark had secured a role with a firm of solicitors in London, and he commuted to London from Cambridge each day by train.

At weekends, we explored Cambridgeshire, visiting museums, galleries and other colleges, punting along the River Cam, and meeting up with friends at many historic and quaint English pubs for a (warm!) beer and a pub meal.

THE RETURN OF THE DEPRESSIVE EPISODES THAT WE TRIED TO AVOID

Over time, the constant stress of the daily commute seemed to grind Mark down. I wasn't sure whether that was the catalyst, or if, as I suspected, he had stopped taking his medicine, but his personality gradually changed. He talked philosophically to me for hours at the kitchen table or insisted on long walks to talk manically about numerous ideas and theories. I indulged his ramblings, as we wandered down chance country roads for miles. We often got lost.

At other times, Mark was introspective, and didn't speak more than a few words for what seemed like days. I tried to engage him in conversation, but quickly sensed he wasn't willing to talk, or more often, just wasn't able to share how he was feeling or what he was thinking. I reasoned that he was trying to protect me from the terrible pain, confusion and gloominess that engulfed him, as it was the only way that I could take any comfort from the endless hours of silence.

Sitting on a park bench in Jesus Green, I asked Mark to tell me how he felt and what he wanted to do. I needed some measure of his wellness and wanted him to be honest with me.

"I can't say how I feel."

"But you need to try, please, so that I can understand what we need to do. I can't work that out if you don't tell me exactly how you are feeling."

I was worried, stressed and anxious. I also felt helpless. On the other side of the world, so far from home, what were we to do? We had embarked on a huge journey to experience the world. Should we leave Cambridge and return to New Zealand? If we did, Mark would have to leave his job, which he seemed to be enjoying, and I wouldn't complete the course.

Eventually he shared.

"I am struggling. I have started hearing voices in my head and I don't know what I am thinking. And I haven't been taking my tablets. I haven't needed them."

I was immediately shocked by how seriously unwell he was. Mark was deteriorating rapidly, and his self-diagnosis had not helped his depression. He had convinced himself that he was well and didn't need any help. But his denial and avoidance had seemingly only worsened his condition.

We talked for hours at Jesus Green, trying to find a solution. Mark wanted me to finish my course and move to Hong Kong and look for work. He had really enjoyed our few days in Hong Kong and felt that he could live there. There was a strong expatriate community in Hong Kong so we would have good prospects of securing work. However, I knew that moving to yet another country, with a totally different culture and language, was not the solution. At that point, I didn't think we could make any substantive decisions. Mark needed urgent medical help, and reluctantly, he agreed to see a doctor who prescribed him medication and convinced him to take a few weeks off work on sick leave. Mark needed the recovery time if he was to ever return to work in London.

Despite being concerned about Mark's mental illness, I still had to pass my final exams, and he encouraged me to study on the basis that we had travelled too far to give up on my course. If I could pass and graduate, we could pack up and head home. I was immensely relieved to pass the exams.

We both attended my graduation, but it wasn't a joyous occasion. Mark was still unwell, and even though I could tell he wanted to make it a great celebration, he was struggling. I also didn't feel any elation as I was so worried about Mark and what we were going to do. We kept the celebrations brief.

After my graduation, we left our university flat, said goodbye to our Cambridge friends and moved to London. It was a welcome relief that Mark no longer had the long daily commutes. Instead, Mark jumped on the underground each morning for the short trip to work. The additional rest and shorter travel times seemed to help, and slowly he seemed to improve, and find his feet again. I was grateful but exhausted. My heart was no longer in our adventures, and I was nervous for how long he would stay well before we would be met with the next health crisis. If he suffered depression again, would it be worse? I felt out of my depth and isolated. Ultimately, we decided to return to New Zealand, and were glad to be home, but were also sad that we didn't stay longer in London.

In Auckland, we both secured legal roles with successful commercial firms. Before too long, Mark told me that he didn't want to continue in his role and had resigned. Mark was struggling with his work and had resigned because of his ill health.

THE CRUCIALITY OF SELF-PRESERVATION

Over time, Mark's health continued to decline. I pleaded with him to see a doctor, but he refused to, on the basis that he was "fine" and that he didn't need medication or any other treatment. I knew that he was seriously unwell. He would have very manic highs and lows, be unpredictable, be awake for hours in the night or asleep all day, be completely disengaged and confused, or talk animatedly for hours about all types of obscure topics that I found difficult to understand. I didn't know what I could do.

At my prodding, he would reassure me that he was not at risk to himself or anyone else. I suggested to Mark that we catch up with his family so that I might be able to reach out to them, but he didn't want to. Everything was starting to unravel. I was torn between respecting his privacy and protecting my own sanity and safety.

Eventually, the situation got totally out of control. One night Mark was in a highly manic phase, deluded and pacing through the house, shouting that I was "Satan" and had to be exorcised from his life. He ran into the kitchen and, without thinking, I followed. In the kitchen, Mark threatened me with a large chopping knife, which I managed to wrestle from him, and I then turned and ran from the kitchen to the bathroom, and shut and locked the door. Mark followed and sat on the other side of the door. We talked through the door until he was calm and had promised me that he knew who I was, and that he wouldn't hurt me or himself. Because of his mania, I don't think he really knew or understood how critical the situation had become, and how he had put my safety at risk. I edged the door open, and he stepped aside. That night, I slept in the spare room.

It was an awful predicament to be in, and I was scared. At that point, something had to be done. I spoke to Mark's parents, explaining what had happened, how unwell Mark was, and how crucial it was that Mark receive professional help and treatment. They needed to know the full extent of what had happened so they could appreciate how unwell Mark was, and that the situation was untenable.

I also needed help and, after more than five years, I could no longer carry this burden myself. I couldn't persuade Mark to seek psychiatric treatment, so his parents stepped in and insisted on making the arrangements to get him the professional help he needed.

It wasn't until my own safety had been put at risk that I spoke about it to my parents, who respected my anguish but were extremely concerned for my welfare. Confused, scared and sad, I was grieving for the man I had lost to a dreadful mental illness. I was also grieving all the plans and dreams we had shared for our married life. My parents insisted that I pack some bags and return to their home.

THE VORTEX OF EMOTIONS THAT CREATES INDECISION

I left Auckland broken-hearted, but Mark was in the safe, loving hands of his parents, his extended family and his many friends. Our lives had fallen apart, and I was filled with a terrible vortex of emotions: love and concern for Mark, guilt in deciding that I needed to protect myself, frustration and despair that there seemed to be no answer to the situation. His reticence was symptomatic of his illness and being in complete denial was part of his condition. But knowing this didn't seem to help.

I didn't want to leave but I also knew that I had to do so for my own safety and sanity. It was a terrible dilemma, and a hard decision to make. I changed my mind many times and agonised over what I was to do. But I couldn't solve the situation and Mark didn't seem to believe in 'us' at that moment.

I reasoned that if I left for a while, it might give Mark space to find the clarity and peace that he needed. It also gave Mark's parents, family and friends the opportunity to provide him with their help, support and love. They might be more persuasive with Mark than I was able to be which might just be enough to help him turn his health around.

I also needed to work out what this all meant for us as individuals, and as a couple. I returned to my parents' home in Napier, lost and defeated. Disappointed in myself that I hadn't been able to help Mark rid himself of the terrible cloak of darkness that was his manic depression, and that the 'happily ever after' had eluded us as a young married couple.

JOURNALLING THE SPAGHETTI

I hoped that Mark would recover and be the man that I had fallen in love with so we could resume our lives and have our future together. I spent a lot of time wandering aimlessly in Mum's garden, taking her dogs for long walks (they would be completely exhausted by the time they came home!) and writing down my thoughts that tangled like spaghetti on the pages in my notebooks.

I found distraction in ripping the used pages out at the book's spine, scrunching them into balls, and from my sitting position on my bed, throwing them like basketballs at the hoop that was my bin on the other side of the room. My writing felt therapeutic; it helped me to remove the muddle of thoughts, feelings and questions in my head onto the paper so that I could rest and find some sleep. In the morning, the scribbled pages were a form of private reflection, and I searched for some meaning in the spaghetti of rambles, as if to sort and sift through everything that had happened.

I spent time with my family and my godmother, Ersi, who helped me understand that no one could 'help' Mark unless he also accepted that he needed help and committed to managing his mental (and physical) health. As it turned out, Mark had significant mental health issues as a teenager, and I'm sure that there were many times in his life when he had concealed his inner turmoil and struggles. His health was far more complicated than I had known when we became engaged, and it was disappointing that Mark had not been more honest with me, or with himself.

CROSSING THE PICTON STRAIT TOWARDS NEW HORIZONS

It took some time for me to find my feet again. When I did, my parents convinced me that I should travel to the South Island. My brother Justin lived in Christchurch, and we were good friends.

Heading to Christchurch, I hoped that once Mark received the medical care and attention he so desperately needed, he would come and find me to restart our lives together in what is a skier's and adventure seeker's paradise. Mark had always been a keen adventurer, and he loved the outdoors, having spent a lot of time tramping through New Zealand's forests and trout fishing on its lakes and rivers. This place held the hope of a new start for us both.

I left Hawke's Bay in a small car packed to the roof with my personal belongings. Belting out Alanis Morissette and Crowded House, I drove to Wellington and caught the car ferry to Picton, in the Marlborough

Sounds, and followed the road south to Christchurch.

Spending time with Justin and his family was delightful whilst I found a flat and secured a job in Christchurch. But at times it was lonely as I had not only left Mark behind in Auckland, but also so much of myself. Everything that made up who I was and what defined me had been tossed up in the air and I didn't know when or where it would land. I missed Mark and all the good things of my old life terribly. But in my heart, there was no going back to Auckland, no going back to an unsafe relationship.

After I moved to Christchurch, Mark and I had contact from time to time, but it soon became apparent to me that there was no chance of reconciliation or transformation.

AN IRRATIONAL ACT THAT DEFIES LOGIC

What I wasn't to know was that, towards the end of the following year, Mark would take his own life.

I was shocked and overwhelmed to be told such excruciatingly painful news, and my heart ached in sadness. I struggled to accept Mark's death for a long time. I couldn't understand why he did it, but I knew in my heart that I would never be able to think of a single reason that would ever be a sufficient answer. There is simply no logic to what can only ever be seen as an irrational act.

My brother was a wonderful support and attended Mark's funeral with me. It was a beautiful but incredibly sad farewell to an amazing young man who left an indelible mark on my life, and on the lives of so many who had the privilege to know and love him.

After Mark passed, I spent many years grieving his death, wondering if I could have done anything to change the outcome.

The questions were endless, and I didn't have the answers. But I knew that without regular and ongoing medical treatment and a steadfast commitment to the sound management of his health and wellbeing, it was an impossible situation for Mark, one that we couldn't solve together.

I have always known that as much as Mark's ill health and death is a tragedy in my life, it was a far greater tragedy to have befallen such a young, intelligent, beautiful man who had a kind spirit, but a terribly tortured soul. Mark had had his whole adult life ahead of him, and by his ill health, he was denied the chance to live a happy life. My only lasting hope is that he is now free of the shackles of his mental illness that so bound and crushed him in his lifetime, and that he has found eternal peace.

INSIGHTS

- Our mental health is fundamental to our overall wellness. When we experience mental health issues or conditions, not only does it affect ourselves, but it can significantly impact our loved ones, extended family and friends, work colleagues and wider social network. Our loved ones need to be included in our diagnosis, treatment and health management processes if they are to understand, encourage, assist and support us in our healing.
- A person's apparent stubbornness or denial of their mental health issue may itself be a serious health issue. 'Anosognosia' is a

condition that means you are unable to 'perceive the realities of one's own condition', i.e. to accept you have a condition that has been formally diagnosed. It can occur despite 'second and even third medical opinions confirming the validity of the diagnosis' and results from 'changes to the brain'.[10] It is common in conditions like schizophrenia, bipolar disorder and major depressive disorder. Referral to a psychiatrist is recommended for both diagnosis and treatment.

- Sudden and traumatic death, particularly suicide, can be overwhelming, and catalysts for an enormous myriad of emotions and painful soul searching, deep sorrow, regret, anger, blame and disappointment by loved ones who have been unable to say goodbye, and who may always struggle to accept the reality of the death.
- It can be difficult to share grief in response to a suicide because of the stigma associated with this cause of death. It is often referred to as 'disenfranchised grief' when your loss does not fit social norms and your grief is not openly acknowledged or supported. Apart from suicide, other examples can include miscarriage, or death from AIDS. Often too, it may be that the grief is experienced, but is overlooked or not supported, such as the grief of children or those with intellectual disabilities. In other cases, the behaviour of the grieving may not fit into society's expectations of what is reasonable or acceptable grief.
- On average men comprise 'seven out of every nine suicides' that occur every day in Australia. The number of men who die by

suicide each year is 'nearly double the [Australian] national road toll'.[11]

There is professional support available in the community to provide help and guidance following the loss of someone to suicide, e.g. see:

- www.supportaftersuicide.org.au;
- www.suicidecallbackservice.org.au;
- other support services include Lifeline (13 11 14),
- Kids Helpline (1800 551 800),
- MensLine Australia (1300 789 978),
- Beyond Blue (1300 224 636),
- Headspace (1800 650 890).

CHAPTER FOUR: LEAN ON ME

Love knows not its own depth until the hour of separation.

—Kahlil Gibran

Justin, or Justie, as I used to call him, or "my little brother", which I didn't get away with very often, was a brave, determined and courageous man. These characteristics were manifest in his childhood. When Justin was three or four years old, he broke his collarbone playing on the seesaw at the local park. Not one to cry, Justin jumped up and kept seesawing, but Mum knew better and rushed him to hospital. Justin was also the fastest kid on the block on his much-loved yellow BMX bike. Perhaps Justin's bravery was built on Vegemite, as nearly every photo of him as a child shows him with a very happy Vegemite grin.

After kindergarten, Justin went to Scots College. Mum took the obligatory first-day-at-school photo with Justin proudly wearing his new uniform, a grey suit with shorts past his knees, socks up to his knees, and a cap over his head that covered his face—you only knew that it was Justin because you could see a huge smile on his face as he proudly stood in uniform. Justin loved wearing uniforms. He was very proud of his full-dress kilt of our Irish clan from Mum's family, which he took great delight in wearing on ceremonial occasions, especially at weddings. I'm still not sure whether he wanted to outdress the bride or whether he just loved not having to wear underwear!

Our family moved to Sydney when Justin was ten years old. It was a significant moment for him as he acquired a long, sun-bleached fringe, a surfboard, a tan and the cheeky, interested looks of young girls. But Justin was still shy and still 'scared of girls'. The surf at Manly was far easier to manage.

A few years later, when our family returned to New Zealand and settled in Hawke's Bay, Justin went to school at Napier Boys High School. This was the beginning of many adventures for the baby in the family who could get away with just about anything, because it was always done with a beguiling, cheeky grin. Justin was a keen equestrian and owned a sixteen-hand horse that he named Paddy, an ode to Justin's Irish heritage. With his Irish Setter and Paddy, he would roam the Hawke's Bay plains from dawn to dusk at the weekends.

Justin was also a keen rugby player, playing for the Napier Boys High first XV rugby team as hooker, and senior rugby for the Colenso Pirates in Napier and the Sydenham Cavaliers in Christchurch. He was also a star player in several touch rugby teams, including one of my work touch rugby teams. He only played five minutes of touch rugby with my teammates for them to see his talent, and name him captain. We played many games together and it was a lot of fun.

Another of Justin's great loves was for animals. It was his affinity with animals that prompted him to pursue a position in the Dog Handling Section of the New Zealand Police. But well before that, Kergen, a Rottweiler, was his first experiment, whom he trained to perfection.

Justin had many recreational experiments. One was brewing beer. Justin loved entertaining his friends poolside at our parents' house, serving his home-brewed beer. The first glass tasted revolting, but the second glass blew your socks off. The beer was so potent that numerous bottles would explode at times, with the caps hitting the roof of the shed. Another of his experiments was car conversion, totally honest, of course. Justin's first car was a Ford Cortina, which he and our brother George proceeded to strip and paint British Racing Green, along with the garage floor. But it wasn't enough to convince him that this had career potential. Justin had his sights set on joining the New Zealand Police.

One afternoon, Justin went to the physical test for recruitment, and completed the physical tests in the time required, but was just an eighth of a centimetre too short in height. The recruitment officer suggested that Justin return to the interview early the next morning. He came home devastated, but I encouraged him to think and feel tall. The next morning, Justin jumped out of bed, and with a very straight spine and a very tall neck, he was measured as having the minimum height.

TRAINING AS A POLICE OFFICER

Justin joined the New Zealand Police as a member of the 121st recruit wing. At Police College, he met a fellow recruit, both young men with similar happy, excitable personalities who would become best friends, both as recruits and as officers over many years of service. They had a real adventure together at Police College. Their antics were legendary.

In the barracks, Justin decided that the spare room on their level should become the team's bar. However, Justin realised that John's room across the hall was larger and would make a better bar, but John couldn't be persuaded to swap rooms. While John was away one weekend, Justin climbed out onto the ledge, shimmied along, and let himself into John's room. He then organised his fellow recruits to help him move all of John's belongings into the smaller room, placing everything where it had been, right down to the photos on the noticeboard. When John returned from his weekend away, Justin was sitting in 'The Bar' with a beer ready for John.

Justin was a terrific recruit who, from his first day at college, fell in love with his career and the police family. On graduation, Justin became Constable D391. He was stationed in Henderson, Auckland, before transferring to Christchurch. He was known as a highly capable police officer who was compassionate and gregarious, with a wicked sense of humour, attributes that endeared him to many.

A LIFE-SAVING HERO BRIMMING WITH HUMILITY AND GRACE

In the small hours one night on patrol, Justin saw a house on fire. Immediately stopping and investigating, he heard a noise from inside the house. Without regard for his own safety, he scaled the wall of the burning house, smashed a bathroom window and pulled himself into the house. He scrambled along the floor amid thick black smoke, searching each room until he found a pair of feet. Justin then dragged the trapped occupant to safety and pushed the unconscious man out of the house. Just as Justin climbed from the house, it exploded into flames. The press became aware of the fire, and a reporter rushed to the scene, securing a photo of Justin and his fellow officers on the lawn of the house, recovering from the ordeal, their lungs filled with smoke. It was a terrific story for the *Christchurch Press* newspaper, and it made front page news the next day.

For his bravery, Justin was awarded the Royal Humane Society Bronze Medal for courage and humanity. At a special meeting held at Christchurch Council, he was presented with the medal by the then mayor of Christchurch, Mr Garry Moore. The Royal Humane Society stated:

"There is no doubt that Justin Gallate's actions resulted in a life being saved at considerable risk to his own."

I was so proud of Justin for saving another man's life. It was the epitome of courage and selflessness, and one of life's greatest achievements. It also made me appreciate that my brother was saving lives in his job every day. But he simply shrugged it off; he was an incidental hero, and it was all in a day's work.

FINDING HIS VOCATION

Justin always felt that the best part about policing was catching the bad guys, and what better way to track them than with a 50kg German Shepherd, and from time to time, watch as the dog stopped them in their tracks and made the arrest. This was Justin's dream, and he was thrilled when he became a member of the Christchurch Police Dog Section.

Justin was incredibly excited about this new stage in his policing career. He had found his vocation in life. He would often say to me, "I love my job, Lise, I just love it!" He was never late, his reasoning being why be late to something you love. "I just can't wait to get there." He was the only person I knew who jumped out of bed to get to work.

Justin had to complete further training at the New Zealand Police Dog Training Centre with his police dog, a ferocious-looking Alsatian called Sabre. On graduation, Justin was given his 'O' stamp, and together they were deemed an operational team. Justin formed strong friendships with his fellow police dog handlers and his sergeant. Following a training session one day, the team finished with a few beverages at a bar in central Christchurch. Opposite this bar was a fancy dress shop. Justin loved organising and dressing up for all sorts of letter-of-the-alphabet and toga parties.

Not one to miss an opportunity to dress up, Justin vanished from the bar and reappeared a short while later in a chicken suit. He was unidentifiable and spent the next few hours following (or perhaps terrorising) patrons and pedestrians. The bar patrons also found him very entertaining and bought him drinks. After a few hours of the chicken dance, Justin came back to his team's table sweating profusely and very tipsy! Justin was a great entertainer, both in and out of a chicken suit!

Justin and Sabre qualified as an Armed Offenders Squad operational team, which meant that they could be put into armed and dangerous situations in which Justin would use Sabre to defuse the situation and take the alleged offender into custody.

During their partnership together, Justin and Sabre would attend over nine hundred jobs and have many catches. His best friend recalls that Justin and Sabre "had an uncanny bond and were an elite crime-fighting unit. Justin loved sharing his war stories with me of tracking offenders at night and then catching them. He loved it and lived it." Justin and Sabre were a formidable pair, and Justin loved every minute of his work.

WHAT LIES BENEATH

Two months after Justin became operational as a police dog handler, he was playing rugby for the Sydenham Cavaliers one Saturday afternoon and hit the ground at the bottom of the collapsed scrum. Justin was rushed to hospital.

Because he had suffered a seizure when the scrum collapsed, Justin's medical team carried out several tests, including head scans. It was only because of this accident, and the medical investigations that followed, that Justin was diagnosed with an aggressive form of brain cancer (known as Glioblastoma or GBM brain cancer).

It was horrific and incomprehensible news. Justin was my baby brother. How could this be happening? It seemed surreal that Justin should now be faced with having to fight such a terrible disease.

The unfairness struck me hard. Justin was such a gregarious and kind man who deserved every happiness in his life. He was married to a loving wife, and together they had two very young, gorgeous children to love and parent. He had also found his vocation as a police officer and dog handler, and together with Sabre and his colleagues, had made an enormous contribution to protect his community. Why was this now happening to him?

Justin's medical team decided that he would require brain surgery, to reduce the impact of the tumour by removing as much of it as possible.

Given it is very delicate surgery with very significant risks, it was a terrifying prospect for Justin and his family. The risks included causing problems with his speech, memory, balance, vision and co-ordination, blood clots or bleeding in the brain, seizures, strokes and brain swelling. It was small thanks that Justin was young, fit and otherwise healthy, and stood every chance of managing the surgery without complications.

Thankfully, Justin got through the surgery, but it was then followed by extensive bouts of chemotherapy to kill the cancer cells, to stop them from growing and dividing into more cells. This was an awful but necessary treatment that Justin managed with dignity, even when it seemed to knock him sideways and made him feel ghastly.

Before Justin's diagnosis, I had no real understanding or knowledge of brain cancer and hoped that my brother would be able to fight and recover from this cancer with the same tenacity and strength he had shown throughout his life.

DRIVING MISS DAISY

Amazingly, after the incredibly invasive treatment that he endured without complaint, Justin recovered enough to return to work. He couldn't wait to be back in uniform with his beloved Sabre, catching the bad guys. Everyone at the police station was as amazed as his family. Although unable to drive, Justin still went to work each day and was driven to each new job, with Sabre excitedly barking in the back of the van. Justin would jump out of the van and do what he did best. It was a standing joke that to be driving Justin, it was 'driving Miss Daisy'. But

Justin didn't care, he was grateful for the help. And his best friend was "lucky enough" one night to be assigned to drive Justin and Sabre in his dog van for a shift. His best friend recalls how "Ces[12] [Justin's nickname] had incredible enthusiasm; his drive to catch crooks was incredible. Ces was a very proud police officer."

Justin was fortunate to spend at least twelve months in his role as a dog handler. But eventually, his declining health forced him from the Dog Section, and Sabre was reassigned. It must surely have been Justin's saddest day in the police force.

THE FIGHT OF HIS LIFE

Justin was now facing the fight of his life—to save his own life. He had a wife and young family that desperately needed their husband and father. Justin had further brain surgery to remove as much of the tumour as possible, buying him more time.

The brain surgery left a significant scar on the top of Justin's now bald head, but it didn't take anything away from his handsome face, and in any case, he didn't care. He would also suffer whatever chemotherapy he had to have, as he was so keen to get back to spending precious time with his own family, to living his life, and getting back to work. Justin did everything he could to beat the cancer. He stood in his kitchen late at night, peeling carrots to make carrot juice (as they are recognised as an important source of natural antioxidants having anti-cancer activity). He also participated in all sorts of natural and alternative therapies, ate a healthy diet, avoided alcohol and other toxins, and stayed physically active. I'm sure that all his efforts and energies to get well helped him to have the best quality of life that he could have, for as long as he could have it.

Justin was eventually able to return to work, but he couldn't resume his duties as a dog handler. Still, he was keen to be back at work even if it meant "driving a desk in recruitment". He continued working in recruitment until just shortly before his death. Such was the character of my brother.

I was in Sydney when I got the call. I should have been emotionally ready for it, but I wasn't. I couldn't believe that my younger brother was coming to the end of a very hard-fought battle, and that there had been no miracle.

There is often no logic, rationale or principle to explain the vagaries of life. Although I knew this, since Zoie and James and Mark had died, I had spent so much of my daily life, and sometimes the middle of the night, trying to make sense of their deaths, searching for some reason or explanation for why they had lost their lives when they were so young; their adult lives were just taking shape and purpose.

WHEN LOVE NEEDS NO VOICE

I flew to Christchurch and met up with my family. My mother was totally bereft, and Dad was struggling to say much at all. They were devastated. We went to see Justin, to say goodbye. My beautiful baby brother was lying in bed, so close to passing, and yet trying to muster all the energy he could to hug me. He was a shell of the man that he had been. Justin, who always delighted in big bear hugs when we met up, was now softly wrapping his arms around me, just as death was quietly cloaking him. My brother couldn't speak, but he didn't need to. It was enough just to feel his love; it didn't need a voice.

After Justin passed, he was dressed in his police dog handler uniform and stayed at his home until his funeral. Over the next several days before his funeral, Justin was kept company by lots of wonderful family, colleagues and friends. It was special time for all of us to be with him, to be near him and to share him, and it helped spending that time with him to come to terms with the reality that he had died. It also gave time for family overseas to travel to Christchurch for his funeral. I knew they would come. Justin was popular with everyone who knew him, including his extended family, and I don't think I ever met anyone who didn't love him. I was so grateful that Mum's sisters, and Uncle Stathi and Aunty Beth flew from Australia for Justin's funeral. It was wonderful to have their support, and I know that Mum and Dad really appreciated it. Many close friends to Justin, and to his family, travelled from all over New Zealand to attend his funeral. Some of my best friends also attended. I was so glad that they were all with us.

Mum and Dad asked me to prepare a eulogy. Aside from wondering if I would be able to write it, I wasn't sure, with all my emotions, that I would be able to read it. Would I burst into tears, find that I couldn't see to read the page for the tears filling my eyes, lose my breath or have a panic attack that stopped me in my tracks? I didn't want to say I wouldn't do it, as I felt it was the least I could do for my brother. After all that he had endured, I felt that I must surely be able to manage a few minutes talking about his wonderful life.

WRITING A EULOGY CAN BE CATHARTIC

As it transpired, it was cathartic time spent individually with family, listening to their memories and adding their stories to our eulogy. After all, these were the family memories that we could easily share. There were many other special memories that we would keep close, but there were so many that it made our eulogy very easy to write. I would have liked to have had time to talk to more of our extended family, so I could share their memories as well. I regret that I did not have the temerity to share more memories of Zoie and Justin together in our family eulogy, but I was only just now folding away some of those memories of her in my own mind, and they were too precious and heartbreaking to share.

A SEA OF BLUE TO FAREWELL A LEGEND

The day of Justin's funeral arrived too soon. I wasn't ready for it, and instead focused my energies on looking after Mum and Dad. Dad was extremely hoarse and desperately sad. Mum was also distraught. I wasn't even sure that she would get through the service. I was so glad that Mum's sisters could take her by each arm and gently lead her into the funeral, although I think they almost carried her. I escorted Dad. Mum wore a black outfit with a beautiful mustard camel coat that she had purchased on an overseas trip with Dad. It was Justin's favourite coat on Mum, and she wore it in his memory. Dad wore his best suit. They were beautifully dressed.

It was an amazing funeral. The commissioner of police, the O.I.C. Canterbury Police District and other dignitaries attended, as well as police officers from Christchurch and all over New Zealand, including officers and operational dogs from Dog Handling Sections in both the North and South Islands. It was a sea of blue. It seemed that there were many hundreds of mourners at Justin's service. He would have been overwhelmed, and very humbled, by the incredible turnout for his farewell.

My brother George read Edgar Albert Guest's poem 'A Child of Mine,'[13] which would resonate with any family that has lost a child. The poem was a stark reminder to all of us that day that even as an adult with his own young family, Justin was himself still a son, still the child of our parents, whose hearts had been forever broken by his untimely death.

CANDLES ARE SYMBOLS OF COMFORT AND HOPE, OF LIGHT OVER DARKNESS AND LIFE ETERNAL

As the celebrant announced that we would now listen to some eulogies celebrating Justin's life, I lit a candle and approached the lectern. Taking some deep breaths, I read our eulogy to the sea of blue without falling apart, and then went back to my seat, relieved but exhausted.

Justin's best friend followed, giving a very sincere and funny eulogy on behalf of all of Justin's friends and work colleagues, recalling some wonderful memories of their friendship, as well as Justin's amazing career in the New Zealand police. "*If the New Zealand police had more people like Ces, we would be invincible at anything. The New Zealand police lost a great copper, an awesome workmate, and a legend."*

The final eulogy was prepared by Justin's wife about their married life and their young family and read on her behalf by a close friend.

The service was a wonderful farewell in honour of my brother. I wanted to stay there in that moment in time, so that we didn't have to face the end, the final goodbye. But before I knew it, we had reached the end of the service, and it was time for Justin to be carried to the hearse.

My father was asked to make a commendation or prayer for his youngest son. Dad stood at the front of the service next to Justin's coffin and prayed for his son in Greek and then repeated the prayer in English.

"To our most precious husband, son, brother, and friend Justinian
With God's blessing proceed speedily now to the
Elysian fields of your ancestors
That beautiful place that is a blazing mass of
flowers and onto life eternal."

Dad was nearly hoarse, and his voice was strangled by his emotions. He could hardly speak. I felt so sorry for him. Just as cruel as it was for Mum, Dad shouldn't have had to carry the burden of losing two of his children as young, vibrant adults with the world at their feet. Dad would carry that burden with him for the rest of his life.

Sabre, with one of Justin's colleagues, then led Justin out of the service. It was a very poignant, symbolic moment. Outside, the driveway was lined with police dogs sitting in position, their handlers next to them. As the handlers and their dogs had been getting ready, we had heard the dogs barking and whining from inside the service. As we exited the service, it was the most incredible scene, so many dogs sitting still and silent, just as my brother's coffin was laid into the hearse to travel to the crematorium.

The next day, I left Christchurch and flew with my parents and aunties to my parents' home in Napier. We were all devastated and spent quiet time out on the deck, going for walks down the country roads, or walking through Mum's vast garden. It was a beautiful garden in which over many years of hard work and love, Mum had created lots of beautiful flowerbeds with hedges and bushes, secret pathways and little love seats. It was an easy garden in which to wander and get lost in thought.

Despite the cocoon of my parents' home and the love of family, I had to return to Sydney for work. I felt broken and alone as none of my Sydney friends or work colleagues knew my brother, and understandably, would not appreciate the enormity of my grief. It was another challenge that lay ahead.

A TOUCHING VISIT FROM THE AFTERLIFE

Some years later, I was on maternity leave and sitting outside my home in the back garden with my three-year-old daughter, Kyra. It was summer and warm. My daughter had never met my brother, and I had never talked about him to her.

Suddenly, she said, "Mummy, Justin is here."

I was spooked by her words. It raised the hairs on my arms, and I thought I would fall off the chair. Surely my daughter wasn't seeing or feeling my brother's spiritual presence?

Instead, I said, "That's nice, honey, what did he say to you?"

She replied, "'Hi, I'm Justin.' Mummy, who's Justin?"

I said, "Oh, he's my brother," as calmly as I could. I couldn't believe it. Could this really be my brother's spirit, making itself known to my daughter? I asked her if he said anything else.

"No, not really. He said to say hi, but he's going now, he's going down the road."

I wasn't fast enough to think of questions for her to ask him, to keep him with us for just a little longer. It was a surreal moment, but young children are often intuitive, and can have psychic ability. I don't know yet if my daughter does, but I would like to think that Justin visited her that day, and that he was with us, even if it was just for a few fleeting moments.

INSIGHTS

- The 'sibling relationship' is a unique relationship and can be one of the most enduring. Often, we are more open and transparent to our siblings than we are to our parents, spouse, children or friends. They are formed in our early years and are amongst our earliest relationships. They will often stay with us into adulthood, and late adulthood, until we are separated by death. They may offer us love, protection, security, reassurance and affirmation of our self-identity, self-confidence and connection. Yet it is one of the most overlooked relationships in our modern society when someone dies.

- There is currently no known cure for brain cancer worldwide. A malignant brain tumour can sometimes be cured if it is identified and treated early, but a brain tumour will often grow back, and may not be able to be completely and successfully removed.
- Around 2000 Australians develop brain cancer every year.[14] Cancer (all forms) is the leading cause of death in New Zealand with more than 25,000 New Zealanders being diagnosed with some form of cancer each year. [15]
- Brain cancer kills more children than any other disease and more people under forty than any other cancer. The worst type of cancer, GBM (Glioblastoma Multiforme cancer) is the most common, with an 'average survival rate of only 15 months from diagnosis'. Brain cancer survival rates have hardly changed in thirty years. Only two out of ten will survive at least five years and less than one out of ten with GBM will be alive at five years.[16]
- There are multiple initiatives in Australia devoted to research, or to supporting research, into brain cancer to improve the lives of brain cancer patients, and to find a cure for brain cancer.[17]

CHAPTER FIVE: LOVE, LOSS AND NEW LIFE

Look for the remedy inside the pain because the rose came from the thorn and the ruby came from a stone.

—Rumi

I had always wanted to be a mother, not least because I owed it to the memory of my sister, Zoie. I also spent most of my adult life thinking that I would fall pregnant easily when I was ready to start a family.

One Saturday, I met Ben through mutual friends at a party in a private suite at the Rosehill Races.

"Hi, there, I'm Ben." Ben was dressed in a dark suit and looked at me with intense green eyes. With his dark hair, tanned skin and a lovely smirk, he had my attention! I immediately thought he looked like a mix between Elvis Presley, Alec Baldwin and Ben Affleck.

"Hi, I'm Lisa."

"I love your hat," said Ben.

"Thanks, so do I."

"It sets off your eyes."

"Umm, thanks," I mused. "But my eyes are brown, and the hat is black."

"Oh yes, you're right! Well, it just really frames your face nicely, brown-eyed girl."

"Haha, thanks! So how do you know Jane and Dave ?" I asked.

"I work with Dave. What about you?" replied Ben.

"Actually, I work with Jane, or at least we work in the same firm."

"Oh, so you're a bean counter as well?"

"No, it's worse. I'm a lawyer." Finally, I had made this funny man laugh.

"Oh well, I guess it could be worse. Can I offer you a tip?" he asked.

"Yes, sure, I think we are up to race three," I pondered.

"Always be good to your mother."

So, he was cheeky as well as funny.

"Gee, thanks, a great tip. I am really good to my mum. But more on that later, race three is about to run. Any BETTING tips?"

"Actually, I do. And I have lots more. Sooo, I think you should stay close to me today, have some champers, and tell me all about your mum."

I was immediately taken by this handsome, charming man and his gregarious nature as he offered me betting tips and flirted with me. His betting tips didn't prove to be successful, but his charm was extremely successful, and although I had to leave the party early, I didn't forget him.

Some months later, our friends organised another race party at their apartment during Melbourne's Spring Racing Season calendar. I was thrilled when I saw Ben arrive. We all had a wonderful day watching the races on a projector and placing our bets. We didn't make any money, but were in great company, and the hospitality was fabulous.

Ben and I started our relationship that day. It went from strength to strength, and we then decided to take the plunge and live together.

We lived in a small apartment overlooking Manly Cove, Sydney, where the Manly Ferry departs for Circular Quay, and bars and restaurants hug the edge of the Cove. They soon became our local favourites, a stone's throw from our apartment, with sensational water views. One day, whilst sitting on our balcony surveying the harbour with my binoculars, I spotted Ben on the Manly Wharf Bar pontoon. I called him.

"Hi, honey, when do you expect to be home?"

"Soon, when the next boat arrives." Interestingly, not a lie, but not the whole truth. As a lawyer, I always sought out 'the truth, the whole truth, and nothing but the truth!'

"Okaaaay, so when is that?"

"Ahh, soon," said Ben as I watched him turning his shoulder to look out to sea and spot the next ferry.

"I think in about ten to fifteen minutes."

"Okay, that's great, that should give you enough time to finish the beer you are drinking on the pontoon."

"What?"

"Haha, you're sprung." It was hilarious, watching Ben as he looked around, and then looked up towards the apartment, as I waved to him from the balcony.

"See you soon, honey."

It became our standing joke. Ben also played the prank on me, if I deviated for a quick drink with friends at one of the bars on my walk home from the ferry.

We also spent many hours on our balcony enjoying the water views, the sunsets and the parakeets in the trees. The parakeets often visited our balcony in the hope of some food. Such friendly, colourful birds, and we loved their company.

From our apartment, we walked to any one of several beaches in Manly, depending on the time of day, the wind direction, the swell of the surf and our energy levels. We also ran regularly from Manly Cove to Forty Baskets, before climbing up a rocky embankment and cliff to Dobroyd Point. From there, we enjoyed fantastic views out to the Heads and the Pacific Ocean, as well as south to Circular Quay and the Central Business District. It was such a relief to get to the top of our run. The sea breeze was so refreshing, and it was a chance to stop and catch our breath.

However, just like any other alpha male, Ben saw every run as a competition, so I always had to run faster than my usual pace just to keep up. Most days I didn't mind, as I was the endurance runner, and whilst he might be faster, he lacked the distance.

One morning as we ran back around Manly Cove towards home, I said we should walk and talk.

"Ben, honey, I have been thinking."

"Yessss, that sounds dangerous. What is it now? What have I done wrong this time?"

"Haha, don't you know?" I retorted.

"Ha, now if I knew that, I would be a lucky man indeed. A bit like Mel Gibson in that movie." He was referring to *What Women Want*.

"Okay, okay, same joke every time. SO, anyways, I was thinking that we should start trying for a family. As you know, I am not getting any younger, but then, neither are you."

"No, that's true," pondered Ben.

"I know that we have only been together for a few years, and we live in a shoebox," I said.

"But it does have a fabulous view," added Ben.

"That's also true. But you can't raise a family in a view."

"No, we can't, but aren't we only thinking of having one child? We have our small love shack by the sea with plenty of room for a baby."

"Well, yes, for the moment at least. So, what do you think?" I didn't want us to get off track talking about numbers of children. We could start with one.

"Honey, I would love for us to have children. And there's no time like the present."

"Okay, great! Are you sure?" I asked, rather worried I had sabotaged our run and pressured Ben into a life-changing commitment.

"Yes, I'm sure, I think! It's a great idea, and you will be a great mum."

"Thanks, honey, I hope so."

We both felt that becoming pregnant would happen easily and naturally, and that it wouldn't be long before we could share the news with our family and friends that we were pregnant. Our optimism was short-lived.

After several months, we found out that getting pregnant is a lot harder than you might think. Or just harder when you desperately want it to happen! Over time, we tried to become more scientific about it, but we had no better luck. I became paranoid by the process, and would randomly take pregnancy tests, in the belief that the test could detect sufficient HCC (human chorionic gonadotropin) days before my period. Over many months, it became an agonising process. Any sense of romance was long gone.

I couldn't think of anything else. Over time, I appreciated how desperate people can become in the quest to have a baby. I had joined their club.

We saw my doctor—a very humbling experience to express our desire to start our family, and how we had failed. He was extremely sympathetic, and encouraged us to keep trying for a further four to six months, after which we would be referred to a fertility specialist. I left the appointment with information on infertility and hope in my heart that all was not lost.

Remarkably, a short time later, we fell pregnant. We were ecstatic! And I had the home pregnancy test to prove it. Even so, I wasn't going to take any chances, and I visited my doctor for a blood test to confirm the result. Showing positive, I was thrilled. I was rather proud of myself and Ben. We decided that we wouldn't share our news with anyone until we had reached the end of the first trimester at thirteen weeks. It was a wonderful secret to hold close to our hearts.

THE QUIET TRAGEDY OF A MISCARRIAGE

Some weeks later, we miscarried. It was the most emotionally agonising experience that had come from nowhere. I had thought that we would be parents with our first pregnancy, but it was not to be. I couldn't help but feel that I had been through enough in my lifetime, and that I didn't deserve this quiet tragedy. The hardest thing of all was that our pregnancy had been our secret, so it made the miscarriage hard to share.

Miscarriage is such an awful phenomenon. Since the causes are still mostly unknown, it is like a curse, and something that no one wants to talk about. I found it incredibly hard to talk about my experience to anyone. It was also the enormity of the loss, which had been made worse by the fact that we had been trying to conceive for nearly eighteen months, and I was fixated on getting pregnant.

We decided to try again for another three to four months. Whilst we nursed our grief and contemplated trying again, I continued to take folic acid and tried to stay as healthy as possible. I ran regularly, swam in the ocean, limited my glasses of wine, and only ate healthy food. I would do all I could to make it happen again.

And happen it did. We fell pregnant for a second time. We were thrilled. But this second time, we knew better than to think too far ahead. After confirming the pregnancy with my doctor, we decided that we would think no further than the twelve-week scan. We knew that there was a high risk of another miscarriage. Even so, that didn't prepare us for when I again miscarried.

We were both so disappointed and it was hard to hide. I was upset to my core. I felt I would never overcome the sense of emptiness and despair that I felt at that moment. It felt brutal. I still couldn't share my grief with anyone.

THE AGONY OF AN UNEXPLAINABLE LOSS

I struggled to understand why I had miscarried again. I would have liked nothing more than for my sister, Zoie, to have scooped me up with her warm embrace and nursed me through my despair. She was such an empathetic person and would have loved to sit and listen as I poured out my grief, shock, anger and sense of unfairness.

Ben was very rational in thinking that there was either a reason for the miscarriage, or that it was just not meant to be. His stoic attitude didn't fit with my emotional response, feeling that maybe I was being punished in some way, that Lady Luck was not on my side, and that this was yet another lesson for me to learn about life, with all its machinations and cruelties.

Our different reactions became another hurdle for us to overcome. After almost two years of trying to conceive, and two miscarriages, we were exhausted by the emotional rollercoaster when we had assumed it was the most natural and easiest thing to do. I had now felt the excitement of being pregnant twice, and as much as I hadn't thought too far ahead, I had allowed myself to daydream, about the idea of one day holding my own baby. Instead, I had suffered the disappointment and emotional turmoil of two miscarriages. I had lost what I had for so long been striving for, and it had been taken away from me so unexpectedly. No one could offer me an explanation for why it had happened not once, but twice. Although there are some recognised common causes, there was nothing to definitively explain our loss.

My doctor urged us to see a fertility specialist if we still wanted to try for a family. By medical standards, I would be an 'old mother', so I had to act fast. Although this thought horrified me, it motivated me to act. I was determined that we exhaust all our options before we gave up.

We attended our appointment with the fertility specialist at salubrious offices in the heart of Sydney City. In the reception, we were met by a very handsome man, dressed in what looked to be an expensive suit.

"Hi, I'm David , please come in."

We entered his office, which had stunning views out to Darling Harbour. I could see the water sparkling in the sunshine, perhaps a good omen.

"So, as you may know, miscarriages are not uncommon. In terms of numbers, we know that fifteen to twenty percent of all pregnancies end in miscarriage. But the difference is that most miscarriages are the loss of a single pregnancy, and the woman will then go on to conceive and have a baby. Given your situation of having experienced more than one miscarriage, you are experiencing a recurrent pregnancy loss, which only occurs to one in twenty couples."

"I see, Doctor. And so, what do you think that means for us?"

"It's likely that there is something wrong, so we should perform some medical procedures before we look at IVF (in vitro fertilisation)."

We both passed the tests. Thankfully, there was nothing unusual to be concerned about. Instead, the specialist thought that our challenge to conceive might just be explained by my age.

As women's fertility peaks at twenty-two years of age and then declines, it becomes an issue at thirty-three years of age when the chance of natural conception is only about 17% and then falls dramatically to about 11% from the age of thirty-eight. By forty years of age, it is about 7%. I wasn't aware of these dire statistics, and of course, the fertility specialist could do nothing about my age.

AUDENTES FORTUNA IUVAT – FORTUNE FAVOURS THE BRAVE

We read the IVF information and decided to take the plunge. My dad has always said that "fortune favours the brave".[18]

I held tight to this thought, deciding that if we were to embark on this journey, I would be as positive as I could be about it, and do everything in my power to make it work.

I also felt privileged that IVF was a medical procedure that was easily accessible to us and relatively affordable. I was conscious that many other couples around the world can't access this service, and that many more couples may try multiple rounds unsuccessfully. I was reassured that we were in good hands as our specialist and his medical team had been engaged in fertility treatment and involved in advancing IVF technology for over thirty years. The result was a very streamlined IVF procedure.

I had to have a blood test before I could start the fertility medications, to confirm that I wasn't pregnant—what a nice surprise that would have been! Sadly, I wasn't.

THE LUCRIN HOUR

I was sent home with my first fertility drug, Lucrin, to begin treatment. Lucrin is a drug that suppresses the pituitary, to prevent the premature release of developing follicles. The drug was contained in vials that I had to insert into the equivalent of an Epi-Pen and inject into my stomach daily, for about three to four weeks, at the same time every day. Nine p.m. each night became the Lucrin Hour. I had to adjust the dial on the Epi-Pen according to how much of the drug I required, based on regular blood tests over the course of the month. It was an emotional rollercoaster.

There was also nothing romantic or simple about the process.

Day thirty arrived.

I had the Lucrin blood test to again check if I had conceived naturally—no such luck!

THE KITCHEN BECOMES MY PHARMACY

The next stage was to start a second medication, FSH (follicle stimulating hormone) to stimulate the development of multiple eggs for in vitro fertilisation. I couldn't help but feel like a chicken on her nest. Since FSH is administered by daily injections, I used the Epi-Pen at home in the kitchen.

Finally, at a designated time and date, I needed to give myself the trigger injection. This required me to play pharmacist and break up and mix certain medications. It was just a step too far for me, so Ben mixed them for me.

We were now on a time frame and would be called into the clinic within the next thirty-six hours.

THE MAGIC OF THE PETRI DISH

Many people used to think that IVF meant test tube babies, but the process just involves bringing the eggs and sperm together on glass inside a lab. The developing embryos are then monitored for several days, before an embryo is transferred to develop inside the mother. If there are any additional healthy embryos, they can be frozen and used at another time.

After the egg retrieval process, we had to wait to find out how our little embryos progressed. It is such a clinical process, and one that was totally foreign to us. On day five, I received THE phone call that we had just one healthy embryo for transfer. Ben wanted to immediately call "all the family".

"No, you can't! It's way too early. We have no idea what's going to happen."

"I know, you're right—again! But I'm just so excited that I want to tell the world."

"I get it, but the world doesn't need to know right now that we only have one healthy embryo sitting in a lab in a clinic! Let's just take it one step at a time and go in for the transfer."

After the transfer, we were sent home with the well wishes of our IVF team. I felt physically and emotionally exhausted by the whole process. I was so glad to go home for some rest and respite, in the hope that we might now be on our way to a healthy pregnancy and become parents.

HOLDING THE LINE

We were advised to have a blood pregnancy test fourteen days after the transfer and to avoid taking a home pregnancy test, in case of a false positive result. I was impatient waiting for fourteen days but accepted that a false positive result would be a cruel outcome. We just had to sit tight.

I was incredibly excited to find out that I was pregnant, but the IVF didn't mean that there was any less risk of another miscarriage. It had just made it an expensive pregnancy! Because of the earlier miscarriages, and my age, my doctor recommended that we see our obstetrician.

Our pregnancy was confirmed with an ultrasound image. It was amazing to hear life inside me—to hear the heartbeat and see this little bean on the ultrasound.

I was so excited and hoped with all my heart that this pregnancy would be successful. I felt so confident that I started buying lots of books about pregnancy, including *Up the Duff* by Kaz Cooke. I wanted to read about the pregnancy process from start to finish, but only read each chapter as I reached that month of the pregnancy. It was a wonderful adventure to be pregnant—to get past the dreaded first trimester, and then to keep learning and growing, literally, as I continued into the second trimester.

THE SERENITY OF A TROPICAL HOLIDAY

At the second trimester, Ben and I celebrated by taking a short holiday to Bali, using a voucher I had 'won' at a corporate cancer charity auction for accommodation at the fabulous Laguna Hotel in Nusa Dua. Now seemed like a perfect opportunity to use it.

We had a fabulous holiday, the highlight of which was that Ben proposed to me! But this was not a standard proposal as Ben had arranged a private outdoors dining experience by one of the pools and the beach, that included tree lights, a music system, our own stage, a flower-strewn path and the most delicious menu. Having missed out on so much romance in our relationship over the last two years, it was perfect. The answer was a very easy yes!

It was great to have a break from the pressures we had imposed on ourselves to get pregnant. Our hotel was such a lovely, serene sanctuary with wonderful hosts and staff, and the holiday really helped us to refresh and ready ourselves for the rest of my pregnancy and the daunting reality of becoming parents. I was now acutely aware that I needed our pregnancy to reach at least thirty weeks, as babies can be born and survive at that stage, even though they will be very premature. If I could stay pregnant until I was full term, it would be a blessing.

Since there aren't many surprises in life once you become an adult, we decided not to find out the sex of our baby. It meant we missed out on a gender reveal party! But it would be a wonderful and complete surprise.

In the last trimester, I continued to work full-time. It was summer and I decided that I wanted to have as much maternity leave after the baby arrived as possible.

BABY NAMES CAN BE LEGACIES OF LOVED ONES

Our little, but completely healthy, baby girl was born in January, at thirty-nine weeks. We named her Kyra Zoie. Kyra is of Old Persian origin and means 'Sun'. It is also of Greek origin meaning 'Of the Lord'. Kyra, my baby daughter, also had to be named after my beloved sister, Zoie. I had contemplated calling her Zoie as her first name, but I knew that this name could only ever mean my sister to our family and friends, and I didn't want my daughter to grow up in Zoie's shadow. If my sister could be my daughter's guardian angel, then that would be perfect.

Kyra was born late at night, so it wasn't until the small hours of the morning that we had quiet time together, when I could watch and enjoy her lying next to me. I was amazed by how little and perfect she was. She was the most beautiful baby, and I was so incredibly proud of her, and of Ben and I as new parents.

We were thrilled to have lots of visitors in hospital from family and friends and were inundated with beautiful flowers. There were so many bouquets in our room that both Kyra and I started reacting to them, and some of our beautiful blooms were moved to the nurses' station, until we were able to take them home. It was a wonderful celebration of new life.

On the way home with Kyra in the car for her first time, we were neurotic parents. I sat in the back seat with Kyra.

"Ben, slow down."

"Honey, I don't think she likes the car."

"Watch the corners, don't take them so quickly."

Ben drove home slowly, much slower than the speed limit of sixty kilometres per hour. It was a first for Ben!

We thoroughly enjoyed being parents to our baby Kyra. But it wasn't long before I started contemplating the idea of trying for another baby. My conversations with Ben regularly included asking:

"Honey, do you think we should try for another baby?"

"Honey, we need to talk about whether we try for a sibling for Kyra."

"Honey, do you want to try to add to our family?"

Ben wasn't as keen as I was to expand our family and needed some convincing. He had seen the emotional challenge of two miscarriages and the IVF treatment, and he wasn't sure that we should try for more children and risk more heartache.

"Ben, let's just try for a short time. I feel that I owe it to Kyra to at least try to give her a sibling. When she is older, I want to be able to say that we tried our best and it wasn't meant to be."

"I know, but I am just worried about you."

"I understand, I get it. But after the loneliness I have gone through from losing Zoie and Justin, I don't want Kyra to be an only child."

"Okay, but I don't want you to be devastated if we aren't successful. We have a beautiful, healthy daughter so we should be grateful for her and just enjoy her."

"I know and I am, she is our little miracle. But let's just try for one more!"

My persistence paid off and Ben agreed. I really wanted my little girl to have a brother or sister with whom she could be best friends as children, and great mates as adults. We knew we might not be successful.

We already felt incredibly blessed to have our little girl, so we would accept with good grace whatever the outcome might be.

LADY LUCK RETURNS

I was encouraged to learn from Dr Google that it's not uncommon for couples to go on and have a natural pregnancy after the IVF. As luck would have it, before too long, we became pregnant again. I couldn't believe it! Wherever Lady Luck had been, she was now back and on our side. We were so thrilled that this might mean a natural healthy pregnancy, and that we wouldn't have to go through IVF.

Our luck didn't last. Within weeks of finding out that I was pregnant, I miscarried. It was so hard emotionally, as it was no longer just my desperate desire for Ben and me, but I also desperately wanted it for Kyra. I was grateful that my daughter was too young to understand what had happened. I ached inside for all the losses that another miscarriage meant for us: the lost baby, the lost child, the lost adult, the lost sibling and all our dreams for the future. I felt totally miserable; I felt I had been selfish and made a huge mistake.

Ben and I talked about it many times, and I spent a lot of time analysing my feelings, thinking that if we had just one more conversation, I could resolve my pain and sadness. We eventually decided to take a break from trying to get pregnant. Instead, we would enjoy our little girl and make the most of our every spare moment with her.

But my yearning to have another baby kept pressing itself upon me. It became just about all that I could think about. I was also at a critical age in my life, so it was now or never.

Over time, I talked Ben into trying again. I wanted my daughter to have a sibling and I felt I had to do everything possible to give Kyra a sister or a brother.

THE MOMENTARY EXCITEMENT OF SUCCESS

One morning, which had the usual scrambles of any other morning before work, I declared to Ben:

"Honey, I think I might be pregnant."

"What makes you think that?"

"Ahh, well, a missed period and I just have this inkling. Maybe Lady Luck is back."

"What? No way!" At this point I wasn't sure if Ben was concerned or excited.

"Do you have any pregnancy tests left?"

"Yes, actually I do, in the bathroom, so we are about to find out!"

We were pregnant! Whilst we were excited, we were both very cynical. By now, we knew the miscarriage risk was very high. Still, the human spirit is amazing. We now felt more resilient from the pain and grief of our earlier miscarriages, determined of our entitlement to enjoy just one more healthy pregnancy.

This time we met the obstetrician early, who confirmed the pregnancy and reminded us of the high risk of another miscarriage. It was a waiting game.

With hope in our hearts, we walked through our daily lives, waiting for time to pass. I was distracted by my secret and daydreamed about another baby. I had had a healthy pregnancy with Kyra and felt sure I could do it again.

We were also thrilled to be preparing for Ben's sister's wedding. It was wonderful to have such a momentous occasion in the family to celebrate, and we were very excited about their upcoming nuptials. It was a great distraction.

Amid all the excitement, as we approached the end of the first trimester, we shared our tentative news with Ben's family. They were all delighted for us.

However, in the week of the wedding, we miscarried. We were devastated, upset and numb that our hopes had been truly dashed.

Time turned on us. We were so looking forward to the wedding, but now had to attend the celebrations knowing that I had miscarried. I was despondent. I knew for Ben and his family that I would have to put my own grief on hold and find my 'smiley face' to enjoy the wedding. It was hard to be circumspect about something so close to our hearts that had occupied our thoughts for so long.

We decided not to tell the family about our miscarriage until after the wedding. But holding on to the secret also made it so much harder to bear. I felt isolated from everyone because of it.

The wedding was an enormous success. The weather was perfect, the bridal couple looked spectacular and it was a wonderful occasion. After a beautiful service and reception, and just as the dancing started, I went home to hide.

Ben and I took some time to recover and work out what, if anything, we were going to do. After all, we had a beautiful, healthy baby girl and perhaps we were just tempting fate by trying for a second baby. We met with our fertility specialist, who was very candid and advised that we could try IVF, but the likelihood of success was very low. We spent some time considering whether we would.

Even though it is a very streamlined procedure, and there was always plenty of support on hand, it is still a very expensive process and an emotional rollercoaster, which has no guarantee of success. I was reminded of that when I travelled interstate for work. The passenger sitting next to me on the flight engaged with me and shared how he and his wife had been through IVF several times without success.

Another round of IVF was a significant decision for us both. I also knew that it would be our last chance to try for a sibling for Kyra. Ben was adamant that I had been through enough emotional strain, and that if we went down this road again, it had to be for the last time. I couldn't help but agree. The first time that I went through IVF was a novel experience, whereas this time, I would know exactly what lay ahead, and how difficult each step would be. I was also very aware that the odds were against us.

We started the IVF process. I was apprehensive and consciously decided that I had to push through my negative thoughts and hope for the best. With my specialist's permission, I also tried acupuncture, which was disconcerting, given the very large needles the acupuncturist strategically placed on me! Still, nothing ventured, nothing gained, and it was an easy enough thing to do, if it might improve my chances.

During the IVF treatment, my stomach became very swollen, and

I had difficulty breathing, symptoms of overstimulation by the fertility drugs. It was ironic that I looked six months pregnant!

Although it was hard to experience IVF for a second time, I was very distracted with my work, and with being a mother to my beautiful girl. The time passed quickly, and we were extraordinarily lucky, given my age and the statistics, to be successful. We were elated when we got the call five days later.

"We have good news for you. We have some healthy embryos. You will need to come in tomorrow for the transfer."

It was magic to our ears. How could we have been so lucky after the journey we had been through to start a family? I couldn't wait to get to the clinic.

The transfer went well, and I returned home, welcoming some rest from the discomfort of the overstimulation. After fourteen days, the blood pregnancy test confirmed that we were positive. We couldn't believe our luck.

THE PROSPECT OF DOUBLE TROUBLE

We met with our obstetrician and after being tentatively congratulated, we had the ultrasound. He took some time moving the transducer over my belly to find images of the baby. I was slightly concerned.

"Now watch this."

"This is the first heartbeat. Annnnnnnnnd (as he moved and prodded me with the transducer), this is the second heartbeat. Congratulations, you are pregnant with twins."

I couldn't believe it. And neither could Ben. He nearly fell over with this news.

The obstetrician said, "Ben, are you okay? You look white as a sheet."

"Yes, yes, fine, it's just a bit of a surprise. We didn't think we would be so successful, but it's great."

The understatement of the year.

We had to wait some weeks for the next ultrasound. Thankfully we were distracted with our plans to get married at the Manly Golf Club. Ben has played and enjoyed golf all his life, so it was an apt venue. The club was founded in 1903 and is one of Sydney's original foundation clubs. The clubrooms are stunning and are one of Sydney's grandest examples of Georgian Mediterranean architecture.

Before the wedding, at just twelve weeks, we attended at the obstetrician's rooms. I was now showing, and my expanding belly had made for many alterations to my wedding dress!

"Well, the great news is that you are still pregnant with your twins. Let's go through these images and their heartbeats carefully. Baby A is smaller than baby B, but both babies are growing well, and have strong heartbeats. I'm quietly confident that your twin pregnancy will continue to go well, and I wish you all the best. It's very exciting and I look forward to seeing you for our next consultation."

We were both so thrilled with the news, and extremely relieved. Just in time for our wedding.

RAIN, RAIN, GO AWAY, IT'S OUR WEDDING DAY!

On our wedding day, and despite it being mid-summer, we woke to rain. It meant a fast change of plans as we had intended marrying on the eighteenth hole and had to settle for the chapel in the clubrooms. We had also planned for Justin's children and Kyra to release butterflies into the air during the ceremony, to flutter above our guests' heads and out across the golf course, a sentimental reminder of weekend afternoons in Mum's garden with Zoie and Justin when we were young kids, chasing butterflies. Instead, the children delighted in half releasing, half throwing the butterflies out the open windows! Not quite the same effect as I had intended, but it was the next best alternative.

We had a wonderful wedding and loved being able to share such a special day with our families and friends. Dad and Mum had travelled from New Zealand and it was wonderful to have them with us, even though Mum was unwell, in a wheelchair, and at times didn't seem to be aware of where she was. Mum's health was declining but I was so glad that she was still with us and able to attend our celebrations.

After the wedding, we honeymooned in the Whitsunday Islands with Kyra. There, I spent some time contemplating our wedding, and the great success that it had been. I also thought that even though the twins were still developing as babies, my own immediate family—the twins in my belly and Kyra—had all been at our wedding. It was a wonderful result.

I felt so privileged to be carrying twins. After our honeymoon, we decided to find out the sex of the twins on the next ultrasound to help us prepare for their births. I also thought it would be very exciting for us, but especially Ben, if we were expecting a girl and a boy. But who would know?

As it turned out, baby A was a girl, and baby B was a boy. I felt like I had won the lottery. Ben was also thrilled. I think that some of the thrill for Ben was knowing that he would not be the only boy in the family! All I had to do now was to continue to carry them for as long as I possibly could to give them the best chance at life when they were born.

I carried the twins to thirty-six weeks. Both Caitlin and Zavier were born healthy babies and we were thrilled.

We now had to adjust to the reality that we had two new babies in our family, and three children under three. Let the games begin!

Finally, after over five years of effort, we had reached the end of an emotionally and physically exhausting journey to have our family and were now starting a very different and exciting journey to care for and love our beautiful, young children. We couldn't wait to take our new twin babies home.

INSIGHTS

- Significant loss events don't just involve the loss of loved ones or 'things' in our lives, but also include the devastating disappointments for what we don't have, or have not achieved, such as having children, and becoming parents. Whilst the wish to have children is a natural and biological aspiration for many, our lifestyle choices in modern society mean that we may delay parenthood, often to our detriment, as infertility becomes an issue.

- Miscarriage can be just as traumatic as other types of loss. However, the grief can be difficult to share if others were not aware of the pregnancy, or are not sensitive to the loss, or its significance. Miscarriage can occur on multiple occasions, and in those situations, it is important to address the grief from each loss.
- Miscarriage (being the spontaneous loss of a pregnancy before the twentieth week) affects up to one in five women,[19] although the actual rate of miscarriage may be higher as some women will miscarry without knowing they were pregnant.

Miscarriage support is available from a number of support services, e.g.:

- Pregnancy, Birth and Baby (1800 882 436),
- SANDS (1300 072 637),
- The Pink Elephants Support Network (www.pinkelephants.org.au),
- Pregnancy Loss Australia (1300 720 942),
- Bears of Hope (13001 HOPE for grief support),
- National Association for Loss and Grief (NALAG) (02 9489 6644).

- The infertility experience is a challenging one. Inevitably, couples will have made enormous and exhausting efforts to become pregnant, only to find they cannot conceive, and this is then often followed by the equally physically and emotionally demanding and stressful rollercoaster that is IVF treatment.
- Whilst there are now multiple organisations in Australia providing IVF treatment, it is time consuming, and can be both emotionally

exhausting and financially costly for families (notwithstanding that Medicare Australia may provide a rebate for some items of IVF treatment).

CHAPTER SIX: AT DEATH'S DOOR

Everyone can master a grief but he that has it.

—William Shakespeare,

Much Ado About Nothing, Act Ill Scene II, Line 26

It's true that 'nothing is certain in life except death and taxes'. It's also true that we are usually totally unprepared for death, whether our own or those of our loved ones. Whilst we know that the natural order is for our parents to predecease us, nothing readies you for that moment when one of your parents hurtles towards the end of their life—and from one defining moment in time, the clock starts ticking an ominous tune. The sound of someone's life fading to black.

I was reminded of the frailty of my father's life on the morning of my birthday. It was like any other morning: I showered fast, dressed faster and raced around the house getting my children ready for school. In the car, I eavesdropped on their conversations, gave them stolen kisses at the school gate and drove like a madwoman to work.

Driving across the Sydney Harbour Bridge to my work in Circular Quay, I rang Dad. My father is an octogenarian, and lives independently by himself in a small two-bedroom bungalow in Napier, Hawke's Bay, New Zealand. Mum was at that time living in a nursing home.

Napier is on the east coast of the North Island and is known as the fruit bowl of New Zealand. Its temperate climate and fertile plains that roll out to the Pacific Ocean make for premium conditions to grow fruits and vegetables. Whilst primary produce is still a significant income producer for the local economy, Napier is now also well known in New Zealand and overseas for its tourism and wine industry. It is a mecca for tourists interested in Art Deco architecture, which was the popular modern architectural style when the cities of Napier and Hastings were rebuilt after the Napier earthquake of 1931. It is also home to many wineries that produce award-winning, export-quality white and red wines, fruity and zesty Sauvignon Blancs, buttery Chardonnays and velvety reds. In the past, with my parents, we've spent many memorable hours lunching at the wineries.

I called Dad using the Bluetooth in my car.

"Hello, Nick Gallate."

"Hi, Dad, it's me."

"Oh, hi, honey, how are you?"

"Good, thanks. Just another year older."

"What? Is it your birthday? Sorry, I forgot. How old are you now?"

"Doesn't matter. Just another year older, that's all. How are you?"

"Lisa, I must say I'm not feeling too well. I haven't been feeling well for days but I really don't know what is wrong."

"Dad, you must go and see your doctor. Give his practice a ring now and see if you can see him today."

"Yes, okay, I think I will."

"And don't forget to ring me later and let me know how you get on."

"Yes, sure."

"Well, I will be calling you back if you don't."

Instead of Dad calling me that afternoon, Dad's neighbour called me.

"Your dad has been rushed to hospital in an ambulance. He asked that I call you to let you know. They don't know what's wrong."

"Thanks, I will call the hospital."

I rang Hawke's Bay Hospital. One of the admin staff took my call.

"Sorry, we don't have your father in A&E. He must still be in transit. Can I suggest that you call back again in an hour or so?"

By now I was at work in the city, and I waited anxiously to call back. An hour felt like a long time to wait.

When I phoned the hospital again, a nurse in A&E confirmed that Dad had arrived, and urgent tests were underway. I played out the scene in my mind, lots of medical staff in accident and emergency surrounding Dad, showing concern, care and kindness. I was told to call back in an hour.

I went home to be with Ben and our children. If Dad died, I wanted to be with them. I couldn't bear the idea of being alone in my office in the city when I learnt my father's fate. Exactly to the minute, one hour later, I spoke to the A&E registrar.

"Hi, Lisa. I understand from the nurse that you are in Sydney. I'm sorry to say that your dad is gravely ill. His metabolic data is deranged, and he is suffering renal failure and his blood sugar and potassium levels are totally off the spectrum. Also, his sodium is very low."

"Oh really, that's terrible. What does this mean for Dad?"

"Well, I'm sorry to say it, but without immediate treatment, your dad is not likely to live."

"Oh, okay, and so will he recover with treatment?"

"Maybe, maybe not, it's difficult to say now. But if you can, you might want to come over as soon as you can."

"Thanks a lot, Doctor, I really appreciate your honesty. I will come across as soon as I can. Please let Dad know that I am coming over, and that I love him."

I was immediately filled with mixed emotions: I was breathing fast; tears filled my eyes. Where was my husband? I called out to him in the lounge room, where he had snuggled in with our children on the couch to watch a movie. He reluctantly stood up and came into the dining room.

"I've now spoken to the doctor; she said he is gravely ill, and I need to go back."

My husband groaned. "Okay, I understand, but do you think you need to go now? Do you not want to wait a little and see what happens?"

I had expected this response.

I was angry and upset. Wasn't it enough that I was reeling from the fact that Dad was on his deathbed on my birthday, and now I had to negotiate my departure with my husband?

"I understand, but he's critically ill. They are transferring him to ICU once they get him stable enough for the transfer. He may not live. I have to go."

Immediately, my husband's face softened.

"Okay, okay. Let's look for flights and get you packed so you can go first thing in the morning."

UNCERTAINTY AND ANXIETY FILLED MY POCKETS

It's always hard to pack a bag for this kind of trip. I had flown back to New Zealand many times over the years on an urgent basis when Justin, Dad or Mum were unwell, uncertainty and anxiety filling my pockets as I travelled across the Tasman. I didn't know what the future held, and whether I was packing for what might be a final farewell. I just hoped Dad would survive and recover from this latest ordeal.

Ben surprised me and was helpful. I knew we had a weekend ahead of sports, play dates and birthday parties, with three young children to navigate through all those activities, so it would be far from easy for him to manage singlehandedly. We cancelled our plans to celebrate my birthday. As much as I was looking forward to our weekend, nothing compared to the anxiety I felt about getting to Dad's bedside. I decided to share a post on Facebook so that family and friends would know what was happening to Dad. It was really encouraging to read so many replies as I travelled. I had the well wishes and kind thoughts of family and friends, willing Dad to survive.

It's often assumed that it is easy and fast to travel to New Zealand because of its geographical proximity to Australia. But because Kingsford Smith Airport in Sydney has a night curfew, the first flight wasn't until the next morning. The connecting flight to Hawke's Bay, the two-hour buffer spent at Auckland Airport, and the two-hour time zone difference would all make for a long day of travel. I was nervous whether I would get there in time.

I rang the hospital while I was waiting at Sydney Airport for my flights. Dad had been transferred to the intensive care unit and was in critical condition. I felt intensely lonely and isolated, full of worry for the life of my father. Life was moving at a frenetic pace around me, but I felt separated from it. I didn't know whether I wanted to get a coffee or read a paper, sit down, stand up or walk. So, I walked around the terminal, mindlessly watching other travellers who were walking with purpose, striding out, confident of their journeys. It reminded me of waiting for my flight after Zoie had died.

With a lot of travel time to occupy, I spent some time reflecting what might lie ahead for Dad. Dr Google was not my friend. I learnt that high blood sugar levels can cause diabetic ketoacidosis, a life-threatening blood chemical imbalance which can cause brain swelling, coma or death. It requires immediate treatment with insulin and fluids, and close monitoring to replace electrolytes. The damage to blood vessels can cause loss of vision, kidney disease and nerve problems. It was an awful picture. 'A little knowledge is a dangerous thing', and I had just sent myself into a spin.

MISSING THE FINAL GOODBYE

I also thought about when my grandmother was nearing her own death. When she passed, it was very sudden. My grandmother had developed pneumonia at the age of ninety-three and was rushed to hospital. Dad travelled from New Zealand, hoping to arrive in time to Sydney to say goodbye to his mum.

When Dad arrived in Sydney, I drove from my grandmother's hospital bedside to Kingsford Smith Airport to collect him. On my way to the airport, my cousin Bernard called me to say that Nana had just died. I cried as I drove to the airport. I was crying as much for my nana as I was for Dad, who would be devastated. I tried to collect myself before I arrived at the terminal. It was a long wait in the arrivals hall. As Dad exited customs and came to meet me, his first words were:

"Is she still with us?"

"Hi, Dad, no, I'm so sorry, she isn't. Bern just rang me on my way out to the airport and she has just died. I am sorry you have missed seeing her. But she knew you were coming to see her."

"Okay, thanks, honey."

"Come on, I will take you to see her now, Dad." I grabbed his arm and his bag, and we left the terminal.

Dad had spent the day travelling to see his mother for the final time and to tell her that he loved her. It was one of the hardest moments I have ever had to share with anyone. I now wondered if I would get to Hawke's Bay in time to see Dad, or whether I would go through the same heartbreaking experience.

It made me think of the power and value of a final goodbye, and how important it is as an early mark in the grieving process. Not being able to say goodbye can often make the grieving process even harder.

I felt like I was waiting an inordinate length of time at the gate to board my flight from Sydney to Auckland. It's at these moments that time seems to drag when you are anxious to get to your destination and are consumed by your own thoughts.

THE MERCY DASHES

After I arrived in Auckland, I flew to Napier in a small turbo-prop plane in which I felt every bump. As we descended towards Napier, through the turbulence and the heavy cloud cover over the Kaweka Ranges, I could see the spectacular Napier Hill which tucks around Hawke's Bay Airport. The houses were lit up with evening lights that sparkled a welcome out to the last plane for the night. I was anxious and couldn't wait to land. My dear friend Alison met me at the airport and rushed me to the Hawke's Bay Hospital.

When I arrived at the intensive care unit, I entered the waiting room and pressed the wall button for permission from the nursing staff to enter the ward. Having spent the day travelling from Sydney, I was tired and impatient. The nurse let me in and sent me in Dad's direction.

What immediately struck me, before even seeing Dad, was the horrible realisation that he was in the very same room that Mum had been, years earlier, when she had also fought for her life.

On that occasion, Mum had developed a chronic illness called colitis and was rushed to hospital. The surgeon called me in Sydney less than ten minutes before Mum went into theatre, to say that she was about to operate on Mum to perform an ileostomy (removing the colon). The surgeon said that if she didn't operate, Mum would die. But even if she did operate, Mum could still die, and I should get back to Napier as quickly as I could. And so began the first of what Ben called 'mercy dashes'.

As I approached Dad's room in intensive care, I had flashbacks of my eldest daughter, Kyra, and I visiting Mum after her ileostomy. Mum slept for very long periods before she would wake up, focus, recognise we were there with a smile and then go back to sleep.

During Mum's recovery, my father and I were asked to meet with Mum's medical team who explained the gravity of her predicament to us, and how they had to remove the entire colon to save her life. Although it is medically possible to reverse an ileostomy, they would only seek to do so in younger, healthier patients. Mum's medical team explained to us that it would not be in her best interests to resuscitate her if she took another turn for the worse. I couldn't quite believe that we were at this point in Mum's treatment. They asked for our comments. Dad was speechless. I said something about Mum always being a strong, energetic lady who wouldn't want to be a burden and that she would hate a life of simple existence. Whilst we couldn't bear the thought of being without her, we wouldn't want her life to be prolonged if it meant she would have no real life at all. At the end of the meeting, after Dad and I agreed that Mum would not be resuscitated, we left the room in tears. Thankfully, Mum did survive and recover from the operation.

In many respects, this visit to see Dad was no different. I knew Dad was at death's door. With trepidation, I walked into his room. Dad was asleep. There were wires everywhere on his body, connecting him to vast machines which engulfed him in the bed. He looked ashen, and I was shocked. I thought I had prepared myself, but I couldn't stop myself from inhaling, wide-eyed and worried. I was greeted by a very kind male intensive care nurse with a lilting Scottish accent.

"Hi, I'm Scott, one of the nurses here, I have been looking after Nick."

"Hi, I'm Nick's daughter Lisa, nice to meet you. How is he?"

"Your dad was delirious and has been gravely unwell. He has been in a deep sleep during my shift from all the medication. We are closely monitoring all his vital signs and metabolic data just now. We need to try to stabilise him, but we also must medicate him carefully. If we give him too many fluids too quickly, it might cause him to have a cardiac arrest. And if we lower his metabolic data too quickly, he could go into a coma."

"I see, it sounds very serious."

"Yes, it is, but at least he is now in the right place. I am just finishing my shift, and the next nurse is coming in now. I hope your dad improves."

"Thanks, Scott, so do I."

As Scott left the room, I felt overwhelmed that Dad was in such a delicate condition, confronting horrific risks. He was facing down death, just as it stood outside the door, tapping quietly on the glass to come in.

I turned my attention to my father. Dad's stature was short but muscular, with solid thighs and buttocks, ideal for running and tackling in a game of rugby. Dad has always been passionate about rugby, whatever the code. He played rugby union as a youngster, but his greatest contribution to the different rugby codes was as a fanatical supporter. He has watched hundreds of Australian NRL (rugby league) matches and just as many provincial and test rugby union matches, with great zeal and focus. A proud supporter of the All Blacks, the Hurricanes and the Christchurch Crusaders—Justin's home team; he loved to follow them, and it was a passion shared. Of course, his loudest cheers were reserved for when Justin played rugby. Dad was a very proud father when my brother played for the First XV at Napier Boys High School, and in the First XV at a senior level with the Colenso Pirates in Napier. But in the hospital bed, surrounded by massive medical equipment, Dad looked diminutive, all his energy and zest for life and his love of rugby stripped out of him.

Over the next four days, Dad had around-the-clock medical care from the ICU team. I have no doubt they saved his life. It was a slow, protracted and nervous journey, but Dad managed it with dignity and his dry sense of humour, which the medical team found very entertaining.

After my first visit to see Dad, I brought Mum from her hospital so she could see him for a brief period. Mum now had advanced Alzheimer's and Parkinson's disease and was confined to a wheelchair. At times, she seemed to understand the gravity of Dad's condition, but at other times, she was terribly confused, wondering why he had not been to see her on his usual daily visit, and what he was now doing in hospital. Even though Dad was on his deathbed, Mum's face lit up to see him.

When visiting the intensive care unit, I had to announce myself into the videocam in the waiting room and wait until the door was opened to permit me onto the ward. Whilst I totally respected that patient welfare was paramount, it was always hard to sit in this room, waiting anxiously to see my father. I flicked through weekly magazines, checked my text messages and blankly looked at the walls. There were often other families waiting. It was hard to know whether to engage them in conversation, knowing that they too were likely to be dealing with a very grave situation. A young man told me that his mother had just returned from Mount Everest and had contracted a terrible infection that was now threatening her life. Another lady told me that she was visiting her seriously ill Kaumatua, an elected elder in the Maori community, who taught and guided current and future generations.

Together, it was a long wait until we were allowed onto the ward. As we entered the ward together, each going our separate ways, we wished the others well for their loved ones.

MAGICIANS WORKING THEIR MAGIC

After four days, Dad was well enough to be transferred to a general medical ward. His metabolic data was still high and abnormal, but he had stabilised. It was an exciting moment for us both, and I was enormously relieved. During the first day on the medical ward, the ICU team handed over Dad's care to the ward staff, and an ICU doctor came to speak to us.

"Nick, you have been very lucky. You have been living with undiagnosed diabetes, and you very nearly died."

"Wow, is that right?" asked Dad from his bed.

"Yes. You were in a very precarious position. We have had lots of younger patients present to the ICU with the same symptoms as you, and they have not survived."

"I see. Thank you, Doctor. I do feel very lucky." It was the oddest and yet most appropriate thing for Dad to say at that moment.

"Please also thank the other doctors and nurses that have looked after me in ICU. They are all magicians and have worked their magic."

The doctor laughed. "Yes, of course I will."

We then spoke at length about what would now happen for Dad, including the need for ongoing monitoring on the ward until the team had stabilised his insulin levels, safely reintroduced his other medicines, helped him to walk again and had him well enough to go home. Dad would now be going home as a diabetic, dependent on insulin injections and regular blood testing. The prospect of Dad managing this new medical condition at home by himself seemed overwhelming to us both. I also wondered how he would manage to care for his wife, commuting an hour every day to visit her in hospital.

After the doctor left, Dad and I agreed that our thanks to the ICU team who had saved his life didn't really seem enough, so I went shopping to buy my two favourite presents that I think are always made to share, chocolates and fudge. I asked Dad if he wanted to write the card of thanks, but he said no, I could do it. As I noted the names of the ICU doctors and staff, Dad said:

"Don't forget Scott. I really think he saved my life."

It was a poignant moment, as Dad was delirious during Scott's shift and hadn't met him. But somehow, Dad knew that this nurse had in part been his saviour. I wrote on the card that Dad thought they were all magicians and had worked their magic, and I took our presents and card to the intensive care unit. Neither words, chocolate nor fudge could ever really be enough thanks, but I'm sure they would have been enjoyed by the team.

I soon had to leave Napier to return to my own beautiful family in Sydney. Ben was flying to Singapore, and I had to get home. I had missed my husband and our three children terribly. My kids knew that their Papou (which they always pronounced as "Pa-poo" with a giggle) was very ill. Although I had wanted to bring Kyra with me, I didn't know whether Dad would survive, or whether they would be joining me for his funeral. As it turned out, I was so grateful that they didn't have to come over to New Zealand to join me. Their Papou was in safe hands.

It was sentimental to see my dad starting to improve, and yet I couldn't stay long enough to see him home, back amongst his own creature comforts. So, I brought some of his creature comforts to him. A TV and a dozen DVDs, some classic movies, even a rugby test or two—he never minded watching repeats—and some 'Spaghetti Westerns' that he had been meaning to watch.

It was hard to say goodbye whilst Dad was still in hospital. At my dad's suggestion, I met with the social worker, who agreed to arrange for the Anglican chaplain to meet with him. I think he felt that he owed God a few prayers. I also knew that he would have a few friends visit him before he returned home. In the end, saying goodbye as he sat in his hospital bed was awful, but it was the same sadness I had felt many times before, the grief of separation by distance across the Tasman, and the worry and anxiety whether this would be the last time that I would see my parents.

INSIGHTS

- Diabetes has been described as the 'epidemic of the twenty-first century' with more than 1.8 million diabetic Australians.[20] Every day, around two hundred and eighty Australians develop diabetes.
- There is no current cure for diabetes, but diabetics can still enjoy

life if their diabetes is managed effectively. The three main types of diabetes are Type 1, Type 2 and gestational diabetes (in pregnancy). All types are complex conditions which require daily care and management.

- If diabetes is not managed well, then potential complications may include heart attack, stroke, kidney disease, limb amputation, depression, anxiety and blindness.[21]
- Support services available for diabetics in Australia can be accessed via the National Diabetics Services Scheme (NDSS)[22] which is administered by Diabetics Australia.

CHAPTER SEVEN: THE LONG GOODBYE

Grief can be the garden of compassion. If you keep your heart open through everything, your pain can become your greatest ally in your life's search for love and wisdom.

—Rumi

It began slowly.

If you weren't watching closely, you might have missed it. The hints increased as time passed. They became more exaggerated and more obvious, until we could no longer ignore it.

Mum forgot important dates and events. She needed to hear the same information repeatedly. She forgot where she was and what she was doing. She misplaced things and couldn't find anything. She forgot the time of day, the day of the week, the date, the season. The clock soon lost all meaning to her. It became harder to hold a conversation with Mum. She would stop mid-sentence, forget what she was talking about, ask the same question repeatedly, or just not know how to express herself. Mum knew what she wanted to say but she had lost her words. She became confused, stressed, anxious.

Mum's driving also became erratic. She would veer into the middle of the road or into the gutter, drive too close to another car or drive too slowly. Her driving quickly became dangerous. I spoke with Dad, and we agreed that she couldn't drive alone. But none of us wanted to be the passenger when we were putting our lives into Mum's hands! Mum didn't like our family decision, but she didn't have a choice. All too quickly, it became clear that Mum couldn't be allowed to continue to drive. She was unsafe, and at risk of having an accident. Dad and I decided to hide her car keys and he became her full-time driver.

Mum also slowly started withdrawing from all her sports, social activities and hobbies. She used to enjoy walking the neighbouring roads and paths down to the nearby river at sunset. But as Mum slowed down, so too did her walking. It became harder and slower for her, until they became shorter walks. Soon her walks were confined to walking around her beautiful gardens. And golf! She wasn't a Tiger Woods, since she had only picked up the sport late in life. But she was a keen novice and had made many friends at the local golf dub. When she stopped her daily walks, Mum also stopped playing golf, and the golf bag soon started collecting cobwebs.

As a keen gardener all her life, Mum had grown the most beautiful gardens in each of her homes. However, maintaining the garden soon became the work of a paid gardener.

THE SLOW CREEP OF DEMENTIA

We weren't certain that Mum's symptoms weren't just signs of old age, but I felt convinced that my mother was suffering from dementia and persuaded Dad that she should see her doctor. Based on her medical history, physical examinations, and memory and cognitive tests, Mum was diagnosed with Alzheimer's disease and Parkinson's disease. Alzheimer's is a disease of the brain that causes a slow decline in the patient's memory, thinking and reasoning skills. It is the most common cause of dementia. Parkinson's is a degenerative disease of the central nervous system, and its symptoms include shaking, rigidity, slowness of movement and difficulty walking. Both diseases are incurable.

Throughout a forty-year nursing career, Mum worked as a registered staff nurse on the orthopaedic wards at Wellington Hospital, later Napier Hospital, and Hawke's Bay Hospital. She was very popular with her colleagues and patients alike as a hardworking and very kind, caring nurse who had a very witty sense of humour. During her career, Mum had also worked in a nursing home caring for the aged and those with dementia. It was an awful irony that now, Mum should be diagnosed as having the same diseases that had claimed the lives of so many of her nursing home patients.

The World Alzheimer's Report[23] records that there were 55 million people globally living with dementia in 2019, but it is projected there will be almost triple that number, or 139 million, with dementia worldwide by 2050. In Australia, there are more than 480,000 living with dementia. Without a medical breakthrough, the number of people with dementia in Australia is expected to increase to almost 1.1 million by 2058.[24]

In addition, Alzheimer's Disease International estimates that globally, 75% of people living with dementia, or 41 million, are undiagnosed dementia sufferers. It is a global health crisis that needs more attention, support and resources.

THE CREATURE COMFORTS OF HOME

Back at her home, Mum struggled to come to terms with her new diagnoses. At times, it wasn't clear how much she really understood. Sometimes, she would ask what was wrong with her, but at other times, Mum tried to hide her confusion and frustration, desperate to hide the extent of her illness. But it slowly and silently creeped into every aspect of her being, becoming my mother's shadow.

We didn't know how quickly the diseases would progress or impact on her ability to continue living at home. Yet, it was clear that Dad would become Mum's primary carer. He would be responsible for everything: the cooking, cleaning, grocery shopping, the making and changing of beds, administering medicines to her, organising all the medical appointments and making the social arrangements. Dad had never been a very good cook or cleaner, but he now had to step up and play the diseases game.

As a family, we wanted Mum to be able to live at home for as long as possible. We didn't want her to be consigned to a nursing home before her level of care demanded it. We didn't want her to live with embarrassment, or in shame, but to live with grace and dignity, and enjoy the creature comforts of her own home. And Dad was willing to do all he could to make sure that she could live at home for as long as possible.

As her cognitive abilities diminished, it became harder for Dad to care for her. She would resist his cajoling to eat, drink water, brush her teeth or to shower. Sometimes, she would resist taking her medications. After Mum had surgery, the hospital arranged carers in the community to attend their home to shower and dress Mum each day. It was some welcome respite for Dad, and I encouraged him to continue this level of care for Mum, and to go out in the mornings and run his errands when a carer was at the house. The carers were only in attendance for an hour or two each day, so Dad was on duty for twenty-two hours, seven days a week. It made it difficult for him to complete simple jobs. Going grocery shopping was arduous as Mum would walk extremely slowly with her walker and often get tired and need rest. Or she would need to be pushed in her wheelchair, which made pushing a trolley nearly impossible. He couldn't run in and out of stores to pay bills or run other errands. He was stranded in his role as carer.

Dad soon became exhausted. Added to the physical exertion were the regular negotiations and arguments with Mum, about anything and everything. Mum didn't fight fair. At times, her mind would drift off or she would stop mid-sentence or change the topic completely. Her voice would often drop to a whisper. At other times, she would become aggressive and defiant. It was a rollercoaster for Dad which he mostly suffered in silence. I often spoke to him about letting go of conversations with Mum, of not correcting her when she was wrong, and of being circumspect with the truth. He had been consumed his entire legal career with understanding the details and getting to the truth, and it was hard for him to let go of an argument or needing to prove that he was right. But he had to understand that the truth no longer really mattered to Mum in her distorted reality.

THE COLLISION OF THE PAST AND THE PRESENT

My mum struggled with the concept of time, as if her past and present had collided. She only had now, but she didn't know where that fitted into her life. Whilst she had some memory of the past, she didn't realise that they were memories, and she thought that they were her reality. And that recollection was very incomplete. Mum would often talk about her childhood, but the memories were mixed up with events of her later life. It wasn't obvious to Mum and her confusion didn't bother me. I just wanted her to enjoy happy memories, even if they were confused jumbles of decades of life.

THE RESPITE OF DAY CARE

Mum started attending a nearby nursing home for day visits, creating much-needed respite for Dad, and some social contact for Mum outside the house. Mum could participate in games and activities at the nursing home and was given morning and afternoon tea, and a cooked lunch each day. She seemed to enjoy this new routine in her daily life just as much as Dad did.

DEMENTIA IS NOT CONTAGIOUS

It is awful to watch the Alzheimer's and Parkinson's take hold. Mum had been a strong, healthy and lively lady who had loved her family, her husband, and her sisters and brothers, and who had adored her children. She had also made a lot of friends, but as the news was shared of Mum's illness, her friends seemed to quietly abandon her, as if her condition was contagious.

She was slowly losing her identity as everything that personified her slowly slipped away. Mum had loved to knit and make jumpers every winter for her children and grandchildren in the most wonderful colours and soft wools, but the knitting quickly became a thing of the past. She had also loved listening to Irish music and opera music, as well as watching operas and movies, but she could no longer concentrate to listen to the music or watch the TV screen. It was as if she couldn't really see or appreciate the visual images. Instead, my mother, who had always been very active and fit, and who never sat still for long, would now sit for hours, often with a blank look on her face and a faraway stare. We were losing Mum.

Mum continued daily visits to the nursing home for months. However, as her dementia deteriorated, so too, did her behaviour. She wandered. She would often be found out in the grounds of the nursing home, or worse still, she would be discovered meandering down the street with her walker. The nurses also reported that Mum was becoming aggressive towards staff. The nursing home did not provide a dedicated dementia ward, and so, with much reluctance, Mum's condition was reviewed and she was admitted as a patient onto a dementia ward.

I was now fully appreciating the ugliness and horror of her diagnosis. It was no longer possible to deny that Mum was seriously ill and would never recover. She was slipping away from us and into the world of her dementia. She would be surrounded by other dementia patients who were at different stages of the disease, and whilst that might almost normalise her condition, it was confronting. Mum was assigned a basic room which we proceeded to personalise for her, with her favourite colourful bedlinen and all her feminine things, her dresses and perfume bottles and make-up, her trinkets and family photos. We tried to make her as comfortable as possible in her new home, but it was hard to let her go, to walk away without her.

Mum would have no more trips over to Sydney to see me or her grandchildren. She wouldn't see them grow, attend their baptisms or first communions, blow up balloons at their birthday parties, watch them learn to ride their bikes, or attend their dance concerts, netball games, or numerous other activities that are the realm of childhood and the joy of grandparents. I was grieving the loss of my mother and the loss of the grandmother to my children. After all that I had experienced, I felt cheated.

THE RELENTLESS TUG OF WAR

The tragedy was happening to my mum, and we were reluctant observers of that tragedy as the Alzheimer's and Parkinson's took hold. It was an awful tug of war, as Mum was pulled in and out of the real world, her mind playing games with her, causing confusion, frustration and despair. I could never wish such a painful and slow demise on anyone.

I decided that if my mum couldn't come to see us, we would go to her as much as our finances and my job would allow. I travelled over from Sydney to visit her as often as I could, acutely aware of the gradual deterioration on each visit.

My daughter Kyra came with me to New Zealand to see Grandma when she was on the ward. Kyra was only seven years old and I was concerned how she might manage attending a dementia ward, but she was happy to visit Grandma and seemed to take the hospital and other patients in her stride. I had suggested she take her guitar to New Zealand so she could keep up her practice.

"Mumma, can I take my guitar to the hospital to show Grandma?" asked Kyra. Yes! Secretly I was delighted; she might even play it for her grandmother whilst we were visiting her.

"Sure, honey, pop it in your guitar bag and let's bring it with us, I am sure Grandma would love to see it."

When we arrived in Mum's room at the hospital, Mum's first question was, "Who's this beautiful little girl?"

"It's your granddaughter, Kyra," I said.

"Hi, Grandma, how are you?" Kyra leant in to give Mum a hug and a kiss, as she sat in her big La-Z-Boy chair.

"Helloo, my, you are a beautiful girl."

"Thanks, Grandma, we've come over from Sydney to see you."

"Oh, that's nice. Who's with you?"

"It's Mumma, Grandma," said Kyra, who looked confused by the obvious question and answer.

"Hi, Mum, how are you? It's so nice to see you," I said as I leant in to give Mum a kiss and a hug.

And then we hit repeat. We must have exchanged hellos several times before I decided it was time to move on to something else.

"Mum, Kyra is learning the guitar and has brought it with her to show you. Kyzie, show Grandma your guitar—get it out of the bag."

"Grandma, this is my guitar," said Kyra as she held her guitar towards her grandma.

"That's nice, darling, what is it?"

"Mum, it's Kyra's guitar. Why don't you play something on it for Grandma, honey, one of the songs you have been learning?" I asked Kyra.

"Okay, well, I can play 'Stand By Me' and 'Smoke on the Water'. But I need to warm up first."

"Terrific, honey, warm up, and then just play whichever one you want to first, I'm sure Grandma would love to hear both."

MUSIC TO TOUCH THE SOUL

Kyra sat on Grandma's bed and started strumming her guitar. As she did, Mum's face lit up with the sound of the strings bouncing around the concrete walls of her room. It was pure magic for Mum to listen to Kyra practising her scales, chords and arpeggios in Mum's room.

A nurse passed in the corridor and popped her head in through the open door.

"Everything okay in here?" she asked as she saw my little girl concentrating hard on her strumming and her chords.

"Oh, how lovely," the nurse said quietly.

"You're welcome to stay," I said. "Kyra is just learning, but Mum seems to love it."

"Yes, she does." We both looked at Mum. Her face had softened, and she was smiling gently, and her eyes seemed to brighten, as she sat in her chair listening to Kyra playing her guitar, not minding that she made a few mistakes.

"Would your daughter like to play the guitar in the lounge? I'm sure the other patients would love to listen to her."

"That sounds great. Kyra, honey, would you like to go into the lounge and play a tune for everyone?"

"Oh really, Mumma, do I have to?"

"Come on, sweetheart, please, Grandma and I will come with you, and you can just play it there like you are here. You don't have to even look at anyone, but I am sure the other patients will love it. We don't have to be in there long."

"Okay, Mumma, but I will only play one song."

"Okay, that's fine, sweetheart."

I had negotiated one song, success! Maybe I could try for one more once we were in the lounge.

We wheeled Mum in her chair to the main lounge and Kyra played 'Twinkle Twinkle' and 'Stand By Me' for the other patients. Many of them seemed to respond to the lyrical sound of the acoustic guitar as Kyra played it with great concentration. She wasn't put off by the other patients—although she lost one patient in her audience who fell asleep!

At the end of her mini concert, the nurses and I, and some of the patients, cheered and clapped with great enthusiasm. I was bursting with pride for my little girl. During the rest of our holiday, we would visit Mum each day, and Kyra would play her guitar for Mum and the other patients. Kyra was a hit. Our visits went well and without incident, until our last day. Kyra and I were in Mum's room when one of Mum's neighbours passed Mum's open door.

"Mumma, he's got no clothes on." Kyra burst into laughter.

I turned around to face the door and saw the naked back and bottom of a male patient walking down the corridor, a nurse's aide running after him. "Bob, you can't come out without your clothes on. Bob, Bob."

Kyra and I laughed together; she didn't seem to mind. I saw Mum studying my face, and then she too laughed. I'm not sure that she knew what we were laughing about, but it didn't matter. It was so nice to watch her laugh.

WHEN ALL REALITY IS LOST

Dad visited Mum daily. He took her out in his car for drives around the area, often for lunch at a winery or cafe. As Mum's mobility deteriorated, it changed their activities, as he could no longer get her out of the car into the wheelchair unaided. Dad would buy takeaway coffees for them to drink in the car, or an ice cream to eat whilst overlooking the beach.

As the dementia progressed, the outdoor trips stopped, and Mum was confined to wheelchair rides around the ward and inspections of the rose beds in the garden. Dad still brought Mum her favourite ice creams and coffees, and it seemed to give Dad a sense of purpose in his old age. He was totally dedicated to her. After all the heartache they had felt in losing two of their children, they had renewed their bonds of love for each other, at the end of their own lives.

THE LITTLE WHITE LIES OF LOVE

For a long time, I felt that Mum still knew who I was when I called or visited her, but over time, she lost her sense of recollection. She would sometimes ask me about my children but couldn't remember their names. It didn't bother me. She also asked after Zoie and Justin many times, where they were and when had I last seen them. Dad was initially adamant that she should know the truth.

"But Dad, it's just cruel."

"It's not, she needs to know that they are no longer here. You can't tell her lies."

"But Dad, it's not fair, it's like she is learning of their deaths all over again every time she asks and every time you tell her. You can't do that to her. You just have to say that you haven't seen them, or you haven't heard from them, or that you will let them know she has asked after them when they next get in touch."

Eventually Dad was persuaded that not all lies were harmful, that little lies could often be better than the truth.

At other times, Mum would call me her nickname for her sister. It also didn't bother me, and I didn't correct her. All I wanted was to have contact with her. Even if she didn't remember, it didn't matter. I know that I loved my mum dearly and that somewhere deep inside, Mum knew that I loved her, and that she loved me. At the end of her very busy, active and full life, what mattered became very simple.

THERE IS NO CHOICE TO DIE WHEN THEY ARE ALREADY DYING

Every family wants their loved one's end of life to be as dignified as possible. But the final months, weeks and days are not kind to the dementia patient or their family. Alzheimer's and Parkinson's are cruel diseases, and the outlook is very bleak. As the diseases progress, they will severely compromise the patient's higher brain functions, balance and co-ordination, and autonomic functions like heart rate, breathing, digestion and sleep cycles will also be severely affected. The patient will have severe difficulty performing the functions that keep the body alive and functioning, unable to sit up or walk at all, confined to bed, and unable to eat or drink. When death comes, it may be caused by any one of many associated conditions such as heart attack, dehydration, kidney failure or aspiration pneumonia.

These are outcomes that shout out for legislation that would permit voluntary euthanasia or assisted dying, not just for the terminally ill who are still competent to make an informed decision about assisted dying, but also for those patients who can make that decision before they become incompetent to do so. Having watched my mother's decline, I know that it was not extraordinary, that it was as ordinary and as horrific as the deaths of so many other dementia patients, for whom there is no cure, with no chance of a different outcome. Whilst we have debated and passed law about euthanasia within many states of Australia,[25] and voted on and passed law permitting euthanasia in New Zealand,[26] we must continue to consider and debate the issue of how and when euthanasia is permissible, and by whom it can or should be administered.

Although it seems natural to hold on to our loved ones and to wish them and ourselves as much time as we might be permitted to share for our final goodbyes, it is the first time in my life that I hoped for a speedy death for my mother. I wanted my mum to pass quickly, to be saved from the agony and excruciating existence that lay ahead of her. We had been blessed with a wonderful mother, wife, sister and friend and, even though we would mourn her death, her slow demise caused us to grieve her passing every day.

I was at lunch with family and friends in Manly, Sydney, celebrating Zavier and Caitlin's First Communion, when the call came. It was Dad.

"Hi, Lisa, it's your mum, she is not doing well, and I think you need to come home. She is not eating or drinking and the doctor thinks that she doesn't have long. Can you home as quickly as you can? The doctor suggested you give him a ring."

"Okay, I will ring him and then see when the next flights are, and I'll let you know when I will get in."

I rang the doctor.

"Your mum is in her final stages, and I really don't think it will be long now, so you should come home as soon as you can if you want to try and see her."

I thanked the doctor and thought how difficult it must be for doctors to routinely have to share such news about their patients with loved ones. It is an invidious responsibility.

I wiped away my tears before I returned to our lunch table. Even with all the advance notice from her years of dementia, it still hurt to know that Mum was now dying, and I wasn't with her. I was also anxious about whether I would make it home in time.

"Ben, that was Dad. Mum doesn't have long, and I need to get home."

"Oh, honey, I'm so sorry; okay, let me help you."

It didn't take long to organise flights, but I could only get on the last flight out of Sydney that evening and had to overnight at Auckland.

THE LOSS OF GRANDPARENTS IS LIFE'S LESSON FOR THE YOUNG

We finished lunch and went home. As I packed, I explained to Kyra, Zavier and Caitlin that Grandma was very unwell, and I needed to go over and see her before she died. They were upset by the news of their grandma, but I felt that I needed to tell them. The deaths of our grandparents are usually a gentle and natural way for our young to start to understand the concept of death and grief, and I didn't want to hide it from them.

After a little while spent processing the news, my children didn't miss a beat. They realised if they came with me, that apart from seeing Grandma, they would get to fly to New Zealand—and they all loved planes!—and it would mean time off school!

"Can we come with you?" asked Zavier.

"Can I come, Mumma? I'm the oldest," retorted Kyra.

"No, we should all go," said Caitie.

"I would love for you all to come, but right now, I need to race over as quickly as I can to see Grandma and I will give her your kisses and hugs. You can send her your love in your prayers. You also need to be here to look after Dadda."

I packed a bag, including some clothes for Mum's funeral, and Ben and our kids drove me out to the airport.

"Let me know when you get to Auckland. I hope you get to Napier in time to see your mum."

"Thanks, honey, I think you should expect to fly over later this week."

"Sure, don't worry about that now. Just know that we can all come over if you think we should, and otherwise I will plan to come myself. I'm sure my family will help us if the kids stay in Sydney."

The prospect of being separated from my children while I would farewell my mum was enough to make me start crying again.

"Honey, it's okay, we will work it out, you don't need to think about it now. It's important that you just get home as soon as you can and see your mum. We all love you very much and will be thinking of you every step of the way."

I broke down, not wanting to leave and not wanting to face what was ahead of me. But I couldn't afford to miss my flight, as it would then delay my arrival by a further day.

The flight over was uneventful. I arrived in Auckland and walked across to the Novotel Hotel at the International Terminal and checked in. I rang Dad and told him I had reached Auckland. Mum was still alive. I would be on the first flight in the morning.

THE LOGISTICAL NIGHTMARE OF THE MERCY DASH

The next morning, the alarm went early, and I jumped out of bed to have a hot shower and get dressed. I packed my bag and headed downstairs to the lobby to check out.

As I passed through the lobby, I noticed that the barista had already started work, and I decided I had time to order a coffee.

As I left the hotel, sipping on my frothy hot coffee, I suddenly realised I was at the international terminal but had to be at the domestic terminal some distance away before check-in closed in ten minutes! It was a stupid error on my part. How had I forgotten?

I looked around but there were no waiting cabs. It was too early. I decided that my best chance was to follow the green line walk between the international and domestic terminals and run/walk as best I could with my bag as quickly as possible. I tried to check in, but the flight had just closed. I was furious with myself. I looked around and decided my next best chance was the service desk. After all, the plane was on the tarmac and there were still twenty minutes before take-off. I waited in line and then explained my predicament to the service staff.

My pleas were ignored. They wouldn't let me on the flight.

By this time, other passengers had started to realise what was happening and a few stepped in, one even saying, "How can you not let her on?" and another saying, "You need to help her."

It was to no avail. The service staff of this low-cost carrier told me that I could get on the next flight in two hours' time.

All I could think of was that my mum might die in that time, and I would not be at her bedside, for my own stupidity! I ran down the terminal to the Air New Zealand desk to see if I could get on an earlier flight. Luckily, Air New Zealand had a flight leaving and I was able to buy a ticket and board.

During the flight, I looked in my handbag for my boarding pass and then looked for but couldn't find my passport. I searched everywhere and realised I didn't have it. How could I continue to be so stupid? I had never lost a passport before, but in my haste at Auckland Domestic Terminal, I had managed to lose it. I had no idea what to do. How would I get out of New Zealand and back into Australia without it?

I decided to own up to my stupidity (again!) and spoke to the air hostess on my flight, who contacted the ground crew. They checked the Auckland service desk. It wasn't there. All I could do was wait until I reached Napier.

Once the plane landed, I tried to ring the Auckland Domestic Terminal to speak to the airport police but couldn't get through. I messaged my brother who was travelling from Dubai. He said he would look for it when he came through Auckland some hours behind me.

I had done this dash—what Ben calls the "mercy dash"—so many times over the years. But on this occasion, when timing meant everything to me, I had messed up my travel. Luckily, my brother, George, was able to locate my passport—at the low-cost carrier's service desk!—and brought it with him to Napier.

THE ELEPHANT IN THE ROOM

It was a relief to arrive in Napier and visit Mum, to talk to her, and hold her hand. Over the next twenty-four hours, my father, my brother, Mum's sister and I spent time with Mum, sharing her final moments and speaking words of comfort and love. They were quiet, peaceful hours together. My mum's sister had flown at very short notice from Queensland and George had flown from Dubai. It was such a relief that we had all made it home in time.

But what of the elephant in the room? That lingering presence of impending death. None of us knew where Mum was up to in her journey, and we really didn't want to know. Instead, we soaked up every minute we could with her, not wanting to be distracted by anything else. When it came, death was quiet and gentle.

My mum was peaceful up until her very last breath, surrounded by her family who loved and adored her. My mother might have died from her illnesses, but I also knew that she had died of a broken heart. She had missed Zoie and Justin every single day since their deaths. I like to think that on the day she passed, they were all reunited.

FINAL WISHES RECORDED IN WRITING, AND RENEWED, AVOID DOUBT AND CONTEST

Soon after Mum passed, the nursing staff asked us whether Mum was to be buried or cremated so they could prepare her. Her final wishes. Dad immediately said, "Burial, please." Mum had apparently prepared a will in which she had requested burial. But Mum had told me several times before she was diagnosed that she wanted to be cremated and have her ashes scattered in Ireland.

I wish I had known what Mum had said in her will before she died, as I would have suggested to her that she make a new will to avoid any later uncertainty, and the very dilemma with which I was now confronted.

Dad was bereft with grief, but I had to try to honour my mum's final wishes. I asked my brother to come into the corridor. As I walked out of Mum's room and waited for him, it made me wonder how many important conversations must have been shared in hushed tones in that hallway.

"George, Mum doesn't want to be buried. She wants to be cremated so her ashes can be spread in Ireland."

"Oh, really? Are you sure?"

"Yes, very sure, she told me several times. I just didn't know that it wasn't in her will. I haven't seen her will though, so I don't know."

"Well, that's what Dad says her will says. We can't very well ask Dad to show it to us now, here at the hospital. I don't even know where it is. He would have to go home and find it, which could take hours, and the nurses are waiting for us to decide."

"Yes, I know, I just can't in good conscience, and out of respect to Mum, not say something."

"Okay, well then, we will have to tell Dad."

"But he is so adamant that she should be buried. It harks back to him thinking that a burial is the only way you reach Heaven."

"Okay, well, that's his belief and he can have that view about his own body if he wants to. But if Mum wants to be cremated, then you will have to tell him."

"Why can't you?"

"Because Mum didn't tell me. So, you need to tell Dad; you just tell him what you know, and we'll work it out. I'll play the bad cop."

"Okay."

And so began a difficult conversation with Dad about Mum's final wishes. It was difficult to reason through this dilemma in such emotional circumstances. I didn't want to disagree with Dad, but out of total respect to my mum, I knew that I had no choice. It was important for the preparation of my mother's body that there be agreement between us.

Ultimately, we resolved that Mum would be cremated. After this decision, it seemed to me that any other issues in preparing Mum's funeral would be easy to resolve.

Mum's sister offered to stay with Mum until she was transferred to the funeral director. My aunty was now the only surviving sibling of thirteen children. I felt her aloneness, her loneliness and her heartache. Reluctantly, I left to take Dad home and help him with the phone calls to family and friends, and to prepare Mum's funeral.

I called Ben to let him know, and to ask him to come over for the funeral.

"Of course. Do you want the kids to come too?"

Another tricky decision to make.

SHARING THE FUNERAL WITH LITTLE ONES

I wanted our children with us. My mother was their grandmother, and I knew that Papou would love to see them. There is something very special about having children at funerals, as they contribute so much by their presence, their hugs, and their interest in what is happening and who is there. It's also an opportunity to help them learn a little about death and the grieving process, an early life lesson. But I was also worried that our twins, Caitlin and Zavier, who had only just turned eight years old, might be a little emotionally overwhelmed by the experience, and by seeing their mum so upset in a way that they had never seen before. I wanted to shield them from my own grief.

I reasoned that only our eldest child, Kyra, should attend.

"Caitlin and Zavier both saw Mum recently, and it would be nice for them to keep those memories. And Caitlin was just here to celebrate Mum's eightieth in April."

"That's true," Ben replied.

"I'm also worried about how well they will cope, and I don't want them to see how sad I feel."

"I think you're right."

"What? I should get that recorded! Okay, well, I was also thinking that it would be great if Kyra wanted to sing at the funeral."

"Isn't that maybe a bit too much for her? Kyzie is only ten."

"I don't know, I think you would be surprised by her strength and maturity. At least at times like this. She sang a song recently for her school at the Vietnam Soldiers War Memorial Service in Manly which I think would be perfect. She won't have to learn a new song."

"Okay, well, I can ask her."

"Thanks, and can you please be gentle with how you tell the children that Grandma has died? They might get really upset."

"Yes, of course I will," said Ben, rather gruffly. I was worried he might be very matter-of-fact and not careful with how the children might react. As it turned out, the twins took it in their stride and agreed between them that they would draw and write sympathy cards for Papou that Dadda could bring over with him to Napier.

THE CANOPY OF LOVE BEFORE THE FINAL FAREWELL

What followed was days of phone calls to family and friends, and meetings with the funeral director and minister to organise the service. It was wonderful to have my aunty with us as she was a wonderful support and guide to me, and a lovely tonic in a week that felt like a wild sea of sadness. My cousin and her son flew over from the Northern Territory and it was so lovely to have their help and support as well. They were great at running errands too! I was also so glad that they were with us as well, in memory of my cousin's mum, Olive, who was Mum's sister and one of the Three Musketeers.

That week was also very special time spent with my dear friend Alison and her children in their beautiful home, having her company to talk into those small hours of the night, sharing memories of Mum and our families, having lots of laughs and tears together. Her home became my sanctuary, and I will never forget her hospitality, warmth and love.

Alison had known Mum since she was a young lady and just like the Three Musketeers, Alison and I had spent much of our lives together, flatting together at university, living and working in the same cities in New Zealand, and often painting the town red together. As our careers took us in different directions, and I moved from Christchurch to Sydney and Ali moved to Hawke's Bay, our friendship stayed strong and true, frequently being topped up with calls and emails and holidays together. Our children are now also friends, and it is so nice for the bond to develop with the next generation.

On Wednesday night, Ben and Kyra arrived from Sydney. I was so glad to see them and so pleased for Papou that he would see Kyra and hear her sing at her grandmother's funeral the next day. Dad, George and I also had the benefit of Justin's wife and his children attending from Christchurch to join the service, as well as Dad's brother Stathi and Aunty Beth. It was lovely to have their company and support.

I collected Ben and Kyra from the airport and took Kyra to meet the musician who would accompany her on the acoustic guitar. He was a music teacher at a local high school and played in a band. He was only too happy to help but was rather bemused that Kyra was taking on the challenge of singing the gospel hymn 'I'll Fly Away'[27] at her grandmother's funeral. The words to this hymn are so prophetic and emotional that it is often sung at funerals.

Listening to Kyra's angelic voice brought me to tears. I wondered if it might be too difficult for Kyra to sing at the funeral, and maybe too much for me!

FUNERALS PROVIDE THE OPPORTUNITY TO HONOUR CULTURES AND TRADITIONS

The next morning, the hearse arrived at my father's house to collect Mum, who, in recognition of her Irish traditions, had been brought home before the funeral. Mum's coffin was in the dining room that had French glass doors opening into the lounge and could be closed when Kyra was at Papou's house. But otherwise, it was lovely to keep the doors open, so even when we weren't sitting in with Mum, she was still part of the activities.

As Mum was carried out from Papou's house, I was taken by surprise. Before I had the chance to, Kyra grabbed Papou by the elbow and said, "Come on, Papou, let's walk Grandma out." It was a tender moment, and a mature gesture by my ten-year-old. I was so proud of her.

It was a sunny Spring day and I had arranged for lots of daffodils to fill the foyer of the church and the pews. Mum had always loved planting bulbs in her garden and watching them burst into daffodils in the spring. The vibrant yellow was now a welcome sight as extended family, friends and colleagues filled the church for Mum's funeral. It was a beautiful farewell for my mum, a wonderful celebration of her life. We listened to some of her favourite opera arias and the song 'You Lift Me Up' sung by the Irish singer Josh Groban. Kyra also sang a beautiful rendition of 'I'll Fly Away'. We also had family share poems and psalms.

I had suggested to Dad that he write a eulogy. If he was unable to stand and share it at the service, it could be read on his behalf. This was a lovely way to honour Dad's wonderful memories of Mum, and for him to be able to contribute in a meaningful way at the service, without the added emotional pressure of having to speak to an audience. It was also a wonderful way to include his brother Stathi, who delivered Dad's eulogy beautifully.

I also delivered a eulogy. I had spent hours writing it in the middle of the night, drinking pots of tea and reflecting on the beautiful mother, wife, friend, sister and colleague that was my mum. As I read the eulogy at the service, my voice did not waver. I was proud to speak of her, to share so many wonderful memories and experiences with Mum, many of the valuable lessons she taught me, and the wonderful sense of humour that she had shared with us all. It was a very different experience to deliver a eulogy about my eighty-year-old mum who had lived a full life.

After the service, Mum was taken to the crematorium in a 1939 Plymouth hearse, made in the same year as Mum's birth. The minister delivered a short committal service. It was wonderful to have family say a few final words at that service, including my Aunty Beth, who I know loved her sister-in-law and her Irish sense of humour.

Kyra joined us for the short service at the crematorium. As we were leaving, she walked up to the minister, and without blinking, extended her hand to shake the minister's hand and said:

"Thank you, Father, for a beautiful service for my grandma."

Hiding his surprise, the minister said:

"Thank YOU, Kyra, you sang beautifully for your grandma."

"Thanks, Father, I think it was good too, but as they say, there's always room for improvement!"

The minister and Kyra shared a small chuckle together. It was a wonderful proud parent moment. And I'm sure Kyra's schoolteachers would have been thrilled.

I have always found the finality of the crematorium or the burial to be very difficult. It is the walking away from our loved ones that pulls at us as we are forced to step back into our lives without them. It was no different with Mum. But I decided that I would do my best to park how I felt so I could be hospitable to everyone at Mum's wake. Mum would want me to do this, and it was the last act that I could do that day to honour her.

THE CAMARADERIE OF COMING TOGETHER IN MEMORY OF A LOVED ONE

We joined together for the wake—at Shed 2 in Ahuriri. It was a lovely bar which was exclusively ours for the afternoon. We could share a drink together and soak up the views out to the Kaweka Ranges and out to sea, or just watch the fishing boats bobbing in the harbour. We were joined by close friends and family and we all stayed for longer than we had planned, but none of us particularly wanted to leave. We didn't want to break the camaraderie of the moment; it was a great comfort and safe harbour for each of us, as we processed the day's events. My dad was so pleased with the service for Mum and the kind words spoken about her by so many. But the time had now come to go home and for each of us to get on with our own lives.

INSIGHTS

- There are almost 500,000 Australians living with dementia and almost 1.6 million people are involved in their care.[28]
- Dementia is the second leading cause of death in Australia but it remains as one of the most "challenging and misunderstood conditions."[29]
- Dementia is the general term or name given to the mental decline that interferes with daily life. Alzheimer's Disease is the most common cause of dementia. Stigma continues to surround Alzheimer's Disease which is due in large part to a lack of public awareness, education and understanding. Often family members may be in denial of the diagnosis, and not want to talk about it, and friends may withdraw from the diagnosed (as happened to my mother).
- There is currently no cure for dementia but scientific research is ongoing to better understand its causes, develop strategies to reduce dementia risk and slow its progression, and ultimately to find a cure. The Dementia Australia Research Foundation (previously known as the Alzheimer's Australia Dementia Research Foundation) is the research arm of Dementia Australia.

Support is available for dementia sufferers and their carers through:

- Dementia Support Australia (1800 699 799).
- Also, the National Dementia Hotline is 1800 100 500.

PART THREE: RENEWAL

CHAPTER EIGHT: MY STRATEGIES FOR HEALING

Grief over things that no longer are,
When all at once we feel far,
Away from memories, one moment after the next,
Of places and people we'll never see again,
Grief is a mixture of both happiness and pain,
Sunny days covered in rain,
To keep in our hearts wherever we go,
Grief is a friend only we know.

—E.H. @Poemboii

My journey of healing and renewal began after Zoie and James died. Their deaths changed my life in an instant. As a young adult, I found their deaths very confronting and difficult to deal with. I struggled with my loss and grief through my university years, and as a junior solicitor. My grief was further compounded with the loss of Mark.

NOVUS ACTUS INTERVENIENS—A NEW ACT INTERVENES

Following Mark's death, I went for a short break to Sydney. After a morning run around Mrs Macquarie's chair, I stopped for a newspaper and a coffee at a café in Circular Quay. Scanning the *Sydney Morning Herald*, I spotted an ad for a legal role with a commercial law firm in Sydney.

When I got back to my friend's apartment, we discussed the opportunity, and I was persuaded to apply for it. After I returned to Christchurch, the job interviews followed, and I was offered the role.

Arriving in Sydney at the end of summer, I settled into my new role and concentrated on meeting the expectations of a new employer in a large cosmopolitan city and learning the laws and multiple systems of government unique to Australia—a welcome distraction to my grief.

Of course, I knew that a change of geography would not erase my grief, but the distractions were helpful. It might have travelled with me, as if neatly folded and tucked into my suitcase, but I had to bear my grief and do something to break the chain of bad tidings in my life, to find a new path for myself. It caused me to think of the legal term *novus actus interveniens*, which is Latin for a new act intervening, i.e. an event or act that breaks the causal connection between a wrong or crime committed by the defendant and subsequent events. I needed a break, and that break might just bring glad tidings for a happier life.

As it turned out, my move across The Ditch was the initial step towards building a new life.

FINDING MY LIFE'S PURPOSE

I also needed to find my life's purpose and create meaning in my life. I knew that I wanted to meet and build a new life with a new partner, and hopefully one day have my own children.

When I moved to Sydney, I wasn't yet sure of my life's purpose.

What was my positive, inspirational and guiding statement that might help me to make the right choices, and direct my actions, to achieve my desired outcomes?

I decided that a good place to start was to set myself some goals that I knew I needed, and wanted, to achieve. I felt that the achievement of those goals would bring me towards identifying and applying my life's purpose.

I had to create my own financial security, so my new job needed to springboard my legal career in a different jurisdiction. I needed to build sufficient personal wealth, so that I might one day own my own home. I also needed to create a new network of friends and colleagues. And I needed to find new activities and pursuits for my free time—I wanted to fill my free time with as much busyness and distraction as possible, so I didn't have too much time to focus on my grief. I had the wonderful distraction of everything around me being new and unknown to me in the bright lights and big city that was Sydney. I still felt my grief and pain, often acutely at times, but at other times, my grief had to fight for my attention. I enjoyed building connections with workmates and creating friendships.

It took time to identify and define my life's purpose and it has changed over time, as my circumstances and my view on life has changed. You will have your own definition of your life's purpose which may be far more elaborate and meaningful than my own. My own definition is:

My life's purpose is to live the fullest and best life that I can, and to be the best version of myself, so that I can help, support and love others and make a positive lasting impact in the world.

This statement is a regular mantra of mine. It has provided me with guidance and a sense of fulfilment and strength in making minor and major choices and decisions, including which of many roads to take, and what to do at the 'T' intersections that we are each confronted with in life.

There are many other benefits from defining your life's purpose. After all, it is a forward-looking statement that is proactive and positive. It should help to motivate you, provide you with a sense of direction and intention about what you want, and can do in your lifetime, whilst creating a sense of achievement and satisfaction for yourself.

SOLACE IN THE CEMENT

Through work friends, I was invited to join different touch rugby and netball teams, and was introduced to Sydney Striders, a running club in Sydney that organised Sunday runs around all different areas in Sydney. It was a great way to see different parts of Sydney whilst enjoying the camaraderie of running with others in the early hours of Sunday morning. Over time, many of my running buddies became my grief buddies, and ultimately, my life buddies. We would talk as we ran around the streets of Sydney, our chatter only interrupted by the sounds of rubbish trucks, and partygoers spilling out of nightclubs.

In Sydney, my early morning Sunday runs were only 10km or 15km, but they were a great introduction to longer distance running as I gradually built my fitness to run more half marathons. I saw so many different parts of Sydney that I might otherwise have never seen. I had been a short-distance runner at university, and then ran regularly up the Rapaki Track in Christchurch with Justin. Over time, I had built up enough endurance to run a half marathon in Buller Gorge, Greymouth. I had to cross the South Island of New Zealand by car to attend the race, so it was my first foray into long-distance running. A running friend had advised me to carb up before the race, so I gorged on a massive pasta dinner the night before the race and woke up to a sore belly and 21.1 km to run! It was and still is my slowest running time ever, but at least I finished.

Running can be a very solitary form of exercise if you are running alone, but I enjoyed the mix of my individual daily runs, local runs with my running buddies and my Sunday morning runs with Sydney Striders. I found solace in pounding the pavement, having a singular focus of being out on the road early in the morning before the rest of Sydney geared into action. It had a meditative, therapeutic quality as I could just focus on how I felt, think about my stride and my breathing, and concentrate on my running route.

At other times, I would use it to process my thoughts and my feelings. It helped me to be able to think freely; if I wanted to, I could feel the sadness and the anguish—which usually meant I would stop running and walk and cry my way back home. I would allow myself this time, but then beat myself up later for wasting a training run! Taking this time also meant that I could come home and get ready for work and 'park' my grief so that I could function and concentrate in my job that day. Some days were easier than others.

My running training guaranteed me some quiet time to think about everything or about nothing. It also offered a slightly different experience on every run. It might be a change in weather, a slightly different route, running into someone I knew, running faster or slower, or feeling fitter than the day before, but I always knew that whatever the weather, the road would be outside my door again tomorrow.

STAYING TRUE TO MY BUCKET LIST—THE CANBERRA MARATHON

After running the Buller Gorge half marathon, I decided that my bucket list had to include running a marathon. As my running fitness increased, I felt that despite my grief, I had to stay true to this goal, commit to the training and choose a marathon course to run. It was simply now or never, as who knew what the future might hold?

In Sydney, some very good running friends and I made the decision to train for a marathon in Canberra. Sydney Striders had a marathon training group (MTG) that was led each year by a seasoned marathon runner. The group was designed to help new runners train for their first marathon. We often met for a mid-week run and ran together for our long Sunday runs.

We also followed a training program that was designed to help us gradually build our weekly kilometres over a period so that our fitness would peak just before the marathon, hopefully without injury or incident. It was a four- to five-month training program. Each night, I would put my training gear by the bed so I could get dressed in the morning and get out the door before I had time to make excuses to myself. I felt I owed it not just to myself but also to my MTG mates to keep up with the program and to stay honest with myself about my weekly training. I knew I would never achieve the end goal of completing a marathon if I allowed myself to skip my training whenever I felt too lazy to do it. A marathon is a real test of endurance and, as I found out, is not something that you can achieve by self-deception.

Over time, I built mileage in my legs in readiness for my first marathon in Canberra. The night before the race, I was careful not to eat too much pasta at the pasta night! But stupidly, I over-hydrated myself before the race and needed lots of bathroom stops on the course! Thank goodness for the portaloos! Whilst I didn't hit the expected 'wall' at the 20km or 25km mark, I found the last 12km extremely challenging, but I made it and was thrilled to cross the finish line.

Before long, I started contemplating a second marathon. I had only intended running one marathon to tick the box on my bucket list but felt there was plenty of room for improvement! After a short recovery, I picked up my training for the Gold Coast Marathon in Queensland. This was a great race option as it was a flat course, so with the right training (and fewer bathroom stops!), I could improve my PB (personal best time). I enjoyed getting away from Sydney with my running buddies for the weekend (ironically 'a short break') and completed the marathon in a new PB. I was elated and felt I was now a legitimate 'marathon runner', having completed two marathons in close succession.

ACTING IN MEMORY AND IN HONOUR OF A LOVED ONE—THE NEW YORK MARATHON

After Justin died, I began running again as a form of self-therapy. I decided that in his honour, I would run one more marathon, but it would have to be the largest marathon in the world. The New York City Marathon. Justin would have loved all the fun, celebration and spontaneity of a major event in New York City, as he had travelled to the USA some years before and had many wonderful memories. I would run the NYC Marathon for Justin as well as for myself.

The trip to New York was an amazing experience for me as a young woman and as a runner. My eyes were opened wide to the most populated city in the United States, home to over 8 million people all jostling for position, power and success in a concrete jungle that is only 784 square km.

During the race, over a million New Yorker spectators packed the sidelines of the course to encourage and cheer thousands of runners, slapping our hands or our backs as we passed, and calling out the names of runners who had written them on their shirts. We started at Staten Island, ran through the five boroughs of New York (one spectator even held a sign 'No walking in the Bronx!') and finished in Central Park.

I had tried to manage my splits as the race signs were posted in miles and yards (rather than kilometres and metres as we are used to in the Southern Hemisphere). As I entered Central Park, I groaned as I realised I had overestimated how far I had reached in the race. The finish line was much further into the park than I had expected. I had thought that the race was only 26 miles, but in fact the additional distance was the 200 yards that I hadn't counted (26.2 miles, rather than 42.195 km!).

The next day, the results of more than 35,000 runners were published on the front page of the *New York Times*. I bought some copies and scanned the page for my name. It was in such small font that you almost needed a magnifying glass, but it was there! And it was a new PB! I knew that Justin would have been so proud and it was so incredibly sad that neither Justin nor Zoie could savour my achievement and share in the celebrations afterwards.

When I returned to Sydney, I was ambushed by some of my running buddies, who persuaded me to run the Melbourne marathon, a flat and fast course. I could improve my sub four-hour time if I concentrated in the race on my splits at each 5km station and ran an even race between the first 21km and the last 21km.

Like all city marathons, it was an early and cool start, which meant we didn't overheat whilst waiting for the race gun. The course took us from beachside Frankston into the Arts Centre in Melbourne City. I followed my time closely during the race, concentrating on where I was up to against my target times for each 5km station. I knew I was ahead of my target time by about five minutes and held that lead at each 5km leg until I reached 25km. At the 25km water station, I decided I needed to get further ahead of my target time before I hit the hardest part of the run, the last 10km. If I could just hold a lead of several minutes coming into the 30km water station, I would have enough time for some slippage at the tail end of the race. I ran hard from the 25km marker, willing myself to hold on to my lead, knowing that this might just be my last marathon.

I held on to my lead until I reached the 40km mark, when my left knee became 'gammy' and I knew I was in trouble. I desperately wanted to stop to a walk, but worried that I might come to a complete stop. I didn't want to give away all that hard-fought lead, and miss making a PB in what might be my last marathon. I kept reciting "*Don't stop, you can do this*" in my head, and then found myself saying it out loud. I thought, wow, I really am a 'rambling runner', but no one noticed, or if they did, they didn't care!

There were many runners and spectators making lots of noise, cheering the runners on from the sidewalks, as we ran in the centre of the road. I took a moment to notice the other runners and the crowd, inspired and motivated by the sea of faces to keep going. I had to finish and not lose my lead. I could worry about my knee afterwards. As it turned out, I finished with a PB, a great sub four hours' time that put me in the top 21% of women marathon runners worldwide.[30] I was so happy with my result and decided that it would be okay to finally hang up my marathon running shoes.

I credit my running for keeping me sane, and for helping me to live with and work through my grief for Zoie and James, Mark and Justin, by allowing me the space to think about it as I ran, and by exhausting me enough physically so that I could get to sleep at night. It was the combination of finding solace in the regular training runs, the company of my friends, the challenges that I set, and the achievements that I enjoyed and endured.

I also credit the physiological benefits of endurance running and exercise, such as strengthening my heart and blood flow, building leg, bone and tendon strength, the serotonin benefits of exercise and the mental toughness from the prolonged training programs to achieve my end goals. These benefits can be achieved from many different forms of exercise and sports. The physiological benefits, physicality and challenges of exercise helped to deplete some of the negative energy that was the angst and pain of my grief, helping me to move forward through it, and helping me to fit it into my daily life.

FOLLOWING THE BLACK LINE

Running can be very hard on your legs, feet, joints, hips and tendons. To bring some balance back and help rid my legs of the lactic acid build-up from periods of concerted training, I started swimming.

I followed the black line on the bottom of the pool, concentrating on nothing more than counting my laps. The repetitiveness of the activity calmed my mind and exhausted my body. I literally wore myself out most nights in the pool after work. It also helped with the constant mind chatter and the flood of emotions and memories that overwhelmed me in the quiet of the night when there were no other distractions.

Some of my running buddies introduced me to a swim group who met on the Northern Beaches of Sydney for ocean swims each Saturday morning. It was a mixed group of different ages and walks of life (and swimming abilities), but between us we all shared a love of swimming. We swam between several different beaches, stopping midpoint to tread water and regroup, and then at the end of each swim, we shared breakfast at a local cafe. It was a privilege to be a part of this group. We became firm friends and, after our swim, shared what was happening in each of our individual lives over bacon and eggs and the delicious smell of coffee.

One Saturday morning, a friend and I were acting as sweepers at the back of our group. We had stopped to regroup, and she told how she loved swimming butterfly, a stroke that I had never mastered. I asked her to swim 'fly' as we headed into Shelley Beach. The sea was calm and there weren't many swimmers around us. She claimed she was rather rusty and then proceeded to swim butterfly like a champion! I was so impressed that I stopped and treaded water for the longest time to watch her. It was a moment that I wished I had been able to capture with a waterproof camera.

Palmie to Bilgola Ocean Swim

Some of our group went on to compete in the various ocean swim races held each summer on the Northern Beaches.

Not to be outdone, a friend of mine, John, and I decided to 'go big' and swim the 3km Palm Beach to Bilgola Beach Ocean race. It wasn't a 'race' as such for either of us, but a challenge to swim (and complete) it!

We all met early morning at the starting gun on Palm Beach. Each age group would race separately so we had the opportunity to stand around and contemplate what on earth we were doing! As my age group started, we set out from Palm Beach following the cliff face, deep dark water beneath us, with thoughts of 'who knows what lies beneath'. As we reached the end of the cliff face, we swam across the cove of Bilgola to the southern end of the beach, before turning at a pink buoy and swimming into the beach. The sea swell made for a choppy swim and dragged us much further south up the beach than the race organisers had intended, adding many metres to our swim. We came into the beach and half ran, half walked up the finish line, exhausted by our efforts and the drag of the tide. We then waited for buses to take us back to the start at Palm Beach, no towels or clothes, just wet swimmers, and tired, barefoot bodies. We were both really satisfied to have completed the race but exhausted by our efforts and the long wait to get back to the car and warm clothes.

On the drive back from Palm Beach, John and I were both so hungry that we couldn't talk, and drove in silence until we reached the infamous Collaroy Pie Shop. We devoured pies for breakfast (not the healthiest option but they were delicious!) and then exchanged a mumble of words as we headed home.

The satisfaction of my physical achievements has been exhilarating and a wonderful distraction from my grief. It has made me appreciate that we can all do what we want with effort, focus, determination, lots of training and, in the case of swim races, following the black line that is on the bottom of every lap pool in Australia. Day after day.

Even beset by emotion, grief, and a host of happy and sad memories, I realised that I could train hard and focus on my goals, converting my anxiety and grief into energy that motivated and propelled me into action. It opened me up to some wonderful new experiences and expanded my environment with fresh faces who have become good friends.

FINDING MY VILLAGE OF GRIEF BUDDIES

It is said that it takes a village to raise a child. I believe it also takes a village to nurture, support and console the grieving. From my many years of grief, I found the most amazing support from the least likely, or least obvious, of people that have crossed my path, and not the most immediate, proximate and closest people to us, our own immediate family and our closest friends. Often, those dearest to us are also trying to come to terms and deal with their own grief and might not be able to provide the support and understanding we need.

After Zoie and James died, I realised that as much as I wanted my parents to help me with my grief, they simply didn't have the capacity as they were struggling themselves. I also realised that my parents' grief was very different to mine. We could share our memories of Zoie together (although my parents always found it hard to speak openly about Zoie after her death), but our grief was very different. My parents grieved the loss of their child, which must surely be the hardest loss to bear, and one that no parent should ever have to suffer. I grieved the loss of my sister and my best friend. We had also lost different futures with Zoie. My parents wouldn't see her marry or have children and she wouldn't be with them at the end of their own lives. To me, Zoie and I wouldn't share each other's lives together, raise our children together or be with each other in our old age.

I found 'grief buddies' in many wonderful people, and just as I seemed to need them. A grief buddy is a confidante and supporter who listens, talks, shares tears and tissues, and holds your hand without judgement or criticism. They can be there for you and understand what it means to grieve. They helped me to understand for myself what it means to suffer heartbreaking loss, and how I might live with that grief and move forward in my own life. They have collectively all been part of my village.

It is this village of 'grief buddies' that has helped me to carry the burden of grief. Whilst my grief might always be with me, I choose the journey, the paths that I travel and the destinations. I also choose how much grief I carry with me and what weight it bears and the impact it has on my daily life. We all have different perspectives on life, love and loss. The benefit of engaging with others with very different perspectives is that it has helped me to find my own perspective.

ADDING A COUNSELLOR TO MY VILLAGE

At different times on my grief journey, I sought support and guidance from kind and trustworthy counsellors who are objective and empathetic, non-judgemental and realistic. Being a confidential and private relationship made it easier to be open and honest, not only with the counsellor, but also with myself. As psychologist Jason Mueller[31] explains:

"*During therapy, I regularly ask my clients to tell me about the 5%, to which I get quizzical looks. As I explain, people tend to avoid being fully open about the things they need to make sense of and tend to keep a portion of their thoughts very private. Developing a good therapeutic relationship helps to build trust and then hopefully the opportunity to discuss these innermost thoughts. As I say to my clients, I want them to be able to have the conversations they need to have to help free up their thinking and emotions. For many, these trusting conversations mark a turning point, leading to catharsis, acceptance, and insight.*"

I could let go a little of my grief by sharing it, giving it a voice, allowing time for it and then parking it in my own mind long enough to let me concentrate on my day. It helped me fit my grief into my daily life. Over time, I found that I engaged with my counsellor and shared my grief each week, each fortnight and then each month, until I only needed to seek support when I most needed it, my six-month update, my annual refresh.

My counsellor understood where I wanted to get to in my grieving, perhaps well before I did.

Jason Mueller comments:

"Working with my clients during a time of grief is often a very positive therapeutic experience for them and defined by emotional growth. Having to confront the reality of death or dying inevitably poses existential questions for which they need answers. It becomes an unexpected opportunity to explore their life's meaning and their purpose as they seek to understand the strong emotions that overwhelm them."

MY OWN TLC

Just as I found physical activity and social contact important, I also found that I needed rest, space and privacy, and quiet time to deal with my grief. The death of a loved one creates countless emotions that can be foreign to us. In addition to experiencing the shock and sadness of our loss, we also must contend with a huge spectrum of potentially new emotions. Dealing with the rollercoaster of emotions can be just as exhausting as physical exercise.

The rollercoaster was easier to manage on some days than on others. I dealt with it well when I had given myself time-out when I needed it, and when I allowed myself to rest. Sometimes, I would struggle to sleep, and other times, I would sleep heavily. I realised that when I couldn't sleep, rest was just as important and could be just as helpful. I would cocoon myself in bed, allowing my body and mind to be quiet and still, to rest, recover and heal.

Being kind to myself and listening to my body kept it simple. It might be some couch time watching non-stop movies or curling up with inspirational and self-help books or trashy novels or some weekly magazines, some pampering time at a day spa, or a Bikram yoga session, or the simple pleasures of a regular massage or manicure. At times of loss, when we are at our lowest emotionally, we are challenged to find out what we can do to nurture ourselves.

When do you feel comforted? What nurtures you, consoles and relaxes you, and helps you breathe? By finding our own forms of nurture, we can identify and build our own toolbox of skills and tools to help us in ways that we know will work.

POWER OF THE WRITTEN WORD

I have applied the art of writing at many different times in my own life as a means of trying to understand and process my grief, and those feelings and emotions that overwhelmed me.

Penning a letter

When Mark died, I felt there was a lot that had been left unsaid. I also had a lot of questions that would and could never be answered, and a lot of heartache that I didn't know how to express or with whom I felt safe sharing it, without judgement and scrutiny. Whilst I had many false starts, I found my voice through writing letters to Mark. I would write in the old-fashioned way of using a pen on paper!

My letters often had sections crossed out and were rewritten, contained doodles and drawings, and were often unfinished. Sometimes, they were just long statements, or were lists of questions that I had no answers for. At other times they were strong, forceful, punchy remarks that were fuelled by my anger, disappointment and frustration.

But you may ask, what to do with them? I often stacked them together, tied with a ribbon or string, and kept them in a shoebox in the wardrobe. When I wasn't writing and adding to them, I would go back and reread them and assess my thought processes and how my moods and feelings had changed (or stayed the same). I also enjoyed the symbolism of burning them in the garden until I started writing again.

My writing encouraged me to think about the importance of the tools of my craft. I found that there was some satisfaction in holding a nice pen, twirling it in my hand as I contemplated my next sentence, or enjoying the colours of the pen case as I stared at the blank page before me. I relished collecting colourful notebooks and journals, although I found them harder to write in, almost as if to do so would spoil the pretty pages.

Keeping a diary

I have kept numerous diaries over the years, often full of descriptive details about my travels, my feelings and other life events, as well as random records of my emotions. I also wrote about my likes and dislikes, new activities, interests and friends. They might be no more than a sentence or two describing my favourite or hardest moment of the day, what I was worried about, what I was procrastinating about in making a decision, a favourite food or new food I had eaten, what I had achieved that day or what I planned to do the next day, what new songs I had heard on the radio, what new film releases I wanted to see, what the morning sky or the night sky looked like, what I had dreamed about in my sleep, what my daydreams were and so it went.

Boxing them in

I also used the tool of writing negative thoughts on a Post-it Note or sticky note and putting them in a box (preferably a box with a lid for privacy, such as a perfume or shoe box), as a symbolic release of those negative feelings by externalising or expelling them onto paper. If I didn't write them down, I was overzealous in analysing my thoughts and feelings. It was easier to consider progress and themes and sense check my emotions by externalising them and reviewing them on paper. As the box filled up, I collected the notes and sorted and leafed through them, and then delighted in ripping them up and throwing them in the bin. It was satisfying as well to empty the shoebox, purging myself of those negative emotions.

Inspirational quotes and positive affirmations

Accidentally, I developed a habit of writing down affirmations and quotes or witty phrases that were motivational, inspiring or just resonated with me at a particular moment. I usually wrote them onto Post-it Notes and put them on the fridge or by the phone (when we used residential landlines!) or on my bedside table, or to the frame of my computer monitor. I then read them during the day as I passed by or as I worked. Eventually I had so many on my computer screen that they started falling off! I couldn't bear to throw them out, so I would pull them off and collate them, and then stack them in my pen drawer and start the process over!

Do you enjoy reading catchphrases and inspirational quotes? Do you have some favourite positive affirmations that motivate you? Often the words of others can offer us comfort and guidance in understanding and reconciling our own emotions. It can also be helpful to verbalise and repeat positive affirmations as we start our day to set our mindset for positivity and growth.

BEING ALERT TO PLATITUDES

Whilst we might want to offer verbal support to someone who has experienced the death of a loved one or other significant loss, all too often we find it difficult to vocalise our concern in kind and gentle ways without judgement. Whilst our words might be said or asked with pure intent or well meaning, some of the more common platitudes that I have heard include:

"*You must be over the worst of it by now.*" (No, and what's the "worst of it"?)

"*Haven't you found that time heals?*" (No, it makes it worse since I haven't seen them for a long time, and it may be even longer before I ever see them again.)

"*At least you must have some great memories.*" (Yes, but I would have loved to have made more great memories with them.)

"*They are in a better place.*" (Are they? How do you know? And where is that?)

"*Don't cry, they would want you to be happy, not sad.*" (They aren't here so why do they get to determine how I am 'allowed' to react?)

"*I know how you feel.*" (No, I'm quite sure you don't—but you may have experienced your own loss and your own grief and know how you feel.)

"*Life goes on.*" (Well, it depends on who you are. It doesn't go on for the ones we have loved and lost, but mine does go on without them.)

"*You have your whole life ahead to live.*" (A similar sentiment to the above, but it reinforces that we are left with our own lives that won't include our loved ones.)

"*Let me know if I can help.*" (I don't know, and I can't think too far ahead in my day or my week or month about what my own needs are or how you can help me with them.)

I know that I don't need words of pity, however well meaning. I also don't need anyone's permission to feel how I do or to express how I feel. I will defend myself and my grief to others, especially to those who may not have yet experienced a heartbreaking loss, whether it is the death of a loved one, or some other life-changing loss. I will protect myself from the judgement of others.

With that sense of self-preservation, there are many ways in which we can help others who seek to support us by our suggestions, such as:

- Thank you for your concern. I really appreciate it.
- Would you like to share your memories [of X] with me?
- I am feeling very sad/hurt/concerned/worried and it seems like this will never end. So please understand that I don't know how others can say that "time heals". All I can concentrate on is right now.
- I need a listening ear if you would like to listen. Perhaps I can tell you how I am feeling.
- Can I tell you what I find so hard right now?
- I appreciate that you say you know how I feel. Do you have any suggestions from your own grief experience that you would like to share with me?
- I appreciate your offer of help. Perhaps you could speak to [my husband, a member of my family, our children] to see what needs to be done and if you can help with any of those things.
- I [don't know yet] or [can't really decide] how you can help me but please have a think and let me know what you can do to help and we can work out if that will be useful.
- I would like to speak with you regularly for a while if you can please work out when you can call me and then I can look forward to our calls.
- I would like to see you regularly for a while if you can please work out when you can pop in/meet for a coffee/go for a walk, etc., and then I can look forward to seeing you.

BE PREPARED

There is no time limit, and no calendar, for grief. I don't just feel my sadness on anniversaries, birthdays or Christmas. Instead, it can and does still sneak up on me, at times when I least expect it.

You may have seen someone like me:

- The woman who hugs her children just a little too tightly every morning at the school gate and who insists on a kiss, a cuddle and an "I love you" from each of her children before she will let them go.
- The woman on the ferry who sits quietly at the window wiping away tears whilst applying makeup on her way to work.
- The woman in the shopping aisle who suddenly bursts into tears whilst reaching for a can of beans (usually because of a random, emotionally charged 'supermarket song').

These women are me. I am less emotional than I used to be, but these moments still happen, and I am simply doing the very best that I can every day to live and function normally within my own changed landscape.

However, I have also learnt that I must avoid situations that will completely unravel me. In New Zealand to visit Dad, I was in his garage and feeding the dryer with washing when I saw it. The shoebox on a shelf with my sister's name, '*Zoie*', written on the lid. I had always known that Dad had kept cards, messages, telegrams and the funeral service sheet from Zoie's funeral, but I didn't know where they were stored. Curiosity got the better of me and I took the lid off the box. Here they were. Beneath the cards and telegrams was a witness statement prepared by the police officer who was first on the scene at the accident site, and my sister's autopsy report. I had never seen these documents before, and whilst I didn't want to read them—I couldn't stop myself. I knew I shouldn't. I sat down on the garage floor as I pored over the statement and autopsy report. It was a moment that I have wished a thousand times since that I could take back. They were filled with very graphic details about the accident, and about Zoie's body. The words stuck to my brain. I couldn't escape them.

What followed were many nights dreaming about Zoie and James, reliving the accident and their funerals, and bursting into tears at random moments throughout the day. When I returned to Sydney, I found that the contents of those reports were embedded firmly in my consciousness and would come to mind whenever I wasn't engaged with my work, in conversation with others, playing with my children or caring for them. Those words, and the violence of their deaths, haunted me for weeks afterwards.

I realised from this experience that we need to take care of ourselves, understanding that our grief is complicated and can be easily triggered. Whilst it is always real to feel the grief, we can also try to avoid our triggers when it is in our own best interests to do so. It isn't to deny how we feel. Whilst we want to fit our grief into our daily lives, it is also a step of acknowledgement of our grief that we are willing to protect our emotional selves.

ACHIEVING SECURITY IN THE REBUILD

After Mark's death and as a single thirty-something woman in Sydney, I could only look to myself to create some financial security and needed to kick-start my financial planning as part of my many goals in rebuilding my life. I decided to start a 'six-month savings session' for a deposit to buy an apartment.

My plan was simple enough. I dodged invitations to restaurant dinners and the many city bars that served exotic cocktails at fancy prices, and instead spent my weekends frugally, occupied with trips to the beach, and runs and swims with friends. I also curbed my miscellaneous spending during the week and saved a deposit on a new apartment just north of the Harbour Bridge. It was a great spot for easy trips to work during the week, and to the beach at the weekend. I was so thrilled to now have my own home (with the help of my bank!) and enjoyed being able to invite friends over for parties, dinners and movie nights.

I was also creating emotional security as I now had four walls that I could call home. It was wonderful to have my own home, and to know that I wouldn't be tipped out by the landlord! I could also personalise it and make as many holes in the walls for my art as I wished. I also enjoyed buying new homewares, as well as adding colours to the white spartan walls. It became my sanctuary, the perfect place to escape from the outside world when I needed it. Because I was on the tenth floor of a secure building that had a twenty-four-hour concierge, I also had the peace of mind of physical security, which was important to me as a single white female living in a large cosmopolitan city.

BEING OPEN TO ROMANCE

Not long after buying my apartment, I started dating Ben. It was very easy to allow myself to be romanced by him. Early in the relationship, we had many wonderful dinners at expensive harbourside restaurants, and weekends away to the Hunter Valley in New South Wales and Noosa in Queensland.

At times, it wasn't easy for Ben to get to know me or to understand me. I had seemingly surrounded myself with a concrete turret as a means of self-protection and mostly came across as a reluctant girlfriend. I also had a complicated demeanour, since I was still processing my grief that I carried from the deaths of Zoie, James, Mark and Justin. I was also trying to work out who I was now, what my priorities were for my own life, and how I could manage being away from my ailing parents who were living in New Zealand with serious health issues.

From all appearances, Ben seemed to take my compounded layers of grief in his stride. Initially, he asked me how I was feeling, but over time, I think he decided it was better not to ask. Instead, I would often volunteer how I was feeling, especially when my sadness was triggered by a memory or moment that reminded me of my family.

At other times, I would find it hard to express how I was feeling and became quiet and introspective. Ben had to wrestle with my short attention spans and changes in mood. At times, he would express his frustration that he didn't know how to help me, or he would feel exasperated and say that he couldn't continue the conversation with me when it just didn't seem to be going anywhere. We had a few blockades to cross.

On my side of the equation, I felt frustrated that Ben didn't understand how I felt. There were many factors that weren't in his favour. Ben was fortunate not to have lost any loved ones—even his great-grandmother was still alive!—and he hadn't had any other major loss experiences in his life to that point. Also, by his own admission, Ben considered himself an alpha male with "limited emotional intelligence", who was brought up to not talk about his emotions. Without the practice of speaking about his emotions, he was uncomfortable with expressing them or listening to the expressed emotions of others (including emotional girlfriends!). Added to this was Ben's attitude that one should reflect and concentrate on all the "happy, positive memories" of loved ones who have passed and "not be so sad", which never resounded well with me.

Ultimately, the most challenging factor of all that makes for difficult conversations about my grief is that Ben never met Zoie, James, Mark or Justin. I have tried over time to share my memories, and to describe their personalities and our adventures and experiences together. Whilst Ben didn't fully understand or appreciate the enormity of what they meant to me, or my grief for them, he now has some insight into my complicated and enduring grief. But I have been circumspect about my memories of Mark and chosen out of fairness and respect to Ben not to share those with him. It is important to consider and choose my audience when dealing with complicated emotions and memories of loved ones, and especially a previous life partner.

Ben has also impressed me with his pragmatism and said how much he would have loved to have known them (especially since he thinks that, from all accounts, he and Justin would have been "good mates"), but he has never allowed himself to be worried by the fact that they never met.

"I can't turn the clock back." And who can argue with that?

Instead, Ben has sought to love and protect me, and always encouraged me to look forward with love in my heart for my past, and hope and promise for all the joy that we can experience together in the present and the future. His optimism and positivity are unwavering and have served to buoy me up in rough waters, when I have been through difficult emotional trials that have tested my zeal that a happy and productive life is possible and deserved.

Together we have been on many travel adventures, experienced different cultures and met many wonderful people who have all impacted our lives in some way. We have also worked incredibly hard in our chosen careers. Our greatest joy has been to become parents to our three gorgeous children. Together they provide us with love and laughter every day, as well as tears and tantrums, long-winded negotiations, pleas and requests, constant demands to be their Uber drivers, unlimited laundry and messy bedrooms, a house that is full of noise and busyness, and the 'joie de vivre'. We feel very blessed and privileged to be parents of these incredible little humans and fully relish our responsibility to help them as they grow to become independent, productive, happy, healthy and kind adults.

CARRYING ON THE LEGACY

Over time, I allowed my grief into the life that I have with our children. Whilst I was nervous about doing this, I knew I had to be honest with myself and them. Although not present in their own lives, I realised that they needed to know about Zoie, James and Justin.

When Kyra was six years old and the twins were four years old, I spoke to them one day about Zoie, James and Justin in the car on the way home from school and long day care. It was easy to mention their names and drop snippets about them in the busyness of the trip and the noise of their mixed-up, interrupted conversations. It turned out to be harder for me to share the facts of their deaths with my children than it was for my children to hear it! Like most young children, they have enquiring minds and had plenty of questions.

"Mumma, why did Zoie die?"

"Mumma, how did Zoie die?"

"Mumma, how old was Zoie when she died?"

"Mumma, why did Justin die?"

"Mumma, how did Justin die?"

"Mumma, how old was Justin when he died?"

And one that has been harder to answer is:

"Mumma, where are Justin and Zoie now?"

Children seem to have their own unique way of understanding complex and difficult concepts by connecting it to what they know. They also asked:

"Does that mean they aren't in their homes now?"

"Are they in a different home now? Where is it?"

"Can Zoie and Justin still see you? Can they see me?"

Questions that aren't easy to answer, but as our children are being educated at Catholic schools, I answered with Christian concepts they understood, such as the funeral and burial, the spirits of our loved ones and going to Heaven. My efforts to be honest have satisfied their curiosity, as they now don't ask as many questions as they used to. They are also comfortable with sharing their knowledge of Zoie and James and Justin and their deaths in a very matter-of-fact way. I don't mind them sharing this news with adults, but I discourage them from talking about it with other children. My open approach to the deaths of my siblings may not be the same choice that other parents would make with their own children.

By teaching my children about their extended family, and not just those who are present in their daily lives, they have come to understand they are the sum of a wonderful, rich ancestry.

It would be easy to ignore the family resemblance. But I have chosen instead to look for it, acknowledge it and appreciate it at every opportunity.

My daughters, Kyra and Caitlin, remind me of Zoie in different ways. Kyra looks a lot like Zoie and has her confidence and wisdom. Many people who have met and spent time with Kyra have said, even from a very early age, that "she is an old soul". Caitlin doesn't look like Zoie, but she has the same personality, exuberance and sense of humour as my sister. She also has the same fire in her belly as Zoie had. My son, Zavier, in personality, is the mirror image of my brother Justin. There are many moments, every day, when I catch my breath because of something Zavier says, or because of one of his expressions or mannerisms that are exactly like Justin. Zavier has a very gentle and kind and loving personality, and I know that Uncle Justin would be so proud of each of my children if he were alive now.

I don't run from these moments, I embrace them. They offer comfort that my sister and brother continue to live on in their nieces and nephew. I like to share these moments with my children, so they know the many ways in which they carry my family with them.

PETS ARE OUR CONSTANT AND OUR CONNECTION

Our pets can be our constant in turbulent lives when we are overwhelmed with our grief and mourning. Often, they can be wonderful reminders of our loved ones. When Zoie and James died, they had a lovely tabby cat called Max. After their deaths, I couldn't take him back to my university flat, so Zoie's best friend became Max's new owner. Max was a wonderful lasting connection to Zoie.

Some years later, Ben and my children became the owners of a White Russian kitten who has one blue eye and one green eye and 'answers' to Jack. He is our 'COVID dog' as we wanted but couldn't find any puppies for sale locally during the COVID lockdown, so we settled for a handsome, low-allergenic and supposedly low-shedding kitten. Jack is still trying to befriend Ben, who just tolerates him. The kids and I love and adore him. He always gives us a big MEOW and nuzzle in the morning, and is always available for pats and cuddles, and even walks on the dog lead. Jack has also been known to chase our neighbour's dog, Pepper, back to his own home whenever Pepper ventures into our garden. When I play with Jack, I often think of Zoie's cat and how much I wished I had been able to give Max a home.

CONTINUING AND CREATING TRADITIONS AND RITUALS

I have continued traditions and created rituals to acknowledge significant dates, events or places that relate to or remind me of Zoie, James, Justin and Mum. They are traditions and rituals that create moments for reflection, remembrance, gratitude, thanks, and appreciation for their lives and for the privilege of having had them in my own life.

Traditions and rituals which include:

- lighting candles on their birthdays and the anniversaries of their deaths
- making toasts in their memory at special family gatherings
- attending carol services and drinking their favourite beverages at Christmas
- adorning our Christmas tree with personalised baubles in their memory
- engraving their names on a wind chime in the window and on a birdhouse that hangs from a tree in the garden
- painting a mosaic tile with one of Mum's favourite Irish poems that sits in the garden bed
- looking at photos of them and showing those photos and talking about them with my children
- drinking my brother's favourite Irish ale on St Patrick's Day
- wearing my sister's favourite scarves in winter and her favourite jewellery on special occasions
- wearing the only ring of Mum's that fits my hand (Mum had long, slim fingers and I do not)

- listening to music by their favourite bands
- watching some of Mum's favourite operas
- watching their favourite movies—James loved Stand By Me[32] and Zoie loved Fame[33]
- taking my sister's favourite flowers to place at the cemetery
- supporting charities by fundraising and making donations in their memory
- talking about them to family and friends

Over time, I have created more rituals, to hold on to my memories and how important my loved ones are to me. It also allows those memories into my daily life, honouring them alongside the traditions and rituals I am now creating with my own family.

My children are included in these traditions and rituals so they learn about how important my 'family of origin' was to me, and how we can honour them in our own lives.

FITTING GRIEF INTO A BUSY LIFE

Modern life is fast and furious. We all lead busy lives. We each receive and send up to hundreds of emails, text messages and calls every day. In such busyness, how do we fit our grief, which demands introspection and reflection, into our lives? It is my work in progress to create time and space for myself, maybe a quiet moment at home, a walk in the park, a run to the beach, watching my children learn to play touch rugby or golf with their dad, a conversation with a friend who knew my family and can share and appreciate the memories. Sometimes, I talk to Ben, sharing the good times as well as the sadness, because this is me and my life, and I must embrace and accept all of me. Because of my grief, I am a different person living in a changed landscape, and doing my best to now live my best life and to be the best person that I can be, and to live those 'unlived years'. If not now, then when?

ACCEPTING THAT MY LIFE TOO SHALL PASS

During our adult lives, most of us will only turn our minds to our own mortality when we prepare our wills and consider what our final wishes might be. Yet we all know that each of us will pass on, that it is the final certainty in our own lives.

After the loss of Mark, I didn't want to leave my apartment for work in the mornings without my bed being made, the breakfast dishes washed (or stacked in the dishwasher) and the apartment tidy. I was subconsciously preoccupied with my own mortality, that something might happen to me during the day and the police would then need to attend my apartment.

Since meeting Ben and being blessed with children, I am less concerned with how our home looks each morning, and more concerned with getting us out of the house on time! It is a welcome relief that I am focused on living my life and less preoccupied with the end of it.

When the inevitable does happen, I hope that I will have shown my family and my children as much love as it is possible for one heart to share, and that they will be filled with lots of lovely, happy memories that will comfort them in their own grief. I don't want my children to be scared or consumed by their grief. I have tried to normalise death and sadness for them by sharing my own grief experiences (as appropriately as I can for their ages), and I hope that this has created a foundation from which they will later understand the meaning of life and death, and the pain that we feel from knowing, loving and losing others. I hope that they will understand that it is normal, that we will grieve those we have lost because of our love for them.

To grieve is human because to love is human.

I hope too that in the darkest hours of their grief, my children will have the support, understanding and love of those closest to them, and that they will continue to live healthy, happy and productive lives in the knowledge that I will always be in their hearts. If they can do this, then it will mean that I have taught them that love, loss and grief are very much a part of life, and they will know how to make their own grief fit their own lives.

CHAPTER NINE: UNDERSTANDING GRIEF

Some of you say, "Joy is greater than sorrow," and others say,
"Nay, sorrow is the greater."
But I say unto you, they are inseparable.
Together they come, and when one sits alone with you at your board,
remember that the other is asleep upon your
bed.

—Kahlil Gibran, The Prophet

Just as grief creates a vortex of emotions, there are many different strategies that, in combination, may help in the healing process, and some may be helpful depending on where you are up to on your own journey.

In the following chapters, I have set out some additional strategies that may assist you in the early days following your loss, as well as in the weeks, months and years that follow. I hope that some, or all, of them may resonate with you.

UNDERSTANDING THE GRIEF PROCESS

We all experience grief differently. It can take very different forms and present itself over different time periods. In her book *On Death and Dying*[34] world renowned Swiss-born American psychiatrist Dr Elisabeth Kübler-Ross identified that there were common stages to grieving by the terminally ill prior to their own deaths: denial and isolation, anger, bargaining, depression and loneliness, and acceptance.

Although they are described as stages, she recognised that they might not all be experienced, or that they might occur together, or even sometimes overlap, as typical emotional responses to learning of actual or imminent death. However, whilst the Kübler-Ross model was also later applied as a model of grief for the bereaved, it was not developed in relation to grief. As such, it is not strictly speaking a model of grief, and, given more contemporary approaches to grief, it is arguably no longer a popular explanation or guide for the grieving process.

In addition, the Kübler-Ross model does not provide answers or guidance to how the pain of loss can be endured. Nor does it reveal to us how we can move through, and past, the pain so that we can move forward with our lives, how we can deal with our own grieving or how we can best support someone who is grieving—someone who may be facing the death of a sister, brother, partner, husband or wife, mother or father, friend or unborn child.

Whilst psychologists and academics have identified other stage- and task-based models of grief,[35] modern approaches to the grieving process recognise that grief does not occur in a pre-determined and finite time frame. Rather, as has been my experience, it may continue to exist in one's life in some form or extent for many months or years, it can be triggered by significant events or milestones or other significant losses, and it can vary widely having regard to individual characteristics of the bereaved, such as their personality, social considerations, ethnic/cultural background, and any religious or spiritual contexts.

These modern approaches also recognise the importance of managing and adjusting to the loss rather than seeking to finally resolve it.[36] Invariably, this entails an acceptance that over time, our grief may dissipate or at least, will start to fit into our lives as we resume some of our usual routines of life, such as cooking and eating, sleeping, engaging with others, household chores and activities, returning to school (or university) or work. We may oscillate between our grieving activities and our other life activities, but hopefully our time will increasingly be more absorbed with daily life. Even so, modern approaches suggest that we can continue our bonds with the deceased by continuing to recognise and appreciate them, in healthy ways, as we move on in our own lives.

From my own experiences, I have recognised that it is also possible to experience what is popularly known as 'anticipatory grief'. As the name suggests, this may occur when, for example, your loved one is diagnosed with a terminal illness (such as cancer or Alzheimer's disease) and the grieving process starts before they pass on. It can arise as the disease or illness progresses, or when it reaches an advanced stage. It may cause similar emotions as grief does, such as denial, frustration, sadness, depression, anxiety and anger.

The news of the impending deaths of Justin and later, Mum, caused me to pause and consider their lives, what they meant to me, the love I felt for them and all the experiences and life that we had shared, all they had done for me, how I had helped shaped their lives and how they had helped shape my own. It was as if I needed to pre-empt how I might feel when they died, how my life would be irrevocably changed, how I would manage without them, and how my life too would come to an end. This period of reflection came to me throughout the periods of their illnesses but was most keenly felt as I spent time with them in their final hours.

Some steps we can take to help us manage our anticipatory grief include:

- Speaking openly, as your loved one is diagnosed or declines, with your family and caregivers about your feelings and sense of loss and how you can manage your feelings and provide support to each other
- Seek support from the hospital or hospice staff who are caring for your loved one
- Obtain updates about the condition and progress of your loved one from their carers
- Seek out your own information about your loved one's condition, the stages of their illness, the symptoms, the available treatments, and their limits, and what the final stages may look like
- Talk to others who are knowledgeable about the illness or condition, e.g. hospital social worker, support groups, hospital or hospice chaplain or church minister, online or hotline services
- Use the time available to have 'those conversations' with your loved

one that are important, e.g. to express any unresolved feelings or issues, or if they can, encourage and support your loved one with their end-of-life plans, their finances and their legal affairs

- Create any lasting memories that you can with your loved one, e.g. walks in the park, trips to their favourite ice cream shop or café, lunches or dinners at their favourite restaurants, visiting their favourite places outdoors, arranging for friends and family to visit, taking new photos of happy gatherings and creating a montage to hang on the wall, sharing and talking about photos of previous family gatherings, listening to favourite bands and musicians, or watching favourite movies, TV shows, operas, etc.
- Look after yourself by taking time out from caring for your loved one, arranging for family to share the caring responsibilities, enjoy your usual activities and connections as a way of having some time out and renewing your energy, and speak to close friends or counsellors about your own grief journey.

KNOW THAT YOU ARE NOT ALONE

Did you know that about 60 million people die globally each year?[37]

It is proof that we are not alone in our grief. Every person who dies has a family (irrespective of whether they are close to their relatives). So we can usually expect that those families have also grieved their loved ones. They are on their own grief journeys, trying to find their own ways to continue to live meaningful and happy lives.

GRIEF IS NOT A DISEASE

Grief is not a disease but a human condition, a collection of emotions and a healing process that is suffered by those who have suffered significant loss, and in the case of bereavement, loved and lost important and special people in their lives. It will be felt by each of us in our lifetimes.

In the case of bereavements, the deaths of our loved ones may affect us differently, but what holds true is that it will always be normal and acceptable for us to feel our grief, as an ordinarily normal and natural reaction to our loss.

However, grief from bereavement that is persistent and disruptive to our normal lives, our identities and our emotional wellness (which is described by reference to multiple criteria but which include preoccupation with the deceased, and severe emotional pain or numbness) for prolonged periods (more than twelve months for adults and more than six months for children and adolescents)[38] may constitute 'prolonged grief' (or 'complicated grief', 'traumatic grief disorder' or 'persistent complex bereavement disorder'). Prolonged grief disorder is recognised as a 'trauma and stressor-related disorder' and was added as a category of mental health disorders by the American Psychiatric Association in the *Diagnostic and Statistical Manual of Mental Disorders V Text Revision* (DSM-5 TR)[39] in March 2022.

The inclusion of prolonged grief disorder as a mental health disorder in DSM-5-TR was controversial and prompted media speculation that it may 'medicalize mourning'. However, in an article addressing an earlier update to the DSM-5 (which removed the 'bereavement exclusion' from those persons with major depression)[40], Dr Ronald Pies[41] considered that that change was unlikely to result in the inappropriate diagnosis of the bereaved with major depressive disorders, and that in most cases, the best therapy may be 'watchful waiting' to see how patients progress on their grief journeys and that talk therapy rather than antidepressants may be sufficient treatment.

Subsequent studies have shown that the definition of and criteria for prolonged grief disorder in DSM-5 are accurate, and its inclusion has not increased the stigmatisation of those persons suffering from prolonged grief disorder.[42]

A LITTLE CYNICISM IS A GOOD THING

We all know the cliché 'time heals all wounds'.[43] But does it really? Isn't time just a human construct to define when things happen, with regard to their duration or the instant when it occurs, and whether as to the past, the present or the future? How can time heal? And if it does, then why do we not all heal in the same way or in the same time frame, if at all?

We will each deal with our own grief experience differently, how transparent we are about our emotions, and how long those emotions will affect our daily lives. I now know that there is no such thing as an 'appropriate level of grief' or an 'appropriate way' to show your grief. Nor is there a 'time limit' to grief. I feel my own grief in a multitude of ways every day. It will accompany me for the rest of my life; it is simply not true that 'time heals'. Instead, it is our own endurance, fortitude, determination, resolve and resilience that help us to find our own way, to continue with our lives that have been forever changed by our loss. We are living changed lives, in our changed landscapes. It is up to each of us as individuals to recognise how we can help heal ourselves—what our own individual journeys of healing and renewal will look like and where they will take us.

CHAPTER TEN: IMMEDIATE AFTERMATH

SHARE YOUR GRIEF WITH OTHERS

When we lose a loved one, we are beset with a myriad of complex emotions that, from the outset, are difficult to feel, process and manage. There is enormous benefit in seeking to share your grief with others. I believe that it helps us to identify how we are feeling, and how we can process and manage it, to cope with the responsibilities that arise following the death of a loved one.

But how do we engage with others about our grief in a rational dialogue when our feelings and thoughts may not feel at all rational to us? We may be overwhelmed by our grief and struggle with expressing it in a way that is relatable to others.

Helping others to help us

Just as we have not been taught how to grieve, we have also not been taught how to console and actively support someone who may be struggling with their grief, whether from the untimely death of loved ones, or other life-changing losses, such as the loss of our marriage or relationship, the loss of our home, our favourite pet, or the loss of income, the loss of our job or our career or our livelihood, the loss of our health such as our mobility or sight or hearing, and other life-changing losses.

We can help steer our conversations with our supporters by using language that invites them to listen to how we are feeling, or by inviting them to share their own memories and feelings. We can encourage them to identify meaningful ways in which they can help us, either with household chores or with the funeral (or other final farewell) arrangements, or by providing us with conversation or company, or comfort that we will find a way to manage and live through our grief and renew our lives.

Let them in

It's hard to know what someone else is feeling or thinking or wants or needs unless they tell us. Whilst we think we may understand and even know others, we truly don't know how any of us will respond to a life-changing loss, or how our lives will be impacted, until it happens. And then none of us will grieve in the same way.

If we are to have others help us, we must let them in. Your network of family and friends may not be aware of your loss, so it is important that you share the message. Others need to know so that they can help. You may decide that you cannot convey the message yourself or that you only want a select few to know. You may want someone else to convey the message. It doesn't need to be you, but it is important to reach out so that those close to you will be able to offer their love and support to you.

We should be willing to share and be open about what has happened, how we are feeling, how we are coping, what we are thinking, how we might be supported, what we want to talk about and when we want to talk. Even when we don't want to talk, we can feel supported by others just being available to us, by being there with us to share the silence.

Perhaps you may also want to make a list of who you need to notify of the passing of your loved one, the details of the service, and who they may need to share that information with so that you can rely on them to let other special people in your network know. You might also want to provide your list to your nominated person who is delegated to contact others on your behalf. Your list might look like the following:

Name of Contact	Relationship to you and to the deceased	Phone/ email/fax details	Other persons that the contact will notify (and any contact details for those persons)	Will they attend/ participate in service or provide message for reading at service

DESIGNATE A LIAISON OR SUPPORT PERSON

You may wish to nominate a spokesperson, liaison or support person for the family. A family member or other relative, close friend or trusted adviser can offer support and guidance to you and your family in dealing with the immediate matters at hand on the passing of your loved one. It is also helpful to have someone to support you as a sounding board, and to provide support in making and negotiating decisions on key issues or arrangements.

You can then decide how much you would like them to be involved, and what they will deal with, including notifying immediate family members of the anticipated passing of your loved one so that they can say or send final goodbyes, formally identifying the deceased, notifying family and friends of the death, assisting with or preparing the obituary, managing the press, assisting with the funeral arrangements, acting as liaison with the funeral director and other service providers, managing accommodation and other requests of extended family and friends.

IMMEDIATE AFTERMATH

When a loved one dies, there are many decisions to make, and practical matters to arrange, almost immediately. There are also practical matters to manage in the short and long term.

Many decisions can be difficult, and some may be delicate decisions for the impact that they will have on others. Invariably too, family and perhaps close friends will expect to be consulted or otherwise involved in the decision-making. It can be a difficult and challenging process to navigate successfully, especially when we are each dealing with our own emotions of shock, denial, anger, sadness, heartache.

Some immediate tasks include:

- Establishing the final wishes of your loved one. Did they express a wish for organ donation? Did they express a preference for a burial or cremation (which will affect the preparation of the body)? Often you may already be aware of their final wishes (or they may be recorded in their will or end of life plan)

- Obtaining the death certificate
- Arranging for the body to be transported to the funeral home
- Making plans for any dependent children or persons under their care or domestic pets
- Taking steps to secure their home, locking doors, turning off appliances or power and water, emptying the mailbox and garbage, etc.
- Locating essential documents such as a will, end-of-life plan, life insurance
- Informing others of your loved one's death—obituaries and telephone calls, posts to Facebook or other social media platforms
- Attending to personal belongings of your loved one (clothing and other personal items such as jewellery, glasses, scarves, hair ties, etc. that you may wish them to wear for their farewell. Usually, the matter of packing up their clothing and personal items and even entire house lots can be dealt with later)
- Confirming how the final expenses will be met
- Arranging for the final farewell including choosing the casket, contacting the celebrant or minister, arranging the venue and date for the service, notifying mourners of the details, considering who will participate in the service, including who will give eulogies, and choosing the music, readings, photos and videos, program of

service, etc. Also attending to the flowers, transport, pallbearers, refreshments (many of which can be arranged by the funeral director)

- Resolving what is to happen with the final remains—did your loved one make plans for their farewell or express a desire about where or with whom they want to be buried or where they want their ashes kept or perhaps scattered?

The above list omits many other ancillary decisions that may need to be made in a short time frame. You may find it helpful to delegate some of these tasks to family members and close friends. It is also a useful way of including them in the process, helping them to feel involved and valued, and will assist them in processing their own grief.

Your designated spokesperson can assist in directing the efforts and energies of the family in making the necessary preparations, moderating any family discussions, liaising with the funeral director, and fielding calls and enquiries in relation to the funeral.

You might want to make a list of all the immediate tasks that need to be completed and who will be asked and/or volunteer to complete them. Your designated spokesperson can speak to those persons and gauge their willingness to assist and participate in the process. It may be that some people are willing to participate but that others might decline to do so, and this is perfectly acceptable as well.

Your list could include the following:

Matter or task	Proposed person to complete	Person who has agreed to complete	Support or information/material they need and who will provide it	Timing for completion

Following the funeral, other tasks and decisions will usually centre around finalising the estate of the deceased. For the executor, this will include reviewing the will and resolving if probate is required and resolving the arrangements for the deceased's property and other assets, as well as finalising all bills and other expenses. The personal belongings of your loved one also need to be collated and stored or distributed. Subject to the deceased's will, it may be useful to give special items of clothing or other keepsakes to family and friends and make donations to a hospice or charity.

In addition to the above, there are also many practical matters to consider.

Meal time

Consider asking friends and family to put together a meal roster/calendar or they can contribute their resources to pay for fresh meals to be delivered to your home. My flatmates organised a roster of meals between them after Zoie and James died and I returned to our university flat, so that I didn't have to share the cooking duties for some weeks. After Justin died, a good friend cooked dinner for me in my apartment in Sydney every Thursday for weeks. It was so nice, not just to enjoy someone else's cooking, but also to have my friend's company while she cooked and shared dinner with me, and I came to relish that special time, and really looked forward to our Thursdays.

If several family or friends are cooking for you, a meal roster might be useful (so you don't have ten consecutive dishes of spaghetti bolognese arrive at your door!). The roster could be on your fridge for friends to add to when they visit, or preferably, your designated support person could email it to everyone to complete and it could look like the following:

	Mon		Tues		Wed		Thur		Fri		Sat		Sun	
	Chef	Dish	Chef	Dish	Chef	Dish	Chef	Dish	Chef	Dish	Chef	Dish	Chef	Dish
Week 1														
Week 2														
Week 3														

Also, your network could be encouraged to cook a little extra or save any extra into a freezer-proof container for you as a frozen meal.

Let them love your little ones

Let trusted friends/family know that you need their help with caring for your children, the school drop-offs/pick-ups, getting to sports practice, birthday parties, playdates and sleepovers. Just as the world keeps turning after we lose our loved ones or suffer other life-changing losses, so too our little ones have lives that need to be lived, and they need to keep their own routines, activities and friendships.

We have a weekly roster on our fridge that sets out our children's activities with a separate calendar next to it for the one-off playdates, birthday parties or extra activities (e.g. end of footy or netball season break-up parties). Your roster could include the following:

Name of Child	Mon		Tues		Wed		Thurs		Fri	
	AM	PM	AM	PM	AM	PM	AM	PM	AM	PM
Jane	Flute, School, 7.30 am, Grandma Contact details for flute teacher:	Netball, Manly Courts, 4.30 pm Grandpa Contact details for coach:								
Bob										
Mary										

Delegate those jobs

Be honest and say "YES" when your supporters visit and ask if they can help. Let them know that as much as you would love to make the millionth cup of tea or coffee, they might make one for you, or perhaps have one with you whilst stacking/unstacking the dishwasher, putting on a load of laundry, hanging out the washing (or bringing it in), making the beds, vacuuming or mopping the floor, feeding the cat/dog/fish/bird, or doing any of those other nasties that count for housework. When you are overwhelmed with and exhausted by your grief, you don't need to be house proud. Let others help you.

Allow others to be your runners

Let your friends and family run your errands for a while. The laundromat won't care who collects the dry cleaning (so long as they have the ticket!), and it won't matter who does the grocery shopping—so long as they have the shopping list! Create a shopping list for the fridge door that others can take with them when they go out or which they can re-order for you online.

Also, allow someone to collect and sort your mail from your letterbox for a while. My parents were inundated with sympathy cards in the mail for weeks after Zoie and James died. I decided to look after the mail, and it was nice to walk their long driveway to the letterbox each day, and to drive to check the post box at the post office, escaping the claustrophobia of their home. I also responded to many messages on behalf of my parents, but whilst we made best efforts, we couldn't respond to them all—hopefully our supporters understood. By being engaged with these tasks, it helped me feel useful and needed, and it was a welcome distraction from my grief.

Your energy levels will also help you to identify what you can manage. It might be that you seek the help of others within your family (or paid help) for jobs that don't have to be done by you personally or in a particular order or time frame, e.g. gardening, cleaning the house, ironing. You might focus your energies on those jobs or demands on your time that are important to you, e.g. parenting, communicating, or spending time with family and friends or enjoying their company, sorting out the personal belongings of your loved one, exercise and your other self-care routines.

BUILD YOUR BORDERS

Whilst we may be willing to share and be open about our loss and grief, we also need to be measured and consider what and how much we share, and with whom. We can decide our own borders with others so that we are comfortable with what and how much others know about us, secure in the knowledge that we will not be judged for what we have imparted, or lectured about what we should or should not do, or how we should/should not feel or think. We may instinctively know our closest mentors and supporters, but we may need to have different borders for different persons in our life, such as family members, extended family, friends, acquaintances, workmates, professional colleagues and others within our network. Our borders help us feel safe; they protect our emotions, decisions, energy levels and values. The level and content of information shared may differ, and so too, our borders may change over time.

Your borders may be quite different in the immediate aftermath of your loss to those that you may have some months or years later. Immediately, you might feel that you need to manage how much time you spend with others, how many people you allow into your home, which of your feelings and emotions you share, how much you support others in their own grief, what decisions you allow others to have input into, and what jobs or responsibilities you are willing to delegate. In time, you may relax your borders, but you may still limit the sharing of your thoughts and emotions, your decisions.

I am now more transparent about my own loss and grief (even writing a book about it!) than I have been in the past. My own borders were important and helped me to feel protected from the judgement, criticism or opinions of others, and to feel comfortable and safe in my decision-making.

So how do we build our borders? You will instinctively know for yourself what you need. Listen to your intuition. You will know who your greatest supporters may be, and those who are not, or with whom you may have a difficult relationship. Decide who will be the good listeners, the good errand runners, those who will be positive and encouraging comforters, and those measured allies who will help you make decisions without taking control. Also, don't be put off by the reactions of others. Instead, keep applying and restating your borders, and keep re-setting them as time, and your circumstances and needs, change.

MANAGE (AND NEGOTIATE) YOUR RETURN TO WORK

Returning to work after the loss of a loved one can be very difficult and stressful. However, it may also be helpful to resume some normality in your life, have the distraction of returning to work and feel some personal satisfaction from performing your job.

In Australia, the federal law affords only two days paid compassionate leave to full-time and part-time employees if an immediate family member or member of the household dies or has a life-threatening illness or injury.[44] It is barely enough time to arrange and attend the funeral or other final farewell. Whilst these entitlements can be, they are often not negotiated with employers where individual contracts of employment apply, and most employer compassionate leave policies will also only provide for a few days' paid leave.

Apart from providing for additional compassionate leave, there are also many other ways in which employers can and should provide support and assistance. In your return to work,[45] you should review any compassionate leave policies in your workplace for any other entitlements or benefits that your employer has agreed to provide. You may also wish to discuss your return to work, and whether there may be flexibility in relation to:

- Additional days being taken as accrued annual leave or unpaid leave either for the days leading up to the passing of your loved one (we know that anticipatory grief can pre-empt the death and be as exhausting as grief after the death) or after the funeral or final farewell (to support yourself or others who are grieving, or you may have dependent children to care for, or you may need to deal with the estate of your loved one)
- A staggered or phased return to work, such as reduced hours each day or reduced days or shifts
- How communications will be managed, including whether your colleagues will be informed of your bereavement, and by whom, and

whether you want to be involved in the messaging/communication of the messaging

- A change in your responsibilities
- Job or task sharing or 'shadowing' on projects, so you have support to meet deadlines
- Access to counselling or other bereavement support
- Working from home or identifying set days in the office
- Attending social activities at work—it may be nice to receive the invitations but may also be nice to be able to decline them without judgement
- Your seating arrangements in the office
- Future dates that you will not be able to work, e.g. unveiling ceremony, anniversary date
- Your work period and whether additional time can be taken as paid or unpaid leave in one month's time, or in three months, six months, one year

Similar considerations apply for those who are self-employed and may have their own workforce.

All of us will experience loss and grief in our lifetimes, and major life events will likely occur at some time during our working lives. Since the grieving process may extend over many weeks and months (and years), it is important that employers recognise and accept that they need to provide ongoing support and understanding to the grieving. Doing this will ultimately help to ensure a compassionate, healthier, happier and more productive workforce.

CHAPTER ELEVEN: BUILD YOUR RESILIENCE

What is resilience and why is it important? You will have your own understanding of what constitutes resilience. To me, it is our ability and capacity to be able to respond to, adapt to, and recover from circumstances of tragedy, trauma, loss and grief, and other difficulties including high levels of stress (or distress). Resilience is important because it gives us the ability and the strength to process and adapt to significant hardship and respond to it in healthy, meaningful ways.

You may have heard of the expression "*Whatever doesn't kill you makes you stronger*", attributed to the German philosopher Friedrich Nietzsche. It is a reference to the science of hormesis, which has to do with the human body's ability to adaptively respond to exposure to toxins or stressors. Although those toxins and stressors are harmful in large doses, the body can respond beneficially to small amounts by triggering cellular repair and maintenance, creating stress resistance. Resilience is all about strengthening our body's ability to respond positively to life's toxins and stressors.

There are many different techniques that we can apply to build our resilience.

EXERCISE

I found that exercise—especially running and swimming—had a very profound and positive effect on my emotional balance and stress management as I learnt to deal with and work through my compound layers of grief.

Exercise is a great trigger for the brain in releasing those feel-good chemicals such as dopamine, serotonin and endorphins, all of which help to balance and promote our mood. Exercise also helps to rid our bodies of stress symptoms and get our bodies and our brains to a state of steady or stable balance necessary for our survival. This is known as homeostasis. If you can exercise in the morning, this will help with motivation levels for the rest of the day. It doesn't need to be as manic as marathon running or ocean swim races. Your choice of exercise should be something that you enjoy, something which gives you some satisfaction, enough to propel you towards repeating your exercise on a regular basis. It may also involve other people. Having a buddy waiting to meet me for my run or walk or swim or yoga or gym session adds another dimension to my motivation. Not only I am accountable to someone other than just myself, but I get to enjoy their company and catch up on what is happening in their lives, and this is a welcome distraction from my grief.

SELF-CARE AND SELF-LOVE

In addition to exercise, my TLC needs to include rest, relaxation work such as meditation or massage, breath work (such as box breathing where you inhale for four seconds, hold your breath for four seconds, and exhale through your mouth for four seconds, as a means of relaxing the body by calming the nervous system and decreasing stress), acupuncture, sleep, good nutrition and hydration (we should now be drinking two litres of water per day).

Looking after our bodies helps us to manage and repair the physical toll that grief, traumatic circumstances and high levels of stress (distress) have on our bodies. We also shouldn't forget sunshine which is extremely helpful for our moods, as vitamin D from some sun exposure (but after the slip-slop-slap!) can help with symptoms of anxiety and depression.

LIMIT THE DEVICES

Our devices can be great distractions from the enormity of our emotions. I have spent many hours at bedtime and in the middle of the night when I couldn't sleep surfing the net. But it is just as important to limit their use, as sleeping is such an important part of our self-care in our grieving.

If we limit our own use of devices prior to bedtime, it will help to prepare our minds for sleep. Instead of picking up the phone in the middle of the night, reading a book or putting on some meditation music may help get you back to sleep. Devices emit large quantities of blue light, which tricks our brains into thinking that it is daytime, and as such, it reduces our melatonin, which is an important hormone to help us relax and get to sleep.

A good quality night's sleep is crucial for our good health and nutrition and to help our brain function. Good sleep will also help maintain hormonal and emotional balance.

GRIEF BUDDIES

Find your grief buddies with whom you can build connections so they can provide you with empathy, support, encouragement and understanding in managing and living with your grief.

FIND YOUR LIFE'S PURPOSE

The loss of loved ones has irrevocably changed me and my landscape. I am very different to the young adult woman who was at university and loving her studies and 'varsity life' before Zoie and James died.

But whilst I accept that I feel pain and loss more deeply and am more aware of how I live my life and my own mortality, I have consciously decided that I will not be defined by my grief. All said, I will not let myself drown in the vortex of my grief, the ache that is inside me that will not heal. I will not let it define who I am or how I live my life. I will love with all my heart and seek out as much laughter and joy in every day as I can. I want to live an authentic and meaningful life and create as many wonderful memories as I can for myself and my family. I also have an innate sense of responsibility to live as full a life as possible, to enjoy those unlived years of my loved ones.

What is it that defines you? What is important to you in your own life? What do you want to achieve, be, do, see, feel, know, understand, have, give, live with and live without? You can find your own life's meaning by letting go a little of your grief, even for just a short time, and looking for, contemplating and visualising your life's meaning or purpose, and what your future looks like to you. Over time, your own life's meaning or purpose may change, but if you can imagine it, you can also define it as a statement of direction and power, and in doing so, make it real in your own life.

You may wish to record your own life's purpose or meaning (which you might later add to or change).

POSITIVE THINKING

Believe in yourself. Visualise how you will manage your loss and grief, including having regard to how you have handled other difficult or tragic situations. Have an optimistic outlook, believe that you deserve a joyful and happy future.

We can consciously direct our thoughts, shifting away from negative and heavy emotions, and concentrate on what is positive around us instead, and in our lives, by creating rituals to express gratitude, and by using regular positive affirmations.[46]

In addition to noting down uplifting quotes and positive affirmations on Post-it Notes (that I stuck on just about any spare space around me!), I have found that expressing (vocalising) affirmations each morning is extremely helpful in setting my brain's framework for a positive outlook for the day.

You may have your own rituals, but I can highly recommend having a morning ritual (whether lying in bed when you wake up, or during your morning shower/run/walk/mediation/yoga/coffee, etc.) of expressing gratitude and positive uplifting affirmations that will train your mind into thinking positively. And first thing in the morning helps to set you up for a positive outlook for the day!

You may wish to list your current favourite positive affirmations and/ or create your own mantra hat you can recite each morning in readiness for the day.

WRITING AS SELF-THERAPY

Loss and grief are universal and timeless human emotions. Although we all grieve differently, loss and grief are emotions that have been written about for centuries.

The Ancient Greek playwright and soldier Aeschylus (born 525/524 BC and died 456 BC aged approximately sixty-seven years old) is credited for several notable quotes, including the following:

"*There is no pain so great as the memory of joy in present grief.*"

"*Even in our sleep, pain which cannot forget falls drop by drop upon the heart, until in our own despair, against our will, comes wisdom, through the awful grace of God.*"[47]

The quote "*Learning is not child's play; we cannot learn without pain*" is attributed to Aristotle (the Greek philosopher who was born in Ancient Greece in 384 BC, nearly 2,400 years ago), which conveys the message that learning processes take time and involve stretching our mind, body and soul.

The Roman writer and poet Quintus Ennius (born 239 BC, died 169 BC) wrote, "*Let no one weep for me, or celebrate my funeral with mourning; for I still live, as I pass to and fro through the mouths of men.*"

Marcus Tullius Cicero, a Roman politician and orator, who was born in 106 BC and died in 43 BC, is quoted as writing: "*The life of the dead is placed in the memory of the living.*"

Nearly 1,650 years later, between 1606 and 1607, William Shakespeare wrote *Macbeth*, which takes place during the reign of King James I, in which Shakespeare writes about grief as needing to be spoken:

"*Give sorrow words; the grief that does not speak, whispers the o'erfraught heart and bids it break.*"[48]

As a modern society, we are willing to share our emotions in snappy lines and sentences that are easily remembered and repeated on the internet and in social media. You only need a quick search of the internet to see that it is now bombarded with lots of pretty landscape photos and one-liner quotes. Whilst many are no more than cheesy platitudes, I have enjoyed browsing the internet for quotes that might resonate with me, offering comfort that other humans in this universe of ours have experienced feelings of grief similar to my own.

There are many different forms of writing that may help you to work through your grief. It is your own self-help, no-cost therapy that is available to you at the end of your pen, pencil, crayon or stylus, twenty-four hours a day, seven days a week.

They may include:

- *writing letters to your loved one*
- *making Post-it Notes and recording quotes to act as self-prompts and positive affirmations*
- *journalling your feelings and thoughts to gain insight and understanding*
- *keeping a diary as a record of your grief journey*

Your writing is for you. It doesn't need to be a literary masterpiece. It is instead your record of your thoughts and feelings, your expression of loss, bereavement, distress and your experiences. It is one of the easiest ways to consider and explore and delve into your innermost feelings and thoughts, a way to unravel your emotions so that on the written page, you can become more aware of them, make sense of, and accept them, and in doing so, find self-love and kindness.

Your writing doesn't need to be expressed in complete sentences, but can be single words, bullet points, phrases, thoughts, lists, pictures, symbols, doodles, numbers and figures. They may not make any sense to anyone else, but they don't need to. You are writing it for your eyes only.

There are many benefits of the written word. They include the catharsis of externalising or expelling our feelings, and thereby helping us to unravel the spaghetti of our emotions. It helps us manage the magnitude and impact of loss on our lives, helps our healing process as we learn about and better understand ourselves and our feelings and emotions. It also acts as a record of our progress and development, thereby creating self-enlightenment, by engaging with ourselves and understanding our own self-identity on our journey of self-discovery.

PREPARE FOR HOLIDAYS AND ANNIVERSARIES

My grief is often triggered by holidays, such as Christmas, New Year's Eve, Easter and birthdays—those of my loved ones who have passed and my own—and other special dates, including the annual dates of their deaths.

Prior to your loss, you may have expected that your holidays and anniversaries would be spent with your loved ones, enjoying their company and having fun, creating new memories by having shared experiences and engaging in various adventures, perhaps exploring new places or trying new activities. So how do you now manage these holidays and anniversaries without your loved ones to share them with you? How do you survive them and, over time, come to find new ways of celebrating these special occasions in your changed landscape?

Consider what you want to do and with whom

- Consider what you want to do on these occasions. What do you want the day to look like? Where do you want to spend the day, and with whom? What would you like to do? How do you want to feel on the day? Giving thought to what is important to you will help you to make plans that reflect your intentions. You shouldn't feel like you must meet the expectations of others (although you may want to consider your immediate family or dependent children and otherwise the only expectations that should matter are your own).
- Be prepared for a myriad of emotions such as sadness, loneliness, aloneness, anxiety, misery or other feelings of depression on the day, even if you have organised for others to share the day with you. Anticipate and accept that how you feel on the day will likely be very different to other years, and that is perfectly normal and reasonable. You may decide to limit or minimise your celebrations or celebrate differently to accommodate different feelings to how you felt on that

day in previous years.

- Consider different options for your celebrations, e.g. instead of hosting a big Christmas lunch, you may suggest that everyone cook a dish for one course, or that they bring a dish towards a potluck meal. You might not offer a traditional lunch, and instead host a BBQ, or have a cold lunch, or change the venue to have the meal at a local park, or beach, instead of at your home.
- Accept the hospitality of others, e.g. accept an invitation to have a Christmas meal at the home of friends or family.
- Choose whether you want to celebrate the occasion at all—you might decide that you do not wish to celebrate Christmas that year (or at all). Perhaps it is enough for you to acknowledge the day and express your well wishes to others (especially if you don't have elderly family or dependent children to consider) and spend the day how you want to. All are equally good. Allow yourself some flexibility. Whilst you might make plans that will reflect your intentions of how you want to spend the day, be prepared for your feelings to change during the day that cause you to want to change your plans or even bring the celebrations to an end. Don't feel that you need to apologise to anyone or do anything that you don't want to do.

To thine own self be true

When I take the time for remembrance before the day's celebrations start, I find that I am better able to compartmentalise my grief. I then feel calm enough to engage in the day and be more present in the celebrations.

You might also want to reflect on your feelings before the day starts in earnest, or perhaps take time during the day to honour the memory of your loved one. It may be enjoying an activity you shared like a special walking track, or cycling or running route, museum or art gallery, shopping district or markets, or going to a special place that you would visit together such as a favourite beach or park, the forest, hills, or mountains, lookouts, or a restaurant or café.

You may choose to do those activities or go to your special places on your own or ask a family member or friend to come with you, so that you have their company and support. You may wish to visit the gravesite of your loved one at the cemetery, or perhaps the site where their ashes were scattered. You may wish to leave or throw some flowers, light candles, say a prayer or special reading or share some special messages. You might decide to visit your local church and attend a service, light a candle, and say some prayers, or spend some quiet time in reflection.

Know your limits

You have probably suffered the same problem that I have at different times of not being able to decline invitations. At times, I have crammed my social calendar full so that I am actively distracted throughout the day or holiday period. Not only am I distracted but I usually end up exhausted, having completely defeated the objective of having a holiday!

It's important to consider how you want to spend your holiday or anniversary time and whether you want to accept a particular invite, without automatically saying yes to every invitation (and then regretting it later). Better to say, "Thanks for your invite, I will check my calendar and come back to you" or "Thanks a lot and I will let you know very shortly if I can make it", creating some space and time for you to consider whether you do want or need to go.

Just be

As a university student, I relished the 'free sessions' in my timetable, which gave me time to regroup from my last lecture, grab a coffee, catch up with friends on campus or spend time in the library preparing for my next lecture. These free sessions are just as important in our lives to create time for debriefs, to organise and prepare for what's ahead, and to just be.

During the holiday periods (or even during our usual week), we can block out time in our calendars which is 'Just Be' time, when we don't make any plans, and it is just downtime to kick back and see what unfolds.

Let them be

Apart from not planning every moment, it's also important to just let your feelings and emotions unfold. Let them be. Just feel them, acknowledge them and decide what you want to do (or not do) with them. Every one of your feelings and emotions is a part of feeling real and being human. They don't need to lead to a breakthrough in your pain and grief. It is just one step at a time in your healing each day.

THE ANIMAL KINGDOM

'Man's (and woman's) best friend is his dog'. When someone we love dies, our pets will be there to offer us distraction, company and affection, and to remind us of our usual routines and responsibilities. They keep us busy attending to their needs, watching them play and giving us glimpses of joy—and often annoyance—as they destroy furniture, smash vases, chew our arranged flowers or dig holes in the garden. They may also hog the bed, monopolise our favourite seats in front of the TV, nibble at our shoelaces, nuzzle against our legs, and demand walks or frolics in the garden. They are also our silent listeners. As strange as it may seem, our pets offer us the opportunity to talk aloud, to verbalise and externalise some of our feelings, much like a walking journal.

Pets are also known to be helpful in increasing our serotonin and dopamine levels, improving our moods, and reducing blood pressure and anxiety, as well as encouraging routine and commitment, companionship and friendship.

Even if you don't have a pet, there is rarely a wrong time to become a pet owner. I now think that at many times in my life as I dealt with the loss of loved ones, a pet would have been a wonderful companion, and I regret that I didn't jump into the animal world sooner. I am pleased to finally be a cat owner (even if we were after a dog!) and able to share the joy, fun, challenges and responsibility of owning a pet with my children.

If the idea of buying a dog or, in our case, a pedigree cat is too much of an investment, you may wish to consider rescuing a pet. The adoption of a rescue pet can be the most rewarding way to secure your own 'fur child'.

Of course, domestic pets are not limited to just cats and dogs but may include birds, guinea pigs, rats and mice, various reptiles, fish, rabbits, chickens, ferrets, ponies and horses, and maybe even goats and sheep! If you cannot take on a pet full-time, there are opportunities to enjoy the companionship and care of domestic pets on a part-time basis.

Consider offering to walk your neighbours' dogs, contact your local pet store and let them know you are interested in offering to help with their clients' pets, contact the RSPCA or other animal welfare organisations (or therapy dog organisations) and volunteer your time.

Therapy dogs can also provide you with support and comfort in managing your grief. Therapy dogs are specially trained to provide affection, comfort and company to individuals and families, and patients in hospitals, nursing homes and palliative care hospices, and there is a growing movement to include them in funeral homes and at funeral services.

CHAPTER TWELVE: EXTEND YOURSELF AND EXPAND YOUR HORIZONS

When we suffer a life-changing loss event, it may seem implausible that we will ever feel happy, content, in love or financially secure again. They can be very traumatic events and the enormity of the impact will often be reflected in the grieving process that follows. Each of us will experience and live with our grief differently and some of us may take longer to traverse our grieving process than others.

But it is possible to bear the grieving process and to start to feel positive emotions and feelings, and a sense of acceptance, that will help you to move forward in your own life. It may be a willingness to accept that our loved one who has passed on will never return, that our romantic/personal/business relationships are at an end and cannot be reconciled, or that we need to find a new job or career or home.

As we move towards letting go and trying to find meaning in our changed landscapes, we cannot ignore that we may still feel sadness, depression, loneliness, defeat, helplessness, fatigue or exhaustion, and that these feelings will interrupt our efforts as we are pulled in a tug of war between our life-changing events and our present and future. There will be days when you may feel or sense hope and peace and optimism and other days when the world around you, and your future, feels bleak and uncertain. These are very normal and natural feelings. For the sake of your own healing, you should let these feelings happen, and feel them as you have them, accepting that for a while, you may be in a pattern of 'two steps forward, one step back'. Even so, you will come to realise that however big or small, there is some forward momentum towards a brighter future.

You may find some of the approaches helpful in creating some forward momentum to find happiness in your own life again.

Accept that you must move through the grieving process to move towards renewal.

Set small daily tasks for yourself, that include your usual routines, but may gradually include some added tasks or activities such as walking the dog (or cat), joining a sports or gym class, joining an activity in your local community or at your local swimming pool or library (such as group walks, beach clean-ups, protecting the penguins, water aerobics, art gallery and museum tours, surf lifesaving), or joining a charity that may be relevant to the cause of death of your loved one (to support fund-raising activities or other aspects of the charity).

STEADY THE SHIP

What are the essential aspects of your life? Who are your loved ones—family, friends, colleagues—that enrich your life and with whom you have close personal relationships? What defines you and what makes you who you are? These things and people are important in your life, and it helps in steadying yourself through your grieving process to recognise and honour them with your focus, appreciation and gratitude. They will be your anchor in which to navigate the rough waters, and your compass when you set sail for new horizons.

HAPPINESS IN YOUR CHANGED LANDSCAPE

It may take time to work out, but it is entirely possible that you can direct your attention and energy towards new things, achieving new goals, developing new skills (e.g. cooking, musical instruments) or trying new activities, places, experiences, hobbies, sports, even people, from which you may find pleasure, satisfaction, joy and even happiness. They don't need to be permanent changes; you may trial different activities, hobbies, sports (even new friendships or romantic relationships) and consider if they are deserving of your time, efforts and energy by what feelings they generate within you. It is what impact they may have on your life that counts. Then plan what, how, when, where and why, or ask family or friends to help you with these details—they will be happy to help you.

EXTEND YOURSELF

After the death of loved ones, I have hit the pause button and considered my own circumstances and how and where I was travelling on my own life journey. By their deaths, I was made acutely aware of my own mortality. Conscious as well of wanting to live the unlived years of my loved ones, I have changed my outlook in life.

I decided I could no longer think, "one day". Instead, it had to be "day one". I had to accept that I needed to engage in everything I wanted to do as well as those things that might help me move to a greater sense of happiness. I also needed to be self-sufficient, relying on myself for my emotional, physical and financial wellbeing. I then extended myself in many different directions. I have tried many different activities, new sports and thrill-seeking adventures. Some of my activities (such as bungy jumping and paragliding) might not be for everyone, but for me, they were catalysts in re-enlivening my sense of adventure and excitement.

EXPAND YOUR HORIZONS

Learning to live and love again in our changed landscapes does not demand that our horizons must stay the same. Although it is important not to make significant decisions and lifestyle changes immediately after significant loss, as you start to heal, you may wish to consider how you might also expand your horizons. What this will look like to you may be different to others.

Retreats

You may be interested to experience the adventure of a retreat, some time out of your normal routine, that aligns with your current interests or hobbies or other pursuits, or which may expose you to new interests or hobbies or other pursuits—photography, creative writing, painting, yoga, wellness, health, cooking and fitness are just a few ideas.[49] Attending a retreat is a wonderful way to escape the everyday and go on an adventure to a beautiful location and facilities where you are pampered head to toe, body and soul, and the only decision you might have to make is which of the multiple program sessions speak to your needs and wants. They are a wonderful option for getting away with friends or family members, and for attending by yourself, some special 'me' time for special care, attention, nutrition and engagement that will help you on your healing journey.

I have thoroughly enjoyed attending retreats with girlfriends that focus on wellness and nutrition. They are opportunities to escape daily routines and enjoy the pleasure and power of rest, recovery, pampering and delicious meals (made even tastier being cooked by others!). These retreats have also enabled special uninterrupted time with my friends that further developed our friendships and understanding of each other. I now plan for bi-annual retreats, either by myself or with friends or family who feel they need some 'me' time (or just want a get-away!).

Most retreats offer the option of gift vouchers that family and friends can purchase for you—they might even come with you!

Change of address

Another option is to consider a change of home, a new residential address, perhaps in the same suburb, or even a new area of the city in which you live. After Justin's death, I bought an apartment north of the Sydney Harbour Bridge in a busy city-side area, which suited my lifestyle at the time with a vast array of shops, bars and restaurants at my doorstep. As my relationship with Ben developed, I decided that it would be wonderful to live in new surroundings on the Northern Beaches, so we were closer to all our weekend activities, and our network of friends. Ben readily agreed—we would be closer to the surf and could catch the ferry to work—so we moved to Manly on the Northern Beaches, and it was a perfect way to create a fresh start.

If such huge lifestyle changes don't suit you or aren't possible, you might also wish to consider whether you want to refresh your home—one or more rooms, or even just one space or zone of your house. They say that '*change is as good as a holiday*'. The size of the change is up to you.

Colour as therapy

It is amazing what a splash of colour to the walls can do to lift your mood and create a sense of newness and freshness. You may have your favourite colours, so why not add them to your walls? Or as a feature wall? In addition to favourites, there are many colours that are known to evoke different reactions or moods. Although it can be very subjective (as the same colour can evoke different reactions in two people because of personal taste or cultural differences), colour experts can advise you on colours that a majority will respond to in the same way, such as:

- Greens, blues and purples are cool colours and evoke a sense of nature, water, raindrops, night sky, calmness and relaxation (you may have heard of the green room for guests at TV sets and radio stations)
- Reds, oranges and yellows may evoke a sense of warmth, joy, energy and passion (especially a hot red!). Yellow is also a very 'happy' colour as it evokes sunshine and warmth (and reminds me of sunflowers!)

- Neutral colours such as browns and beiges, creams and greys are often used in combination with other colours that act as accents. Sometimes neutral colours can be used by themselves to create a minimalist, contemporary look
- White is often associated with cleanliness, light and purity. It is an uplifting colour that can make spaces feel bigger and brighter and works well with just about any other colour. (In Eastern countries, it is often associated with death and bereavement.) White can create warmth if it is matched with warm colours (pinks, oranges and yellows) or can create a sense of coolness when matched with cool colours (blues, greens and black)
- Black can be symbolic of majesty and formality or officialdom. It may also be a strong contrast when used with white. (In Western countries, it is also typically associated with death and mourning.) Because of the negative connotations associated with black, it may be best to use it sparingly as a framing colour or as an accent.

Soft furnishings and furniture

Another refresh option that can be very cost effective is to mix up your accent colours or change your furniture by moving pieces around the house or by just reorganising your room.

It has been very refreshing for me to change my soft furnishings. Changing the cushions, throws, rugs and art in my lounge gives the room a lift and a refresh. It is easy to pick out different colours from your wall art, curtain fabrics or furniture and use these in your soft furnishings, so the changes don't have to be expensive. I have also been known to regularly move furniture around and change pieces of furniture or art in and out of the attic, so much so that Ben often comes home wondering what the lounge will look like when he opens the front door! I have also proudly hung photos of my loved ones, even art painted by my sister, Zoie, and moved these around the house to find the right spot for them.

You will also find places for your treasures, the special keepsakes of your loved ones that are wonderful memories that you can keep close by, and by positioning them in favourite spots of your house, they will be a part of your daily life. They also make for great conversation starters, a lovely way of sharing your memories with visitors to your home.

Travel

At some stage on your grief journey, you might decide that you are ready to pack your backpack (or suitcase) and embark on some globetrotting adventures. Perhaps you have always wanted to go overseas to bask in the sunshine on an exotic island, go surfing in Indonesia, tour through Europe, travel by train across the United States or Canada, ski in Japan, visit Antarctica, or trek in the Himalayas. The world really does offer a 'pick your own adventure'.

The recent COVID-19 pandemic may have significantly interrupted global travel, but the interruption reminds us of the myriad of destinations to travel to within our own countries as well as across the globe. It reminds us of the privilege that we each have as humans to decide our own travel adventures, the course of our own life journeys and our destinations.

RESOUNDING LESSONS

The great wonder of our world is that there are limitless opportunities for us to choose how we live our lives, what we do in them, and how we enjoy and reflect on the lives of others. When we suffer loss, whether of a loved one or some other life-changing event, we are presented with a defining moment that we must work out how to survive, how to carry with us and how to continue in our changed landscapes. Life-changing events teach each of us different lessons.

A resounding lesson that has been shared with me by many who have suffered major life-changing loss or bereavement is the acceptance that we indeed have finite lives in this world, and that we must make the most of them. It may be so obvious that it goes without saying, but it is not until we are confronted with life-changing events that our own mortality is understood.

My own resounding and enduring lesson from the death of my loved ones and other life-changing loss events is that I must live the best life that I can, make each and every day count, do my very best to live the unlived years of my loved ones with meaning and purpose, and be open about my own grief as a means of helping others with their own. Just Because.

EPILOGUE

What we have once enjoyed and deeply loved we can never lose, for all that we love deeply becomes a part of us.

—Helen Keller

Since writing this book, my father has died. Dad was unwell with cold-like symptoms and took a RAD test, and his COVID-19 diagnosis was later confirmed with a PCR test. After his diagnosis, my father had two trips to hospital. The second visit would be his last, and he passed away on a COVID ward.

After spending many months, if not years, diligently managing his chronic health conditions, it was devastating that COVID-19 should be his downfall.

I was 'fortunate' to be able to travel to New Zealand to spend time with Dad in hospital before he passed. The charge nurse of the COVID ward gave me permission to attend as a visitor, and I went onto the ward in full PPE gear to see Dad. I will never forget walking onto that ward and seeing the desperate faces of patients looking out at me as I passed their rooms, their tired and exhausted bodies heaving with the brutality of COVID symptoms, that literally sucked all life and oxygen from them.

My dad was in just as bad condition and struggling to breathe. He was eighty-seven years old and chronically unwell. His medical team had decided that he would not be intubated. I initially thought that this must have been a hard decision for them to make, but as I spent time speaking with his doctors, I appreciated the enormity of their roles, which is not just to help their patients recover and live whenever reasonably possible, but it is also to help their patients die with dignity, and without pain. The 'two sides of the same coin'. I was extremely upset to know that Dad would not recover, but I was comforted by the fact that his doctors were acting in Dad's best interests, providing palliative care until his last breath.

They were difficult, but sentimental days spent bedside with Dad, as COVID ravaged his body. Dad seemed pleased to be visited by the hospital chaplain, and to have me read to him from the Bible. Despite the deaths of two of his children as young adults, Dad had remained steadfast in his faith, believing that God was always walking with us, supporting and guiding each of us in our grief. He also keenly shared his faith with anyone who was brave enough to ask and had an hour or two to spare! I truly believe that Dad was convinced and relieved that he was to be reunited with Zoie, Justin and Mum in Heaven.

In his final days, by virtue of his steely determination, my father held on for my older brother and I to travel back to New Zealand to be with him, and to pass on the anniversary of Justin's death. I have no doubt that he wanted to reconnect with his youngest son and ensure that they would always be remembered together.

We had a beautiful funeral for Dad in his favourite church, the Waiapu Cathedral of St John the Baptist, surrounded by many family and friends, and his fellow parishioners. We celebrated his life at Shed 2 in Ahuriri, where we had also held Mum's wake. It was a fitting end to his farewell.

Having seen patients cling to life (and meet their deaths) on a COVID ward, my lasting hope is that I will never again have to experience the cruelty of COVID-19, or its many variants.

With the passing of both my parents, I am now an 'orphan' (in its broader sense). This new term feels strange and unfamiliar to me, but I know I will get used to it. For that is life.

ENDNOTES AND REFERENCES

Introduction

1 https://covid.19.who.int: As of 6.36 p.m. CEST 12 August 2022, there were 585,950,085 confirmed cases of COVID-19 globally, including 6,425,422 deaths. The WHO World Health Statistics Report (2022) records that due to many countries having 'limited testing capacity and lack functioning vital statistics or registration systems to provide accurate and complete mortality data and causes of death' the global number of COVID-19 cases and deaths are underreported and that the likely mortality estimate between 'January 2020 and December 2021 was 14.9 million worldwide – or 9.5 million more deaths than the initially reported 5.4 million COVID-19 deaths during that period'.

2 'Incomplete grief' is 'emotion that is frozen in time, making it difficult for the mourner to move through the phases of grief that lead to healing' (www.beyondthedash.com, 'What Is Incomplete Grief?' 24 February 2021). In relation to 'complex grief' see Harris D.L and Winokuer H.R (2016) 'Principles and practice of grief counselling' (2nd ed) New York, NY: Springer Publishing Company.

3 Harold S.Kushner *When Bad Things Happen to Good People* (1981), Schocken Books, New York, USA.

4 Mitch Albom *Tuesdays with Morrie* (1997), Doubleday, USA.

Chapter Two

5 Queen Elizabeth said "Grief is the price we pay for love" in a message of support for those who lost loved ones during the September 11 terrorist attacks in the United States. The quote comes from Dr Colin Murray Parkes, in *Bereavement: Studies of Grief in Adult Life* (1972), Penguin Books Ltd, UK, part of which is 'The pain of grief is just as much part of life as the joy of love; it is perhaps the price we pay for love, the cost of commitment.'

6 Karla FC Holloway, 'A Name for a Parent Whose Child Has Died', Duke Today, 2022, University Communications [Durham, NC (919) 684 2823].

7 Bill Withers (April 1972), but a cover version popular at the time was played at the service.

8 'Nessum Dorma' was the aria that Luciano Pavarotti popularised with the modern music world by his rendition that the BBC used as its FIFA theme song for the 1990 World Cup.

Chapter Three

9 'The Church has survived centuries of buffeting by the elements and the earthquake on the high windswept uplands of Ithaca.' Mark Ottoway, *The Most Beautiful Villages of Greece and the Greek Islands*, Thames and Hudson Ltd, London, 1998, page 203.

10 Tim Jewell: 'What is Anosognosia' 27 February 2019: https://www.

healthline.com/health/anosognosia

11 www.beyondblue.org.au

Chapter Four

12 A nod to Cecil the Ram from *Footrot Flats* by Murray Ball, the iconic cartoon strips that were famous to New Zealanders and Australians alike, first appearing in the *Evening Post* in 1976, and which would go on to appear in over 200 papers in New Zealand and Australia. Compilation books then followed and *Footrot Flats: A Dog's Tale* would be released as New Zealand's first animated feature film in 1986. See www.footrotflats.com.

13 Edgar Guest was an English-born American poet in the first half of the twentieth century.

14 https://www.health.gov.au/initiatives-and-programs/australian-brain-cancer-mission

15 www.health.govt.nz/your-health/conditions-and-treatments/diseases-and-illnesses/cancer

16 https://www.charlieteofoundation.org.au ; https://www.whitematterbraincancertrust.nz/about/brain-cancer-facts/

17 For example, in Australia, refer to The Charlie Teo Foundation – see https://www.charlieteofoundation.org.au; and The Australian Brain Cancer Mission – see https://www.health.gov.au/initiatives-and-programs/australian-brain-cancer-mission. Also the Cure Brain Cancer Foundation, https://curebraincancer.org.au

Chapter Five

[18] A translation of the Latin proverb, *audentes Fortuna iuvat*, where Fortuna is the goddess of luck.

[19] https://www.thewomens.org.au/health-information/pregnancy-and-birth/pregnancy-problems/early-pregnancy-problems/miscarriage

Chapter Six

[20] Diabetes Australia see https://www.diabetesaustralia.com.au

[21] https://www.diabetesaustralia.com.au

[22] See https://www.ndss.com.au

Chapter Seven

[23] 'Journey through the Diagnosis of Dementia', *Alzheimer's Disease International*, 2021.

[24] Dementia Australia (2018) Dementia Prevalence Data 2018-2058, commissioned research undertaken by NATSEM, University of Canberra.

[25] Euthanasia has been legalised in Victoria, Western Australia, and legislation passed in Tasmania, South Australia, Queensland and New South Wales are expected to become effective between October 2022 (Tasmania), January 2023 (South Australia and Queensland) and November 2023 (New South Wales). Voluntary euthanasia and assisted suicide are currently illegal in all territories of Australia.

[26] End of Life Choice Act 2019 (New Zealand)

[27] 'I'll Fly Away' is a hymn written by Albert E. Brumley in 1929 and published in 1932 by the Hartford Music company in a collection titled *Wonderful Message.*

[28] www.dementia.org.au

[29] According to Dementia Australia – see https://www.dementia.org.au

Chapter Eight

[30] https://www.livestrong.com/article/13763749-marathon-statistics

[31] Jason can be contacted at jasonm@solutionfocus.com.au

[32] A coming-of-age film about four boys who go on a hike in 1959 to find the dead body of a missing boy (1986, Columbia Pictures).

[33] A movie about four teenagers who must prove their talent as they start their journey at the New York High School of Performing Arts (1980, Metro-Goldwyn-Mayer).

Chapter Nine

[34] Elizabeth Kübler-Ross M.D *On Death and Dying : What the dying have to teach doctors, nurses, clergy and their own families* (1969) Scribner, New York, NY.

[35] Models such as the 'Attachment Theory' of John Bowlby, the Six Rs of Mourning of Dr Therese Rando, and William Worden's 'Four Tasks of Mourning'.

[36] E.g. see the Dual Process Model (M Stroebe & H Schut (1999) 'The

dual process of coping with bereavement: Rationale and description' *Death Studies* 23(3), 197 – 224) which recognises the movement between loss orientation (coming to terms with loss) and restoration orientation (adjusting and attending to life's daily demands post loss).

37 https://www.theworldcounts.com/populations/world/deaths

38 The minimum time criteria is six months in the International Classification of Diseases (ICD-11) published by the World Health Organisation in relation to mental health and other health disorders, which included prolonged grief disorder in ICD-11 in 2018.

39 American Psychiatric Association (Fifth Edition, text revision) Washington DC 2022, a publication used for the classification of mental health disorders using a common language and standard criteria. See also https://en.wikipedia.org/wiki/Diagnostic_and_Statistical_Manual_of_Mental_Disorders

40 See Dr Pies 'The Bereavement Exclusion and DSM-5: An Update and Commentary', *Innov Clin Neurosci*. 2014 Jul-Aug; 11(7-8): 19-22. Published online Jul-Aug 2014: https://www.ncbi.nlm.nih.gov/pmc/articles/PMC4204469. The effect of the change was to no longer exclude those persons who were bereaved from the set of persons with major depression, if they otherwise met the criteria for major depression, i.e. DSM-5 recognises that persons who are bereaved can also be suffering major depression (even if the cause is not the bereavement), but the fact that they are bereaved should not exclude them from being recognised and treated for major depression.

41 Professor of Psychiatry at SUNY Upstate Medical University Syracuse, New York, and Clinical Professor of Psychiatry at Tuffs University

School of Medicine in Boston

42 https://en.wikipedia.org/wiki/Prolonged_grief_disorder#cite_note-:1-17. Also that many 'bereaved who met the criteria for PGD were receptive to treatment' and a 2020 study found that 'labeling PGD symptoms with a grief-specific diagnosis does not produce additional public stigma beyond the stigma of these severe grief reactions alone'.

43 According to Grammarist, this cliché has been attributed to the Greek poet Menander who lived around 300 B.C and said "Time is the healer of all necessary evils" per https://grammarist.com/proverb/time-heals-all-wounds

Chapter Ten

44 The Fair Work Act of Australia (2009). Casual employees are only entitled to unpaid leave. Organisations that employ Aboriginal Australians and Torres Strait Islanders are encouraged to be more flexible because of the cultural importance of Sorry Business in these communities.

45 What follows are general comments only and should not be taken or construed as legal advice.

Chapter Eleven

46 The app 'I am' can provide you with regular affirmations: day.apps.apple.com/us/app/i-am-daily-affirmations/id874656917

47 Quoted by Senator Robert F Kennedy during his presidential campaign

in 1968 on the night of the assassination of Martin Luther King Jr.

48 William Shakespeare, *Macbeth*, Act 4 Scene 3.

Chapter Twelve

49 In New South Wales you may for example wish to visit Brightlands Retreat – www.brightlandsretreat.com (Leura, Blue Mountains), Elysia Wellness Retreat, www.elysiaretreat.com.au (Hunter Valley), Gaia Retreat – www.gaiaretreat.com.au (Byron Bay), Elements of Byron – www.elementsofbyron.com.au (Byron Bay) or Gymea Eco Retreat and Spa – www.gymearetreat.com.au (Uki, Mt Warning). In Queensland, you may wish to consider Spicers Tamarind (Maleny) or Spicers Clovelly (Montville) or Spicers Balfour Hotel (New Farm, Brisbane) – www.spicersretreats.com; Gwinganna Lifestyle Retreat – www.gwinganna.com (Tallebudgera Valley, QLD) , Eden Health Retreat – www.edenhealthretreat.com.au (Currumbin Valley, QLD), or Living Valley Health Retreat – www.lvs.com.au (Kin Kin, QLD). In New Zealand perhaps see www.manaretreat.com (Mana Retreat, Coromandel), www.aro-ha.com (Aro Ha Wellness Retreat in Glenorchy, Queenstown), www.tewahiora.co.nz (Piha, West Auckland) , www.earthenergiessanctuary.com (Mangatarata, Waikato), www.anahata-retreat.org.nz (Takaka, Golden Bay), www.rcr.co.nz (Papamoa Ranges, Waikato), www.tehinruru.com (Russell, Bay of Islands), www.capesouth.co.nz (Cape Kidnappers, Hawke's Bay).

ACKNOWLEDGEMENTS

This book would not have been possible without the support of many people in my village.

My unending gratitude to my husband, Ben, and our adorable children, Kyra, Zavier and Caitlin, for their love, support and patience, and for making life with them so full, fun and fantastic.

I also thank many extended family and friends who supported me through my grief, and created and shared new beginnings with me, especially my 'Sydney parents' Stathi and Beth, George and Tanja and the other 'US Gallates', Bernard and Jason and Angela, Olive, Phyllis and Sarah, Harry and June, Dennise and Jean, Peter and Belinda, Denis, Jane and Xavier and (more recently!) Sylvie, Sam and Brody, Ersi, Genia and Christina, Andreas, Dennis and Anna, Alison and Charlotte and Sebastian, Monique and Garry, Cathy and Cam and Andrew, Gilly and John, Lynn and George and the Striders MTG crew, Samantha, Kate and Patrick, James Bond (and the swim gang), Sue and Mark and the Redskins, Shaan and Martin, Jason, and Lisa, Judy, Ruth and Tanya.

I especially appreciate the encouragement (and patience) of my publisher Pepper Press, and the support of family who always believed in the importance of writing about loss, death, grief and renewal. Special thanks also to my good friends Bec and Kate for their feedback, and also to my dad who was the most diligent commentator on this book and would have loved to have read it in hard copy.

ABOUT THE AUTHOR

Lisa trained as a lawyer, and is a senior commercial litigator specialising in class action litigation and corporate insolvency. She holds a Master of Law from the University of Cambridge, undergraduate degrees in law and commerce from Victoria University, New Zealand, and was a finalist for the NSW Women Lawyers' Association 'Woman Lawyer of the Year'.

Lisa is a member of the Australian Centre for Grief and Bereavement, the National Association for Loss and Grief, the Australian Counselling Association, and has contributed to Diversity Council Australia podcasts about grief support in the workplace. Lisa is on the executive committee of the Northern Beaches Community Cancer Charity (NBCCC) and, through her marathon running, has raised funds for many charities. Born in New Zealand, Lisa now lives on the Northern Beaches of Sydney with her husband, three children and Jack the Cat.

A proportion of author proceeds from the sale of this book will be donated to NBCCC.org.au.

See www.lisagallate.com for more information on speaking engagements and other services.

OTHER BOOKS FROM PEPPER PRESS

When A Soulmate Says No

Manjits and the Tandoor of Secrets

Coming soon

Shirley's Story

www.fairplaypublishing.com.au | www.pepperpress.com.au

PEPPER PRESS

PEPPER PRESS

CPSIA information can be obtained
at www.ICGtesting.com
Printed in the USA
BVHW041757160223
658686BV00012B/261

HOUSE RULES

SURVIVAL TIPS FOR GETTING SH!T DONE

50 TIPS TO CONQUER YOUR TO-DO LIST AND ACHIEVE YOUR DREAMS

STEVEN ALMEIDA

HOUSE RULES

SURVIVAL TIPS FOR GETTING SH!T DONE

50 TIPS TO CONQUER YOUR TO-DO LIST AND ACHIEVE YOUR DREAMS

STEVEN ALMEIDA

Autumn House Entertainment LLC
www.autumnhouseent.com

For my sons, Anakin Nasir & Bryce Jude, so they always have a way to find a way.

"The world is a possibility if only you'll discover it."
– **Ralph Ellison, Invisible Man**

INTRODUCTION

Amidst the flurry of our modern lives, we can easily find ourselves submerged in the relentless tide of responsibilities, ceaselessly sapping our time and vitality. We're all dreamers with lofty aspirations, yet the conversion of these dreams into tangible reality becomes an uphill battle amidst daily distractions and the never-ending carousel of to-do lists.

But what if there was a method to cut through the complexity, seize control of your day, and inch steadily towards your dreams? What if you could harness a system that empowers you to focus your energy and resources on priorities that truly resonate?

Enter "House Rules: Survival Tips For Getting Sh!t Done". This book stands as your comprehensive blueprint to unlocking your productivity and transforming your dreams into reality, irrespective of their scale. We'll navigate through a plethora of tips and strategies, specifically engineered to help you zone in on what's crucial, streamline your process, and enable decisive action towards your goals.

Regardless of whether you're an overworked professional, a swamped student, or simply an individual yearning to maximize your time and energy, this book has something in store for you. Whether you aspire to elevate your professional journey, enrich your relationships, or simply squeeze more zest out of life, you'll discover the arsenal of tools and strategies you need right here.

So let's embark on this journey. It's time to unleash your potential, simplify your journey, and truly get things done.

RULE #001

START NOW

Writing a book is a journey, a long and arduous one at that. It took me two years to get to where I am today. I started on small yellow post-it notes, jotting down motivational quotes that applied to my life and sticking them all over New York City. From buses to trains, to coffee shops and restaurants, I didn't care where I placed them. All that mattered was that I started. And that's the key, my friends. Starting is the hardest part. But without a beginning, there can be no end. So, if you're struggling to start a project or bring an idea to life, my advice to you is simple - START NOW! Don't wait for the perfect moment or the perfect idea. Just start and work out the kinks along the way. Experience is the greatest teacher, after all. Remember, every tree was once a seed.

TIP: *Set a clear goal - Define your objective clearly and precisely. This helps you break down your plan into tangible and achievable steps. Write it down on a yellow sticky note, everyday for a year if you have to.*

"BEZOS STARTED AMAZON.COM IN A GARAGE WITH A POTBELLY STOVE. HE HELD MOST OF HIS MEETINGS AT THE NEIGHBORHOOD BARNES & NOBLE."
- Avery Hartmans, BusinessInsider.com

RULE #002

EMBRACE FAILURE

Embrace failure as a crucial part of the adventure to success, a mindset adopted by some of the most triumphant souls on this planet. It's recognizing that failure ain't a dead end, but a stepping stone towards growth, learning, and eventually, success. The secret to wielding the might of failure is to see it as a chance for growth, not a reason to throw in the towel.

One of the most precious lessons failure teaches us is humility. It's a reminder that we ain't flawless, and there's still a whole lot to learn. This humbling experience can be the spark for growth, nudging us to reevaluate our methods and strategies, and to hunt down fresh knowledge and skills. It also pushes us to be more receptive to feedback and criticism, essential ingredients for betterment.

Another vital lesson failure imparts is resilience. The capacity to bounce back from setbacks and keep going despite roadblocks is a crucial skill in chasing success. It's through the process of conquering challenges that we develop the mental and emotional grit needed to reach our objectives.

Failure also cultivates creativity and innovation. When things don't unfold as we hoped, we're forced to think unconventionally and cook up new solutions to problems. This can lead to earth-shattering ideas and breakthroughs that may have never come to light had we not encountered failure in the first place.

In a time when gas lighting ruled the world, Thomas Edison knew there had to be a better way. He had his sights set on creating an electric light that'd flip the script and change the game forever. The journey wasn't smooth, though - he had to battle through failures, doubt, and haters.

Edison was all about that trial and error life, testing everything from platinum to carbonized plant fibers to find the perfect filament for his light bulb. Each time he came up short, he learned a little more, getting closer and closer to that winning formula.

The world wasn't exactly cheering him on, though. As Edison's list of failed attempts grew, so did the doubts from his peers and the public. But Edison didn't let that noise bring him down. He famously clapped back, "I have not failed. I've just found 10,000 ways that won't work."

Homie was relentless. In 1879, after countless experiments, he found the magic ingredient - carbonized bamboo. That discovery led to the birth of the practical incandescent light bulb, and it changed everything, from the way we live to the way we work and play.

Here's the thing: Edison's success came from a foundation of failures. With each setback, he learned, adapted, and inched closer to his ultimate goal. By embracing failure as part of the process, Edison shook up the world and earned his spot among the greatest inventors in history.

So, next time you face failure, remember Edison's story. Embrace it, learn from it, and use it as fuel to keep pushing forward. You never know when your own carbonized bamboo moment might come along.

TIP: *Change your mindset - Rather than viewing failure as a setback, view it as an opportunity to learn and grow. Embrace failure as an integral part of the learning process. Take calculated risks - Don't be afraid to take risks. However, be sure to assess and calculate the risks involved, so if you fail, you'll have a plan to come back from it. Analyze your failures - Analyzing your failures will help you identify the areas that need improvement.*

"WE GOT TURNED DOWN, WE FAILED, HAD SETBACKS, HAD TO START OVER A LOT OF TIMES. BUT WE KEPT GOING AT IT. IN ANYBODY'S CASE THAT'S ALWAYS THE DISTINGUISHING FACTOR."
- Nipsey Hussle

RULE #003

NURTURE CONSISTENT PROGRESS THROUGH UNWAVERING PROCESS

"FOR ME, THERE IS A GUIDING COMPASS THAT JUST LIVES INSIDE OF ME. EVERY TIME I'VE GONE AGAINST IT, SOMETHING BAD HAS HAPPENED. AS LONG AS I STAY IN LINE AND HONOR IT, IT HAS REALLY BEEN LIFE-CHANGING."
- Tyler Perry

Life is a series of transformations, much like the metamorphosis of a larva into a butterfly. We all experience moments of being a larva, cocooning ourselves, and eventually emerging as a changed individual. The journey of personal growth is never a smooth one; it is filled with countless challenges, heartaches, and discomfort. However, it is by facing these adversities that we can truly progress and evolve.

Just as I took a leap of faith in writing my first book, we all have opportunities to take risks and push ourselves outside of our comfort zones. The road to success may be bumpy and filled with obstacles, but it is by overcoming these hurdles that we can truly grow and transform. It is essential not to give up when the going gets tough or when others doubt our abilities. Instead, we must continue to persevere and navigate through the challenges life throws our way.

In an interview, Jay-Z once said, "I'm not a businessman, I'm a business, man." This statement encapsulates his approach to life and his commitment to constant progression. By consistently pushing himself and striving for greatness, Jay-Z has achieved a level of success that few can even dream of.

In the early '90s, Jay-Z faced rejection from major record labels. Undeterred, he started his own label, Roc-A-Fella Records, alongside Damon Dash and Kareem "Biggs" Burke. This move demonstrated Jay-Z's commitment to his craft, and the business.

Throughout his career, Jay-Z has been a model of consistency, releasing album after album, each time pushing the envelope and redefining the sound of hip-hop. His determination and persistence, matched with his incredible talent, enabled him to build a musical empire. But he didn't stop at music; he ventured into various businesses, including clothing, sports, and streaming services. His success in these domains can also be attributed to his consistency and relentless work ethic.

Embracing the process of transformation and personal growth is vital for achieving our goals and reaching our full potential. We must not resist change or shy away from difficulties, for it is through these experiences that we can truly evolve and progress. Just as a caterpillar must undergo the painful process of metamorphosis to become a beautiful butterfly, we too must face our challenges head-on and embrace the changes that life presents to us.

TIP: *Create an environment that promotes progress by minimizing distractions that may hinder your focus and consistency. Surround yourself with* *people or things that inspire you. Find sources of inspiration in books, podcasts, or motivational videos to keep you motivated.*

RULE #004

THE 80/20 RULE

"HE LEFT HIMSELF NO POSSIBLE WAY OF RETREAT. HE HAD TO WIN OR PERISH! THAT IS ALL THERE IS TO THE BARNES STORY OF SUCCESS!"
- Napoleon Hill

Picture this: you're knee-deep in a sea of tasks, feeling swamped and overwhelmed, trying to juggle everything that's coming at you. Sound familiar? Well, it's time to flip the script and learn the art of the 80/20 Rule, a game-changing technique that'll help you focus on the tasks that truly matter, supercharge your efforts, and leave those time-wasters in the dust.

The 80/20 Rule, also known as the Pareto Principle, is a powerful concept that asserts that 80% of your desired results come from just 20% of your efforts. Yep, you read that right. This golden rule can be applied to almost every aspect of life, from work to relationships and beyond. So, how do you harness the magic of the 80/20 Rule to maximize your productivity and get the most bang for your buck? Strap in, and let's dive right in.

Sift Through the Chaos: Start by analyzing your daily tasks, goals, and commitments. Jot 'em all down, and don't leave anything out. The aim here is to identify that 20% of tasks that yield 80% of the results. This could include high-value projects at work, quality time with your loved ones, or even self-care routines that recharge your batteries.

2. **Rank and Reevaluate:** Once you've got everything laid out, it's time to rank those tasks based on their impact and value. Focus on the tasks that bring you closer to your goals and align with your values. Those tasks that rank low on the impact scale? It's time to reevaluate their importance in your life.
3. **Cut the Dead Weight:** The 80/20 Rule ain't just about identifying what's important – it's also about having the courage to let go of the tasks that ain't worth your time. Be ruthless in eliminating or delegating low-impact tasks to free up time and energy for what truly matters.
4. **The Power of Saying "No":** Learning to say "no" can be a game-changer. By turning down tasks or commitments that don't align with your priorities, you're carving out more space for the tasks that bring you closer to success.
5. **Time Blocking Like a Pro:** Now that you've got your high-impact tasks sorted, it's time to give 'em the attention they deserve. Allocate dedicated chunks of time for these tasks, and protect that time like it's your most valuable possession.

Remember, the 80/20 Rule is all about zeroing in on the tasks that pack the most punch, and letting go of the rest. By embracing this principle, you'll be making the most of your time and energy, catapulting you towards success at lightning speed.

TIP: Stay focused on that golden 20% by regularly reviewing and adjusting your priorities. Life ain't static, and neither should be your goals. Continuously assess and tweak your approach to ensure you're always locked onto that sweet spot of maximum impact.

RULE #005

SEEK HELP WHEN YOU NEED IT!

In this breakneck world of hustle and grind, we often feel the weight of success solely on our shoulders. We believe that if we just push a little harder, if we're relentless enough, we'll make it. But let me tell you, this belief, although well-intentioned, is a little off course. The true magic lies in realizing that seeking help when needed is one of the most potent tools for success.

Let me lay down some reasons why seeking help is vital for the journey:

First off, when you extend a hand to others, you open doors to their unique wisdom and expertise. This can be priceless when tackling a problem, making a decision, or chasing a dream. Learn from the journeys of others, and you'll find yourself working with grace, not just grit.

Second, asking for help can lead to wiser decision-making. When you bounce ideas off others, you catch fresh perspectives and insights that help you sidestep pitfalls and make more enlightened choices.

Third, seeking help can be the key to unlocking challenges that might seem insurmountable. No matter how self-reliant you are, there will be moments when you need a hand. Embrace the willingness to ask for help, and you'll discover solutions to problems that might have thrown you off track.

Fourth, seeking help can create connections with like-minded souls who share your goals and values. These bonds offer support, encouragement, and a sense of belonging that keeps you inspired and focused.

Asking for help can amplify your confidence and self-esteem. By showing you're open to collaborating with others to reach your goals, you radiate confidence in your own abilities and commitment to doing whatever it takes to succeed.

Steve Jobs, co-founder of Apple Inc., and the driving force behind some of the most groundbreaking innovations in technology was known for his vision and unyielding pursuit of excellence, he also recognized the value of teamwork and collaboration. One of his most significant partnerships was with Steve Wozniak, who co-founded Apple with him. Together, they created the Apple I and Apple II computers, which laid the groundwork for Apple's future successes.

As Apple grew, he continued to surround himself with brilliant minds, such as Jony Ive, who designed iconic products like the iPhone and iMac. Jobs was known for fostering a culture of innovation and collaboration at Apple, where employees were encouraged to share ideas and work together to create groundbreaking products. When developing the iPhone, he enlisted the expertise of AT&T, as well as various hardware and software partners, to make his vision a reality.

Seeking help ain't a sign of weakness or incapability – it's quite the contrary. It takes courage and wisdom to recognize when you need a hand and ask for it. It shows that you're bold enough to acknowledge your limitations and dedicated to finding creative answers to life's challenges.

TIP: *Build a diverse team with complementary skillsets for greater success: Begin by honestly evaluating your own skills, talents, and areas where you need improvement. Knowing your limitations is crucial for assembling a well-rounded team. Look for individuals who possess the skills and expertise you need to complement your own. Consider reaching out to your existing network or attend industry events and conferences to meet potential collaborators. When selecting team members, ensure they share your values and work ethic. Assess their personalities, communication styles, and approach to problem-solving to make sure they align with your vision and culture. Clearly define each team member's role and responsibilities, ensuring that each person's skills are used effectively and that there's no overlap or confusion about tasks. Encourage team members to communicate openly and honestly about their ideas, challenges, and progress. Establish regular check-ins and meetings to facilitate communication and collaboration.*

"THE MARVELOUS THING ABOUT A GOOD QUESTION IS THAT IT SHAPES OUR IDENTITY AS MUCH BY THE ASKING AS IT DOES BY THE ANSWERING."
- David Whyte

RULE #006

NEVER COMPARE

"REMIND YOURSELF NOBODY BUILT LIKE YOU, YOU DESIGNED YOURSELF!"
- Sean "Jay-Z" Carter

In a world where chasing greatness is the norm, it's tempting to get caught up in comparisons. We glance at the legends, the Spielbergs and Joyces, believing we must mirror them to taste success. But here's the truth : comparison is an admission of unoriginality.

Nope, your short film will never be a Spielberg masterpiece. And that ain't because you lack the skills; it's because Spielberg is SPIELBERG. He's got his own distinct voice, style, and storytelling flair. The same holds for you. You're incredible in your own right, no need to lean on comparisons for validation.

Some might say, "no idea is original." But I beg to differ. Every idea is original. We draw inspiration from our surroundings, the people we encounter, and the tales we share. And in turn, we inspire others.

My writing style is an upcycled blend of my favorite authors, but I never stack myself up against them. I study Nas like I study Ralph Ellison, but I don't aspire to be either of them. I yearn to become myself, to forge my own unique voice and share my stories.

You'll never be them, and they'll never be you. That's the beauty of uniqueness – that's what makes your ideas original. Even if your work is a patchwork of influences, you're the one weaving it together.

As a young basketball player, Micheal Jordan was often compared to the legendary basketball player Julius "Dr. J" Erving, who was known for his acrobatic moves and high-flying dunks. Many people thought Jordan would never be able to live up to Erving's legacy and doubted his potential as a basketball player.

However, Jordan continued to work hard and hone his skills. He developed his own unique style of play, which combined incredible athleticism with precision and finesse. He became known for his signature moves, such as the "slam dunk" and the "fadeaway," which were completely his own.

Jordan went on to become one of the greatest basketball players of all time, winning six NBA championships and numerous individual awards. He was inducted into the Basketball Hall of Fame in 2009 and is widely regarded as a legend in the sport.

So let's flip the script: "Every idea is original." Embrace your individuality and sidestep the trap of comparison. Be authentically you, narrate your own story, and create something genuinely original.

TIP: *Create a vision board. Fill it with your ideas, your goals, your dreams, put up the people, and the things that inspire you. Write down who you are today, the things you've accomplished, the things you are working on, then write down who you were, follow the same process and finally write down who you aspire to be, and the things you are on your way to do. Take the time to identify the stages, appreciate the process, because its YOUR process. Compare yourself to YOU, that's your only competition, compare your present work to your past* *work, is there growth? Have you gotten better? Are you further along on your journey? Are you closer to your goal than you were before?*

"JUST DO IT."
-NIKE

RULE #007

SHOW DON'T TELL

One of the most straightforward success principles appears to be the toughest to embrace: just DO it. Sure, it's a breeze to chatter about what you'll do, but actually doing it? That's a whole different ball game. In a world where faking the grind and flexing on social media is the norm, the real doers are the ones who shine.

We've all heard sayings like "all bark and no bite" and "the quietest in the room is the most lethal." The truth is, those caught up in the doing don't have time to talk. They're consumed with putting in the work, day after day, inch by inch, until they hit their targets.

It's all too tempting to point fingers at others for our lack of success. We might argue that our loved ones don't back us or that the world is conspiring against us. But let's be real, we're often our own biggest roadblock. We talk a big game about our dreams but don't take the plunge to make them come true.

The journey to achieving our goals can be long and arduous. It demands patience, commitment, and sweat equity. But that's the only way to move forward. You can't sit idly by, waiting for opportunity to strike or for others to hand you success on a silver platter. You've got to get out there and seize it yourself.

Maybe no one's investing in your big idea. Maybe you're lacking the support you crave. But that's no excuse to throw in the towel. Instead, bet on yourself. Have faith in your abilities. Show up for yourself every day and take tangible steps to turn your dreams into reality.

At the end of the day, action is what counts. Talking about your ambitions won't get you far. Only by taking action can you advance, step by step, until your dreams are within reach. So quit talking and start doing. The world is waiting with bated breath.

TIP: *Make a daily action plan: Identify the specific actions you need to take each day to work toward your milestones. Incorporate these actions into your daily routine to make them a habit. List your tasks and goals: Begin by writing down all the tasks and goals you need to accomplish for the day. This list should include both personal and professional items, as well as any specific actions related to your long-term goals.*

6. *Prioritize: Review your list and rank each task by its importance and urgency. Consider using a priority matrix or the Eisenhower Matrix to categorize tasks into four quadrants: urgent and important, important but not urgent, urgent but not important, and neither urgent nor important.*
7. *Estimate time: Assign a realistic time estimate to each task. This will help you allocate sufficient time to complete each item and avoid overcommitting.*
8. *Schedule your day: Using your prioritized list and time estimates, create a daily schedule. Allocate specific time blocks for each task, starting with the most important and urgent ones. Remember to include breaks and buffer*

time for unexpected events or tasks that might take longer than anticipated.

9. *Batch similar tasks: Group similar tasks together, such as answering emails, making phone calls, or running errands, to increase efficiency and minimize context switching.*
10. *Plan for peak productivity: Schedule tasks that require deep focus and concentration during your most productive hours. For most people, this is typically in the morning, but it can vary from person to person.*
11. *Incorporate routines: Establish morning and evening routines to bookend your day. These routines can help set the tone for your day and provide a sense of stability and structure.*
12. *Set daily goals: Identify one or two key goals for the day that align with your long-term objectives. Focusing on these goals can help ensure you make meaningful progress toward your bigger aspirations.*
13. *Review and revise: At the end of the day, review your action plan and assess your progress. Reflect on what worked well, what didn't, and any adjustments you need to make for the following day.*

"FOR AS THE BODY WITHOUT THE SPIRIT IS DEAD, SO FAITH WITHOUT WORKS IS DEAD ALSO."
- James 2:26 | King James Version

RULE #008

MAKE SMALL COMMITMENTS AND KEEP THEM

"INSTEAD OF TRYING TO BUILD A BRICK WALL, LAY A BRICK EVERYDAY, EVENTUALLY YOU'LL LOOK UP AND YOU'LL HAVE A BRICK WALL."
- Nipsey Hussle

Think massive. Dream colossal. There ain't no shame in reaching for the heavens. After all, the Great Wall of China emerged brick by brick, one tiny commitment at a time. The trick is to stay true to your word. Each time you do, you deposit into your psychological vault of confidence, trust, and follow-through. When you're known as someone who gets stuff done, others who share the same vibe will flock to you like moths to a flame. Confidence is the juice that propels your vessel, while trust and execution are its bones and gears. Without all three, your ship might float, but it won't be cruising toward anything magnificent.

Tiny commitments lay the groundwork for self-discipline. Rising at 5 A.M. every day, hitting the gym every evening, clocking in at work punctually, and grinding through some overtime are all tiny commitments that compound over time. When I penned this book, I struck a deal with myself to honor a small commitment: WRITE A PAGE A DAY. It was plain, sharp, and achievable. If I upheld that small commitment daily, eventually, I'd have a complete book – my first book. And if you're reading this, you're holding tangible evidence of what can be accomplished by applying this principle to your own life.

Keep in mind, every grand dream kicks off with a modest commitment. Don't shy away from setting your sights high and dreaming vast. Just ensure you've got a strategy to arrive there, one small commitment at a time. Because, in the end, the only thing that distinguishes the dream-chasers from the dream-fakers is the ability to keep their word, one small commitment at a time.

TIP: *Make a note FIRST thing in the morning of what you are accomplishing for the day, make your commitment and DO NOT argue with the plan! When you begin the process, do not question it, do not hesitate, you cannot back down! You MUST work hard every single day at your maximum capacity to reach your dream. You need a "no-matter what" mindset, no matter what, you will accomplish the things when you said you would. Create pressure for yourself, let it push you, otherwise nothing will get done. Create a routine that becomes second nature and COMMIT to it, but be careful in choosing where you will spend your time and energy, because once invested it will become difficult to quit. The follow through will get you to the end. Understand the transformation process. Your body and brain will resist change and growth. Laziness is natural but you have to power through it. The hardest part about discipline is maintaining the actions needed to achieve your dreams and goals.*

Most importantly FIND PLEASURE IN THE HARD WORK.

RULE #009

SET STANDARDS OF ACCOUNTABILITY

"OUR GOALS CAN ONLY BE REACHED THROUGH A VEHICLE OF A PLAN, IN WHICH WE MUST FERVENTLY BELIEVE, AND UPON WHICH WE MUST VIGOROUSLY ACT. THERE IS NO OTHER ROUTE TO SUCCESS."
-Pablo Picasso

In the kaleidoscope of ceaseless temptations and boundless prospects, the distinction between dreams and goals can fade into a blur. Dreams often feel like elusive, unattainable figments of our minds, while goals are etched onto our planners and whiteboards as we plot a path to reach them. Yet, they share more in common than we might think.

A flashback to my school days unveils the AIM written atop our papers, which, at the time, seemed purposeless. Now, I perceive its true essence: a beacon guiding us towards our daily aspirations, holding us responsible for our deeds. Each day either saw us hitting our AIM or falling short.

For a multitude, dreams soar to immeasurable heights, appearing unachievable and devoid of responsibility or action. But holding ourselves accountable is the key to making dreams come true. The distance to our dreams is determined by our own strides.

So, my friends, pen down that dream, embrace accountability, and take steps towards it. Shatter it into manageable pieces and pursue it relentlessly. Don't let your dream linger as a mere figment of your imagination—seize it and manifest it into reality.

TIP: *Articulate your goals and the step by step process it's going to take to achieve them, then turn them into a creative and artistic visual. Write at least a paragraph on how it feels to achieve your goal, acting as if you've achieved your goal. Setting goals that truly motivate you takes a clear understanding of your motivation and WHY you want to achieve your goals. Once your goals have been written down, take action immediately! During the progress don't be afraid of celebrating the wins and tracking your process. Share your goals, sharing them holds you accountable! It's a great way to make an unknowing commitment.*

RULE #010

NEVER LET EMOTIONS OVERPOWER INTELLIGENCE

"EMOTION CAN BE THE ENEMY, IF YOU GIVE INTO YOUR EMOTION, YOU LOSE YOURSELF. YOU MUST BE AT ONE WITH YOUR EMOTIONS, BECAUSE THE BODY ALWAYS FOLLOWS THE MIND."
— *Bruce Lee*

As we sail through life's intricate seas, it's all too simple for our emotions to steer our ship. A familiar snare, it can lead to catastrophic outcomes. Indeed, history's pages are strewn with tales of those governed by unbridled emotions. Yet, here's the catch: emotions aren't innately evil. They're the essence of our human journey. The secret lies in cultivating emotional intelligence, mastering the harmony between sentiment and reason.

It's a nuanced waltz, no doubt. But as a survivor of numerous emotional tempests, I assure you, it's an endeavor worth undertaking. Reflect on instances when you've made choices driven by fleeting emotions. Frequently, such decisions hindered your progress. But rejoice in this truth: each of those moments imparted wisdom, revealing the path to avoid next time.

Admittedly, it's challenging to rein in our emotions. Often, the catalysts lie buried deep within our psyche, concealed from our awareness. Yet, self-awareness is the key. Identifying our emotional triggers empowers us to command our responses.

Fear, a potent emotion, is etched into our DNA—an age-old survival tool. However, like any emotion, fear bears its flaws. It can immobilize us, obstructing risks and inhibiting our fullest lives. Hence, mastering fear is paramount.

I don't advocate for fearlessness. Fear is a natural reaction to specific circumstances. But to achieve our ambitions and lead fulfilling lives, we must learn to forge ahead in spite of fear, embracing risks even when trembling.

Ultimately, balance is the goal. Emotions form our identity, and suppressing them is futile. Simultaneously, we must steer our emotions, not be driven by them. So, when facing a difficult choice, pause and check in with yourself. Assess your emotions and juxtapose them against your rational mind. It may be arduous, but it's an attainable skill. Trust me, the effort is worthwhile.

TIP: *When facing a situation that triggers strong emotional reactions, take a moment to pause and take a deep breath. Allow yourself enough time to react thoughtfully. Identify the emotions you're experiencing and acknowledge their connection to your behavior. Understanding the root cause of your emotional response can aid in processing your feelings and not reacting impulsively. Challenge any irrational or illogical thoughts. Evaluate whether your current behavior or response is practical, and don't make assumptions about other people's motives.*

Engage with the analytical part of your brain in assessing and processing the situation, and make decisions that are based on objective reasoning. Develop mindfulness practices that can be used to calm and center yourself. Activities such as meditation or physical exercise can help to balance your emotions and reduce stress. Surround yourself with positive and supportive people. This support system can assist in providing perspective and guidance towards a peaceful and unbiased solution.

RULE #011

WORK WOUNDED

In the heart of struggle lies the seed of greatness. Adversity, like a blacksmith's forge, shapes and molds us into stronger, more resilient beings. But it takes more than just weathering the storm to achieve true greatness. It takes the courage to rise above it, the willpower to grow from it, and the inspiration to flourish beyond all expectations.

Like a seedling fighting to break through concrete, those who dare to embrace adversity often find themselves blooming in ways they never thought possible. They crash through the glass ceilings of their own limitations, leaving behind scars and lacerations as proof of their unyielding determination.

But progress and success come at a cost. Sacrifice, loss, and failure are inevitable, yet it is precisely in these moments that we must dig deep and work wounded. Even when we want to quit, when we feel like giving up, that's when we must push harder, strive further, and live on the edge of our own limits.

Michael Jordan, one of the greatest basketball players of all time, embodied this spirit of relentless determination. In the now-infamous "Flu Game" of 1997, he played for 44 minutes and scored 38 points, despite suffering from food poisoning and being visibly weak and ill. He later said, "I felt the obligation to my team, to the city of Chicago, to go out and give that extra effort."

It is moments like these that define greatness. When the world is a dangerous place, and the odds seem insurmountable, it is up to us to rise above it all and carve our own path to success. Yes, there will be bad days and challenges that test our limits, but it is precisely in these moments that we find our edge and become great. So let us embrace the grit and the mud, let us work wounded, and let us thrive in the face of adversity.

TIP: *Taking care of yourself is non-negotiable, and your body and mind need to be nurtured.* Maintain your schedule but also understand when to take breaks. Be realistic with deadlines and manage your time. Prioritize the essential tasks and shift less urgent work to a later date.

"SOMETIMES YOU NEED TO GET HIT IN THE HEAD TO REALIZE THAT YOU'RE IN A FIGHT."
- Michael Jordan

RULE #012

NARROW YOUR FOCUS

That classic proverb teaches us, "a jack of all trades is a master of none." But, many overlook that the saying extends to "but oftentimes better than a master of one." In our dynamic, ever-evolving world, possessing a range of talents isn't just applauded, it's almost imperative. Still, to truly prosper in diverse endeavors, master one first.

At the outset of your odyssey, multitasking may impede progress. It's essential to concentrate on refining a single skill, creating the bedrock for future accomplishments. Malcolm Gladwell's Outliers claims around 10,000 hours of practice are needed to excel in any field. Have you dedicated that time to any pursuit? It's a challenge, but vital for true mastery.

Picture your ambition to become the world's preeminent pastry chef. How many cakes must you perfect? How many hours should you devote to the kitchen? It's an intimidating mission, but achievable through focus, discipline, and experience. Mastery demands time, effort, and unwavering tenacity.

The initial phase of your adventure may be riddled with confusion and skepticism, but these are the moments of profound growth. Sharpen your focus, establish discipline, and utilize your experiences. Through perseverance and commitment, you can conquer many trades—but it all begins with mastering one.

TIP: *Identify potential distractions (e.g., phone notifications, social media, noisy environments) and take steps to eliminate or minimize them. Create a conducive work environment that supports concentration and focus. Allocate specific time slots for each task, and stick to the schedule as much as possible. Establish deadlines or time limits for each task, and strive to complete the task within the allotted time. Commit to following your schedule and maintaining focus on the task at hand. Remain disciplined and hold yourself accountable for completing the tasks within the set time frame.*

"SUCCESS IS A FUNCTION OF PERSISTENCE AND DOGGEDNESS AND THE WILLINGNESS TO WORK HARD FOR TWENTY-TWO MINUTES TO MAKE SENSE OF SOMETHING THAT MOST PEOPLE WOULD GIVE UP ON AFTER THIRTY SECONDS."
- Malcolm Gladwell

RULE #013

DROWN OUT THE NOISE

Our world is vast and brimming with endless opportunities, yet many of us fail to embrace these possibilities. We settle into familiar routines, oblivious to the fact that there is more to life than our current experiences. This reluctance to explore can result in a distressing loss of opportunities that cannot be reclaimed.

The rewards of embracing the world around us are countless. Stepping beyond our comfort zones exposes us to new ideas, cultures, and viewpoints. We develop a deeper appreciation for and understanding of people who differ from us, fostering open-mindedness and tolerance. Conversely, when we confine ourselves to our known environments, we restrict our global awareness and our capacity for empathy. Such limited understanding can give rise to misconceptions and even bias against those unlike us.

Exploration unveils new passions and interests, revealing potential pursuits we might never have contemplated. As we sample novel experiences and destinations, we unlock a realm of possibilities. We might find ourselves captivated by a previously unconsidered hobby, art, or vocation. Without exploration, our true potential remains untapped.

Moreover, neglecting to explore can breed regret in later years. As we reflect on our lives, we yearn for a sense of accomplishment and contentment, knowing we seized every opportunity. However, when exploration is absent, we grapple with "what if?" questions and wishes for what could have been. By venturing into the unknown and embracing novelty, we forge lasting memories and experiences.

Admittedly, various factors may deter individuals from exploring—fear, anxiety, financial constraints, or personal and professional obligations. Nevertheless, it is crucial to recognize the immense value exploration offers in comparison to its risks.

In conclusion, the forfeiture of experiences due to a lack of exploration is a preventable tragedy. By stepping beyond our boundaries and delving into the world, we immerse ourselves in fresh ideas, cultures, and perspectives. We uncover new passions and interests, accumulating memories and experiences to cherish forever. So, the next time the chance to explore arises, grasp it wholeheartedly. The world eagerly awaits.

TIP: *Build a rapport with colleagues, co-workers, or fellow professionals to stay engaged and motivated at work. These social connections can provide a support system, leading to better focus and productivity. Engage in mindful listening where you can genuinely connect, understand, and contribute during conversations. This approach can help you interact more effectively, stay engaged, and be less distracted.*

"THE WAY WE INTERACT WITH OTHERS IS THE WAY WE INTERACT WITH LIFE."
- Paulo Coelho

RULE #014

TURN POISON INTO MEDICINE

Life's journey can be arduous, laden with obstacles and hardships we must confront. Yet, imagine if we could transform these adversities into something advantageous—that's the essence of the ancient principle of turning poison into medicine. This Eastern philosophy urges us to choose between succumbing to our challenges or harnessing them to our benefit.

You might wonder how to achieve this feat. It begins with embracing a growth mindset, which entails believing in our capacity to enhance our skills and abilities through perseverance and determination. By adopting this perspective, we can tackle challenges with an optimistic and proactive attitude, viewing them as catalysts for growth and development.

The idea of turning poison into medicine originates from Laozi's ancient Taoist philosophy. In his seminal work, the Tao Te Ching, Laozi discusses discovering joy and contentment even amid difficulties. He asserts that the wise and virtuous can find satisfaction in any circumstance.

This principle also resonates in traditional Chinese medicine, where numerous potent remedies are derived from toxic substances. With proper preparation and care, poison can be converted into powerful medicine.

So, how can we incorporate this concept into our daily lives? One crucial step is cultivating gratitude.

By concentrating on our blessings rather than our deficiencies, we can foster a positive outlook and boost our resilience when facing challenges. By acknowledging the good in our lives, we can divert our attention from our struggles and uncover innovative ways to transform them into opportunities.

TIP: *Accept that you are in a difficult situation and allow yourself to feel any emotions that arise without judgment. Look for any positive aspects or opportunities within the situation. Ask yourself, "What can I learn from this?" or "Is there anything beneficial that can come from this experience?" Create a clear plan of action, and regularly evaluate your progress and adjust your plan as needed. Be open to change and adapt your strategies if they are not yielding the desired results.*

"THE LOTUS FLOWER BLOOMS MOST BEAUTIFULLY FROM THE DEEPEST AND THICKEST MUD."
- Buddhist Proverb

RULE #015

TAKE ACTION

The belief that "anything not growing is dead" goes beyond a memorable saying; it embodies a potent principle that can revolutionize our lives and help us conquer anxiety. In today's fast-paced society, it's easy to succumb to complacency and routine, which can lead to stagnation and dissatisfaction. Growth, however, is vital for our physical, mental, and emotional well-being.

Growth is more than just exploring new endeavors or taking risks; it encompasses embracing change and constantly striving for improvement. This can be intimidating, and feeling anxious about the unknown is natural. Nevertheless, taking action is the antidote to overcoming anxiety and confronting our fears. By taking action, we confirm our dedication to growth and demonstrate our willingness to welcome change.

Action also neutralizes anxiety by providing a sense of control and purpose. Actively pursuing our objectives leaves less room for dwelling on fears and worries, reducing stress and enhancing our well-being. It's crucial to recognize that growth and action can be difficult and challenging at times, but embracing these trials as opportunities for development is essential.

In essence, growth is indispensable for our survival. Ceasing to grow equates to ceasing to live, resulting in a static and unfulfilling existence. Continuously seeking novel experiences and challenges that encourage growth and development is crucial. By taking action and championing growth, we can overcome our fears and anxiety, leading to a more rewarding life.

Don't hesitate to step beyond your comfort zone and embrace new experiences and challenges. Your growth and happiness rely on it. Bear in mind that anything not growing is dead, and you deserve a life brimming with growth, transformation, and boundless potential.

TIP: *Regular exercise can help reduce stress and improve your mood. Even a quick 10-15 minute walk can help clear your mind and reduce anxiety. Deep breathing exercises and other relaxation techniques such as progressive muscle relaxation, meditation, or yoga can help calm your body and mind, reducing anxiety.*

"THE BEST WAY TO NOT FEEL HOPELESS IS TO GET UP AND DO SOMETHING."
- Barack Obama

RULE #016

CREATE STANDARDS, NOT EXPECTATIONS

In the pursuit of success, we all hold certain expectations. We imagine reaching specific milestones, gaining recognition for our efforts, and accomplishing personal and professional objectives. However, solely relying on expectations can lead to a precarious situation, resulting in disappointment and frustration. In this discussion, we delve into why establishing standards serves as a more effective approach to success.

Expectations are subjective and frequently unrealistic, shaped by our biases and convictions. One person's expectations may vary from another's, making it challenging to achieve a shared goal. Unmet expectations can result in disappointment, aggravation, and even failure.

In contrast, standards are objective and quantifiable. They offer a definitive aim to work towards, grounded in facts and data. Standards enable us to allocate our time and resources efficiently, monitor our progress, and maintain focus on crucial aspects. Meeting our standards instills a sense of achievement and motivation to continue progressing.

Emphasizing standards also benefits our mental health. Unrealistic expectations can induce pressure, leading to anxiety, stress, and burnout. Concentrating on standards allows us to feel more in control, reducing stress and bolstering our self-esteem.

Moreover, implementing standards streamlines collaboration among individuals. When there is a mutual understanding of expectations, we can combine our efforts to reach a common goal. This promotes improved communication, cooperation, and teamwork – all essential components for achieving success.

TIP: *Set boundaries with work and personal time to maintain a healthy work-life balance. Take care of your physical health by getting enough sleep, eating well, and exercising regularly. Practice mindfulness and meditation to reduce stress and increase focus. Schedule time for creative hobbies and activities outside of work to recharge your energy.*

"THE WORLD NEEDS DREAMERS AND THE WORLD NEEDS DOERS. BUT ABOVE ALL, THE WORLD NEEDS DREAMERS WHO DO."
- Sarah Ban Breathnach

RULE #017

USE THE POMODORO TECHNIQUE

"PRODUCTIVITY IS NEVER AN ACCIDENT. IT IS ALWAYS THE RESULT OF A COMMITMENT TO EXCELLENCE, INTELLIGENT PLANNING, AND FOCUSED EFFORT."
- Paul J. Meyer

Are you finding it difficult to maintain focus and complete tasks? Do you frequently feel as though there aren't enough hours in the day to accomplish everything on your agenda? In today's fast-paced society, remaining productive and concentrated on our objectives can be quite challenging. This is where the Pomodoro Technique can be of assistance.

The Pomodoro Technique, developed by Francesco Cirillo in the late 1980s, is a time management method designed to help you divide large tasks into smaller, more manageable segments. Named after the tomato-shaped timer Cirillo employed to time his work sessions when he initially devised the method, the technique centers on working in 25-minute concentrated intervals, followed by brief breaks, with longer breaks after several sessions.

TIP: *To effectively utilize the Pomodoro Technique, adhere to these straightforward steps:*

1. *Select a task to work on.*
2. *Set a timer for 25 minutes and begin working on the task.*
3. *When the timer rings, take a 5-minute break.*

4. *After completing four Pomodoros (25-minute work sessions), take an extended break lasting 15-30 minutes.*
5. *Repeat the process, starting with step 1.*

Working in 25-minute focused intervals can help you avoid distractions and maintain productivity. The brief pauses between sessions offer your brain an opportunity to rest and recharge, making it easier to concentrate during the subsequent work session.

The Pomodoro Technique offers several advantages:

- *Enhanced productivity: By dividing tasks into smaller portions and working in focused intervals, you can accomplish more in less time.*
- *Diminished distractions: The Pomodoro Technique encourages you to eliminate distractions during work sessions, helping you remain focused on the current task.*
- *Improved time management: By monitoring your Pomodoros, you can gain a better understanding of how long specific tasks take and adjust your schedule as needed.*
- *Decreased burnout: Short breaks between Pomodoros can help prevent burnout and improve your overall well-being.*

To effectively apply the Pomodoro Technique, consider these suggestions:

- *Choose tasks that can be finished in 25-minute intervals. This will help you stay motivated and make progress.*

- *Eliminate distractions during work sessions. This can involve turning off phone notifications, closing unnecessary computer tabs, and finding a quiet workspace.*
- *Utilize your longer breaks to rest. Use this time to stand up, stretch, or engage in something enjoyable to help you recharge.*
- *Keep track of your Pomodoros. This can help you stay accountable and monitor your progress over time.*
- *Experiment with the duration of your work sessions and breaks. Some individuals find shorter or longer sessions more effective, so don't hesitate to adjust the timing to suit your needs.*

RULE #018

SIMPLIFY THE SOLUTION

In this wildly intricate universe, brimming with limitless prospects and mind-bending complexities, we're often weighed down by the enormity of our challenges. Overwhelmed, intimidated, and feeling utterly defeated. But what if I told you there's a straightforward key to unlocking even the most intricate enigmas?

It starts with dissecting the beast into digestible chunks. Pinpoint the heart of the matter - the single obstacle standing between you and your grand objective. Then, take a step back and soak in the panorama. What are the crucial elements fueling this issue? What are the underlying causes of each of those components?

Imagine this: You're running a business, aiming to elevate customer satisfaction. Your mind's racing, contemplating everything that could be amiss. But hold up! Inhale deeply, and sketch a mind map or flowchart. Jot down every factor contributing to customer satisfaction - product quality, customer service, pricing, and so on. Then, group similar factors and expose their root causes.

Here's where the magic happens - discovering easy answers for each piece of the puzzle. Brainstorm a list of potential solutions for each factor group. Weigh the practicality, potency, and cost of each proposition. For instance, if subpar customer service is the crux of the problem, consider ramping up employee training, enhancing communication channels, or introducing a customer feedback system. Assess each solution based on its impact on customer satisfaction and cost-effectiveness.

Finally, it's time to roll out and evaluate your solutions. Monitor your progress and tweak as necessary. Keep communication lines wide open with stakeholders, and lend an ear to their input.

To wrap it up, addressing convoluted problems is all about embracing a step-by-step method. Divide and conquer, uncover straightforward solutions for each portion, and evaluate their efficacy. By maintaining focus on your ultimate goal, you can triumph over even the most formidable of obstacles.

TIP: *Focus on the most important aspects of the task and let go of the rest. For example, if you're planning a party, focus on the key elements like the guest list, menu, and venue, and don't worry too much about small details like decorations.*

There are many tools and resources available to help simplify complex tasks. For example, project management software can help you break down a large project into smaller tasks, while templates and checklists can help ensure you don't overlook important details. Don't be afraid to leverage these resources to simplify your work.

"IF YOU CAN'T EXPLAIN IT TO A SIX-YEAR-OLD, YOU DON'T UNDERSTAND IT YOURSELF."
- Albert Einstein

RULE #019

CLIMB AND MAINTAIN

In the quest for success, it's tempting to think of it as a finish line we can finally cross. However, the reality is that success isn't a final destination. Instead, it's a voyage that involves both ascending and sustaining in various aspects of our lives. Ascending entails setting objectives, making headway, and achieving greater levels of success. Sustaining involves preserving that success and preventing regression. Here are some pointers on how to ascend and maintain success in different areas of our lives:

Career: *To ascend in your profession, establish clear objectives and concentrate on your strengths. Pursue opportunities for professional growth, and consistently develop your skills and network. To maintain your success, remain engaged and motivated in your work. Keep honing your skills, broadening your network, and stay open to fresh challenges and possibilities.*

Relationships: *Ascending in your relationships means actively listening, communicating effectively, and demonstrating genuine interest and empathy. To maintain your success, strive to build trust and respect. Invest time and energy in your relationships, and provide support for those you care about.*

Finances: *Ascending in your finances involves creating a budget, monitoring your expenses, and seeking ways to boost your income. To maintain your success, exercise discipline in your spending habits, steer clear of debt, and persist in saving and investing for the future.*

Personal Development: *Ascending in your personal development requires setting explicit goals, discovering new learning opportunities, and working on your mindset and habits. To maintain your success, keep focusing on personal growth. Embrace challenges and opportunities for learning, and stay engaged and motivated in your personal development journey.*

*S*uccess isn't a destination that we can eventually attain. It's a journey that demands both ascending and sustaining in various aspects of our lives. To accomplish success, we must establish clear goals, emphasize our strengths, and labor to create and uphold our progress in each of these areas. By doing so, we can continue to rise and maintain our success over time.

"SUCCESS IS A JOURNEY, NOT A DESTINATION. IT REQUIRES CONSTANT EFFORT, VIGILANCE, AND REEVALUATION."
- Mark Twain

RULE #020

THE EISENHOWER MATRIX

Are you feeling overwhelmed by the constant demands of modern life? Do you struggle to prioritize tasks and often find yourself scrambling to catch up? Don't stress, my friend. In today's fast-paced world, managing our time effectively and efficiently is a challenge we all face. Luckily, there's a solution that can help: the Eisenhower Matrix.

Named after Dwight D. Eisenhower, the 34th President of the United States, this matrix is a powerful tool for prioritizing tasks based on their level of urgency and importance. It's a simple yet effective way to help you focus on what matters most and make the most of your time.

The matrix is divided into four quadrants, each with its own set of tasks:

Quadrant 1: *Urgent and Important tasks that require immediate attention and have a significant impact on your goals and objectives. These are the tasks that you should tackle first.*

Quadrant 2: *Not Urgent but Important tasks that contribute to your long-term goals and require planning and strategy. These tasks should be prioritized based on their level of importance.*

Quadrant 3: *Urgent but Not Important tasks that should be delegated or eliminated. These tasks may be time-sensitive but have little impact on your overall goals and objectives.*

Quadrant 4: *Not Urgent and Not Important tasks that can be eliminated or postponed. These are the tasks that do not contribute to your goals and objectives and can often be distractions.*

The benefits of using the Eisenhower Matrix are numerous. It provides clear prioritization, improves time management, enhances decision-making, and reduces stress. By focusing on tasks that are most important and have the greatest impact on your goals and objectives, you can manage your time more effectively and efficiently.

To use the Eisenhower Matrix effectively, it's crucial to be honest with yourself when evaluating the urgency and importance of tasks. Use the matrix regularly to manage your workload and stay on top of your tasks. Delegate tasks in Quadrant 3 to others if possible, and review and update the matrix regularly to ensure that you're making progress on your goals and objectives.

TIP: *Using the Eisenhower Matrix is simple. First, write down all the tasks that need to be done. Then, place each task in the appropriate quadrant based on its level of urgency and importance. Tackle the tasks in Quadrant 1 first, prioritize tasks in Quadrant 2 based on their level of importance, delegate tasks in Quadrant 3 if possible, and eliminate or postpone tasks in Quadrant 4.*

"WHAT IS IMPORTANT IS SELDOM URGENT, AND WHAT IS URGENT IS SELDOM IMPORTANT."
- Dwight D. Eisenhower

RULE #021

PLAN & EXECUTE

"A GOAL WITHOUT A PLAN IS JUST A WISH."
- Antoine de Saint-Exupéry

Listen up! If you want to achieve success in any project, big or small, you gotta start with the planning phase. It's the foundation that sets you up for victory. By planning, you make sure your resources are used efficiently, goals are clear, and challenges are identified and addressed beforehand. People who plan before they act on their ideas are more likely to succeed and avoid failure.

One reason why planning is crucial is that it helps clarify your goals and objectives. When you know what you want to achieve, you can figure out the steps to take to make it happen. This level of focus helps prioritize resources and optimize efforts towards those objectives.

But that's not all. Planning also helps you identify potential challenges and risks. When you're prepared for obstacles and have a plan in place to overcome them, you increase your chances of success and reduce the likelihood of failure. Do your market research, assess the competition, and get feedback from stakeholders - that's how you mitigate risks.

Effective resource allocation is another essential part of planning. When you create a detailed plan, you can identify the resources you need to achieve your goals, like time, money, personnel, and materials. That way, you can make sure you have the necessary resources and allocate them in the best way possible.

Lastly, planning increases accountability and ownership. With a clear plan, it's easier to assign responsibilities and track progress. You make sure everyone is working towards the same goals, and progress is monitored effectively.

Planning is the key to success in any project. It helps you clarify your objectives, anticipate obstacles, allocate resources effectively, and increase accountability. So before you jump into anything, take the time to plan. Your future self will thank you for it!

TIP: *There are many tools available that can help make planning and executing ideas easier. Here are a few examples:*

> ***Mind Mapping Software:*** *This type of software can help you visualize ideas and concepts in a more organized and structured way. It allows you to create diagrams, flowcharts, and other visual representations of your thoughts and ideas.*
>
> ***1.*** *ClickUp is one of the highest-rated productivity tools and mind mapping tools used by productive teams in small and large companies.*
> ***2.*** *XMind is a simple mind mapping software that helps generate ideas, goals, and tasks.*
> ***3.*** *ConceptDraw MINDMAP is an idea management and diagramming tool that can help organize your free-running ideas.*

2. **Project Management Tools:** These tools can help you organize and manage projects more efficiently. They often include features such as task lists, calendars, and collaboration tools to help you stay on track.

1. *monday.com — Best for building custom workflows across teams*
2. *Wrike — Best project management software for scaling organizations*
3. *Smartsheet — Best for low-code project management automation*

3. ***Note-Taking Apps:*** *These apps can help you capture and organize ideas quickly and easily. They often include features such as tagging, search, and collaboration to help you find and share your notes with others.*

1. *Bullet is a bullet journal app lets you add tasks, notes & events all in one place.* https://bulletjournal.app/
2. *Capacities is a place for all your information. It stores your knowledge and can resurface it, right when you need it.* https://capacities.io/
3. *Clover is your daily workspace: Notes, Tasks, Whiteboards and a Daily Planner in a streamlined workflow.* https://cloverapp.com/

4. ***Time Management Apps:*** *These apps can help you track your time and stay focused on your goals. They often include features such as timers, calendars, and reminders to help you manage your schedule more effectively.*

1. Todoist is a great checklist app that will help you prioritize your tasks and manage time.
2. RescueTime is a productivity reporting tool that you can use to see how much time you're spending on certain apps and websites.
3. Toggl Plan is a great checklist app to manage your tasks and optimize your time management tactics.

5. ***Feedback Tools:*** *These tools can help you gather feedback from others, such as colleagues, customers, or stakeholders. They often include features such as surveys, polls, and reviews to help you collect and analyze feedback in a structured way.*

1. *Marker.io is a website feedback tool that's perfect for QA testing and client feedback.*

2. *Hotjar helps you understand user behavior on your site.*

3. *Qualaroo This tool surveys specific users in context while they browse various pages on your website.*

RULE #022

BE EMPOWERED BY EMPOWERING OTHERS

"THE GREATEST GOOD YOU CAN DO FOR ANOTHER IS NOT JUST TO SHARE YOUR RICHES BUT TO REVEAL TO HIM HIS OWN."
- Benjamin Disraeli

Empowerment is that game-changer that flips the script not only in our lives but also in the lives of those we touch. When we give people the keys to unlock their potential, we're lighting a fire that'll help them conquer their dreams. And guess what? It ain't just about being selfless; we get to taste that empowerment magic too, feeling a sense of fulfillment that money can't buy.

One of the dopest things about lifting others up is that it creates those unbreakable bonds and connections that last a lifetime. By investing in their growth and happiness, we're weaving a fabric of trust, respect, and a love that's all about giving and supporting each other.

But there's more to it than that. When we empower others, we're also taking ourselves to school. We learn, we grow, and we pick up new skills that help us level up our own game. We ain't just making a difference for others, but we're also becoming the best version of ourselves.

And let's talk about that self-discovery, because empowering others makes us dig deep and find the gold within us. As we push them to soar, we discover our strengths, our weaknesses, and the skills we never knew we had. Plus, we get to see the world through new lenses, understanding the stories and struggles of others that we might've missed before.

Now, here's the cherry on top: empowering others brings that sunshine into our lives. When we're out there, making the world a better place, we're also finding our purpose, our meaning, and that happiness we all crave. By lifting others up, we become part of a tribe that's all about that shared goal and vibe.

So, in a nutshell, empowering others is like a two-way street of transformation. Whether we're looking to build unbreakable connections, learn new things, or leave a positive mark on this world, lifting others up is the golden ticket to a more fulfilled and satisfied life. That's the power of empowerment, and it's a gift we can all share.

TIP: Allow the individuals you are working with to make decisions and take ownership of their tasks. This gives them a sense of responsibility and control over their work, which can lead to increased motivation and commitment. Provide clear expectations and guidelines, but also give them the freedom to find their own solutions.

Example: Instead of micromanaging every detail of a project, set clear objectives and deadlines, but give team members the flexibility to determine the best way to achieve those goals.

Ensure that individuals have access to the necessary resources, tools, and information to be successful in their tasks. Offer your expertise and assistance when needed, but also encourage them to seek help from others and learn from their experiences.

Example: Make sure your team has access to relevant training materials, software, and equipment, and offer to connect them with experts in their field for additional guidance.

Foster a sense of teamwork and unity by encouraging individuals to work together on projects and share their knowledge and skills with one another. This not only promotes a supportive environment but also helps to build trust and camaraderie among team members.

Example: Assign group projects that require collaboration, or create a mentorship program where experienced team members help develop the skills of their less-experienced colleagues.

RULE #023

CREATE PROGRAMS OF COMMUNICATION

"TO EFFECTIVELY COMMUNICATE, WE MUST REALIZE THAT WE ARE ALL DIFFERENT IN THE WAY WE PERCEIVE THE WORLD AND USE THIS UNDERSTANDING AS A GUIDE TO OUR COMMUNICATION WITH OTHERS."
- Tony Robbins

Effective communication ain't no buzzword. It's the heartbeat of success, the lifeblood of our personal and professional worlds. We're talking workplace vibes, love connections, and the way we come together as a community. Communication ain't just about flapping' our lips, it's about tailoring' the way we talk, sharing' what we know, and listening' like our life depends on it, 'cause sometimes it does.

When we tune into the rhythm of our people, we can vibe on a deeper level. We all got our unique style, and when we understand the beat of someone else's drum, we can dance together in perfect harmony. Tailored communication programs cut through the noise, bringing' clarity and focus. It keeps confusion at bay and keeps us on the same page, riding' the same wavelength.

Trust and credibility grow when we make others feel heard and valued. We're all just lookin' to be understood, and when we tap into that, we're nurturing' stronger relationships, lifting' morale, and creating' a workplace where everyone feels like they belong.

We can't forget about engagement, that magical spark that fuels communication. When we show we care, when we're invested in the process, we inspire productivity, creativity, and collaboration. It's that secret sauce that drives success for both individuals and organizations.

So, my friends, let's put in the work and create communication programs that are tailor-made for the people around us. Let's groove to the beat of each other's hearts, and together, we'll create a world that sings in perfect harmony.

TIP: *Identify your target audience: Understand the demographics, preferences, and needs of your target audience. This will enable you to create tailored messages that resonate with them and address their specific concerns. Select the most appropriate channels to reach your target audience. These could include traditional methods such as print, radio, and television, or digital channels like social media, email, and websites. Ensure you choose a mix of channels to maximize your reach.*

Develop compelling content: Craft engaging, relevant, and informative content that speaks directly to your audience's interests and needs. Use storytelling techniques, incorporate visuals, and optimize your content for SEO and conversations to make it more accessible and shareable. Maintain a consistent tone and voice throughout your communication program to build a strong brand identity. This helps in creating familiarity and trust among your target audience.

Use feedback and analytics: Regularly monitor the effectiveness of your communication program by gathering feedback from your audience and analyzing key performance indicators (KPIs). This will help you understand what works and what doesn't, allowing you to make necessary adjustments for better results. Open up conversations with your audience, encouraging them to interact with your brand. This could be through social media comments, email, or even in-person events. This will not only help you better understand your audience but also foster loyalty and trust.

Set a realistic budget: Create a budget for your communication program, taking into account the costs associated with creating content, hiring staff, and deploying various communication channels. Ensure you allocate resources wisely to maximize the return on investment (ROI). Ensure that your team is well-equipped with the necessary skills and tools to execute the communication program effectively. Provide them with regular training and updates on the latest industry trends and best practices.

Review and optimize: Continuously evaluate and optimize your communication program to stay relevant in the ever-changing market landscape. Keep an eye on emerging trends and technologies and be ready to adapt your strategies to stay ahead of the curve.

RULE #024

FOCUS ON PROGRESS, NOT PERFECTION

Chasing perfection is like trying to catch a cloud. It looks all shiny and pretty from a distance, but up close, it's nothing more than an illusion. Instead of going after that mirage, let's focus on making progress, 'cause that's where the real magic happens.

Here's some wisdom to help you shift gears and ride that progress train:

1. Keep it real: Don't aim for the moon when you ain't built your rocket yet. Set goals that make sense, and celebrate the little wins you score along the way.
2. Give mistakes a hug: Messing up is part of the game, so embrace it. When you trip, learn to pick yourself up and grow from the experience, instead of beating yourself down.
3. Dance to the small victories: Every step you take is worth a celebration. So let loose, and groove to the progress you're making'.
4. It's about the journey, baby: Success ain't just a destination, it's the whole ride. Soak in the moments, feel the growth, and enjoy the scenery as you make your way.
5. Show yourself some love: Nobody's perfect, and that's a fact. Be kind to yourself, and remember that progress is a journey, with its ups and downs.

In a nutshell, chasing progress over perfection is the way to win at life. By keeping it real, embracing your mistakes, celebrating your wins, loving the journey, and being kind to yourself, you'll be cruising towards your dreams with a smile on your face and joy in your heart. So let's get moving, and remember, progress, not perfection, is the key to a life well-lived.

TIP: *Take time to regularly review your progress, acknowledging the positive steps you've taken and the challenges you've overcome. By setting checkpoints and reflecting on your journey, you can celebrate your achievements and maintain motivation to continue moving forward.*

"PERFECTION IS NOT ATTAINABLE, BUT IF WE CHASE PERFECTION WE CAN CATCH EXCELLENCE."
- Vince Lombardi

RULE #025

WRITE EVERYTHING DOWN

"THE ACT OF WRITING IS THE ACT OF DISCOVERING WHAT YOU BELIEVE."
- David Hare

Aight, let's talk about this secret weapon we've all been sleeping on—writing. It's that magic key that unlocks the door to organizing your thoughts, clearing your mind, and stepping into the world of success. From scribbling your ideas in the boardroom to mapping out your daily tasks, getting those words on paper levels up your focus and productivity.

Now, let me break down why you gotta start putting pen to paper:

1. Let your thoughts shine: Writing is like turning on the high beams in your brain, giving your thoughts purpose and direction. Plus, it takes those massive ideas and turns 'em into snack-sized, easy-to-handle morsels.
2. Tidy up that mind: When you jot it all down, you're organizing your thoughts and keeping crucial intel close at hand. That means more time and less stress when you gotta dig up those vital details.
3. Accountability is key: Penning down your goals and plans creates a roadmap to your dreams, helping you hold yourself accountable and ensuring you follow through with your commitments.

4. Reflection, baby: Reviewing your notes is like taking a pit stop on your journey, allowing you to see how far you've traveled and adjust your route if needed. This self-assessment keeps you fired up and ready to grow.
5. Memory game strong: Writing is like activating a secret power-up for your brain, engaging different areas of your mind and making it a breeze to remember the important stuff.

So here's the deal, writing everything down is like unearthing a hidden gem that helps you stay organized, focused, and pumped. It's all about bringing clarity, getting things in order, staying true to your commitments, reflecting on your progress, and boosting that memory of yours. Grab that pen, and let's take on the world one word at a time, together.

TIP: *Start by deciding what you want to write down—ideas, tasks, goals, or maybe even daily reflections. Having a clear vision will guide you in making this habit stick:*

▸ **Find your sweet spot:** Choose a time and place that works best for you. It could be in the morning with a cup of joe or at night when the world's winding down. Find that cozy nook where you can write in peace.

▸ ***Set a reminder:*** *Until it becomes second nature, set reminders on your phone or use sticky notes around your space to prompt you to write. Consistency is key, and these cues will help keep you on track.*

▸ ***Start small:*** *Don't go overboard right away. Begin with just a few lines or bullet points each day.*

This way, you won't feel overwhelmed, and it'll be easier to stay committed to your new habit.

- ***Make it personal:*** *Customize your writing experience by adding some flair. Use colored pens, stickers, or anything else that makes it feel like an extension of you. The more personal it feels, the more you'll enjoy the process.*
- ***Review and reflect:*** *Take some time each week to review what you've written. This will help you appreciate the progress you've made and motivate you to keep the habit going strong.*
- ***Be patient:*** *Rome wasn't built in a day, and neither is a new habit. Give yourself time to adjust, and if you miss a day, don't stress—just pick up where you left off and keep going.*

RULE #026

EMBRACE BALANCE AND REALISM

The siren song of success and the looming shadow of failure often send us spiraling to the edges, blinding us to the truth. When we're caught up in extremes, we can lose sight of reality, cooking up false perceptions and setting ourselves up for a letdown. It's all too easy to get trapped in that web of sky-high standards, thinking that anything less than extraordinary ain't worth a dime.

We might see someone basking in the glow of success and think we can breeze our way to the top just like that. It's like we're slapping labels on everyone—either you're a winner or a loser, with no in-between. This tunnel vision focuses on the wild success stories without giving a second thought to the blood, sweat, and tears that made 'em happen.

There's a different path we can take. Instead of gettin' tangled up in the world of extremes, we can choose a more balanced, grounded approach. Let's keep it real by considering what's possible and what's actually within reach, rather than just fixating on the wildest dreams. By doing this, we can sidestep the disappointment that comes from chasing the unattainable and set ourselves up for the kind of success that sticks around for the long haul.

TIP: *Avoid an all-or-nothing mentality, as it can lead to extreme beliefs and behaviors. Instead, strive for balance in your thoughts, actions, and goals. Recognize that success often lies in the middle* *ground, where you can maintain a healthy, sustainable lifestyle while pursuing growth. Treat yourself with kindness and understanding when faced with setbacks or challenges. Acknowledge that you are only human, and it's natural to encounter obstacles along the way. By practicing self-compassion, you can foster a more resilient mindset that focuses on growth rather than perfection.*

Take time to reflect on your past experiences, both successes and failures. Use this insight to identify patterns, learn from your mistakes, and set more realistic expectations for the future. As you progress on your self-improvement journey, be open to adjusting your expectations when necessary. Life is dynamic and ever-changing, so it's essential to remain flexible and adapt your goals to align with your current circumstances.

"FALSE EXPECTATIONS ARE THE THIEF OF JOY."
- Theodore Roosevelt.

RULE #027

PRIORITIZE YOUR TIME AND ENERGY

"TIME IS A CREATED THING. TO SAY 'I DON'T HAVE TIME,' IS LIKE SAYING, 'I DON'T WANT TO."

- Lao Tzu

Time—it's a riddle wrapped in a mystery, a head-scratcher that we all feel ticking away, but can't quite pin down. Still, there's no denying the weight it carries. Time is our most treasured possession, as the wise ol' Theophrastus once said. What makes it so precious? It's a limited, non-renewable gem, unlike cash, real estate, or even our health. We've all got 24 hours a day, and when they're gone, there ain't no gettin' them back. That makes time the ultimate leveler, handing out equal helpings to everyone, no matter their social standing, fortune, or influence.

But time ain't just about leveling the playing field. It's the bedrock of our lives, the soil from which all our experiences, chances, and connections sprout. Everything we do is a dance with time—our goals, passions, and the lives we crave all play out on its stage. The way we juggle and manage our time can make or break the quality of our lives and how high we soar.

Since time's a finite treasure, it's crucial we treat it like gold. It's a resource that demands we use it with intention, making every moment count and living life to the max. This means taking a good, hard look at what really matters to us, setting our priorities straight, and mapping out how we wanna spend our days. It's about being mindful of the moments, choosing actions that align with our values and dreams.

To sum it up, grasping the true value of time is the first step towards mastering it and making our aspirations come true. Time is, without a doubt, our most valuable asset, and it's on us to spend it wisely and with purpose. As Theophrastus dropped that timeless truth, time is the most valuable thing a person can spend.

TIP: *Identify what is most important to you and allocate your time accordingly. Create a schedule that reflects your priorities and stick to it as much as possible. Learn to say no to activities and commitments that are not aligned with your priorities. This will free up your time and energy for things that are more important to you. Identify the activities that give you the most energy and focus on them. This could be exercise, spending time with loved ones, or pursuing a hobby you enjoy.*

Pay attention to your energy levels throughout the day and try to match your activities to your energy level. For example, if you have a lot of energy in the morning, schedule your most important tasks for that time. Make sure to take breaks throughout the day to recharge your energy. This could be taking a walk outside, meditating, or simply taking a few deep breaths.

Simplify your life: Eliminate unnecessary activities and commitments that drain your time and energy.

RULE #028

LIMIT DECISION FATIGUE

"CLUTTER IS THE PHYSICAL MANIFESTATION OF UNMADE DECISIONS FUELED BY PROCRASTINATION."
- Christina Scalise

We all know that life can be a whirlwind of choices, tossing us between trivial matters and momentous decisions like a pinball. But, have you ever pondered about the impact of all those daily decisions on your mental energy? Well, buckle up, my friend, because we're about to dive into the magic of limiting decision fatigue, an ingenious technique to simplify your life and save that precious brainpower for the big leagues.

Decision fatigue is a real deal – a sneaky thief that snatches your mental energy away, leaving you feeling drained and unfocused. When you're caught in the labyrinth of countless decisions, your ability to make sound choices dwindles, and your productivity suffers. So, how do you combat this invisible energy bandit? The answer lies in cutting the clutter and streamlining your decision-making process.

Start by identifying the areas of your life where decisions pile up like dirty laundry. We're talking about those mundane, everyday choices that sneakily sap your mental energy – what to wear, what to eat, or which route to take to work. Once you've got these culprits lined up, it's time to devise a game plan to tackle 'em.

The secret sauce to conquering decision fatigue is to create routines and habits that automate these pesky daily choices. By doing so, you free up mental space and keep that brainpower locked and loaded for the more critical tasks. Remember, the key to mastering the art of limiting decision fatigue is to simplify, simplify, simplify! Once you've streamlined your daily decision-making, you'll notice the fog lifting, and your mental energy will be laser-focused on the tasks that truly matter.

TIP: Dress for Success: *Simplify your wardrobe by picking a "uniform" for daily wear. Choose clothing items that suit your style and are easily mix-and-matchable. By reducing the time spent on selecting outfits, you save precious mental energy for the day ahead.*

Eat Smart: *Plan your meals in advance, or adopt a meal rotation that keeps things simple and tasty. Meal prep ain't just for fitness buffs – it's a valuable weapon against decision fatigue that'll also save you time and money.*

Make a Roadmap: *Establish a daily routine for your personal and work life, and stick to it like glue. When you know what's coming next, you'll be better equipped to focus on the task at hand without getting sidetracked by indecision.*

Delegate or Automate: *Don't be a hero, and don't try to do everything yourself. Learn to delegate tasks to others when possible or use technology to automate repetitive chores. This way, you can free up mental energy for more critical decisions and creative thinking.*

Prioritize Like a Boss: *Learn to separate the wheat from the chaff, and focus on what truly matters. By prioritizing your tasks and decisions,* *you'll become more efficient, and decision fatigue won't stand a chance.*

RULE #029

PATIENCE, DISCIPLINE, AND A EAGERNESS TO LEARN

"PATIENCE AND FORTITUDE CONQUER ALL THINGS."
- Ralph Waldo Emerson

Success ain't a prize you can just snatch up overnight. Nah, it takes a blend of time, hustle, and the right mix of qualities and skills to make it happen. There are three game-changers you need in your corner: patience, discipline, and an unquenchable hunger for knowledge.

Patience is where it's at when we're chasing our dreams. It helps us stand tall and keep pushing when the going gets tough, and that's what makes success a reality. Without patience, it's all too easy to feel fed up and lose heart, leading us to throw in the towel. By learning to be patient, we pick up a priceless skill that helps us tackle hurdles and keep our eyes on the prize.

Discipline's another heavyweight in the ring of success. It keeps us locked in and focused on the mission, laying down the groundwork we need to make strides. Whether it's sticking to a daily grind, carving out time each day to work on our goals, or simply dodging distractions, discipline's a key player in helping us stay the course and march on.

And let's not forget that burning desire to learn. We gotta stay open to fresh ideas, new perspectives, and out-of-the-box ways to crack the code. It's our ability to learn from what we've been through and bounce back from our slip-ups that sets the winners apart from the rest. We gotta be hungry for knowledge and game to try out new things if we wanna see real growth in our lives, both personally and professionally.

Patience, discipline, and a never-ending thirst for knowledge are must-haves if you're lookin' to score big in life. By nurturing these skills, we can climb over obstacles, take it one step at a time, and ultimately hit the heights of success we've been dreaming of.

TIP: *Embrace the power of the "pause." When you find yourself in situations where impatience is creepin' up, take a step back and hit the brakes. That's right, just pause for a moment. Inhale deeply and exhale slowly. This simple act of conscious breathing will help you calm your mind and shift your focus from those impatient urges to the present moment.*

By taking this breather, you're giving yourself space to reflect and remind yourself that good things take time. And, with each pause, you're flexing that patience muscle, making it stronger and more resilient. So, next time you feel impatience nippin' at your heels, remember to take a beat, breathe, and watch that patience grow.

DISCIPLINE IS THE SOUL OF AN ARMY. IT MAKES SMALL NUMBERS FORMIDABLE; PROCURES SUCCESS TO THE WEAK, AND ESTEEM TO ALL."

- George Washington

RULE #030

INNOVATE

In the fast-paced, dog-eat-dog world we live in today, innovation is the secret sauce that keeps progress and success cooking. Without new ideas and creative solutions, we risk getting stuck in the mud, as progress crawls to a halt, and the competition zips past, leaving us in the dust.

This innovation drought hits hard, especially for organizations that are stuck in their ways and putting up walls against change. When businesses get all cozy with their current processes and products, they risk losing sight of the need to level up and stay ahead of the game. That's when market share slips away, customers start frowning, and the money train slows down.

Stagnation's the name of the game when innovation ain't on the table. As progress grinds to a halt, organizations dig their heels in, becoming less open to change. This can lead to employees checking out, morale taking a nosedive, and a dip in overall productivity.

To dodge the pitfalls of stagnation and innovation drought, we gotta crank up the volume on change and creativity. That means getting employees to be curious, take smart risks, and toy with new ways of thinking. It also means pouring resources into research and development, nurturing a "never stop growing" mindset, and building a team that's all about communication and collaboration.

A lack of innovation and the stagnation that follows can put the brakes on success for individuals, organizations, and entire industries. The key to busting through these barriers is to hug change tight and create an atmosphere that's all about fresh ideas and creative energy. By doin' that, we make sure our businesses, our careers, and our lives stay vibrant, innovative, and on the up-and-up.

TIP: *Keep up with industry trends, emerging technologies, and global events. Being informed will help you identify opportunities for innovation and anticipate potential challenges.*

Test your ideas, gather feedback, and refine your approach. Iterating and refining your ideas will help you discover new and improved solutions. Look for inspiration in diverse fields, industries, and cultures. Drawing from different sources can help you create unique and innovative ideas. Focus on the bigger picture and consider the long-term implications of your ideas. This will help you develop innovative solutions that are sustainable and impactful.

"INNOVATION IS CREATIVITY WITH A JOB TO DO."
- John Emmerling

RULE#031

DEVOURING THE DREAD: EAT THE FROG

We've all been there – staring at that one task on our to-do list, feeling the dread bubble up as we try to ignore it or push it to the bottom. But, what if I told you there's a way to conquer that beast, and not just conquer it, but own it like a boss? Enter the "Eat the Frog" technique, a tried-and-true method to face your most challenging or dreaded tasks head-on, kick anxiety to the curb, and bask in the glow of accomplishment. Let's dive into the art of devouring the dread.

"Eat the Frog" is a metaphor coined by the great Mark Twain, who once said, "Eat a live frog first thing in the morning, and nothing worse will happen to you the rest of the day." While we ain't advocating for the consumption of actual amphibians, the message is clear: tackle your most daunting task first thing in the morning, and the rest of your day will feel like a breeze.

So, how do you master the "Eat the Frog" technique and start crushing those fearsome tasks like a pro? The "Eat the Frog" technique is all about facing your fears and challenges head-on, and conquering them with confidence and determination. By tackling your most dreaded task first thing in the morning, you'll alleviate anxiety, create a sense of accomplishment, and set the stage for a productive and fulfilling day.

TIP: *Identify Your Frog: Look at your to-do list and pinpoint that task that's causing the most anxiety or dread. That's your frog, the task you'll want to tackle first thing in the morning. Remember, the goal is to face the challenge head-on, not to hide from it. Prepare the night before, set yourself up for success by planning your frog-eating session the night before. Outline the steps needed to complete the task, gather any materials, and mentally prepare yourself for the challenge ahead.*

Jump right in, when the morning rolls around, don't waste time dilly-dallying. Dive right into your frog task, giving it your full attention and energy. The sooner you start, the sooner you'll experience the sweet taste of accomplishment.

"EAT A LIVE FROG FIRST THING IN THE MORNING AND NOTHING WORSE WILL HAPPEN TO YOU THE REST OF THE DAY."
- Mark Twain

RULE #032

STUDY THE GAME TAPES

"THE PAST IS NOT A BURDEN TO CARRY, BUT A TREASURE TO MINE. STUDY IT WITH CURIOSITY, EXTRACT ITS GEMS, AND USE THEM TO PAVE YOUR WAY TO GREATNESS IN THE FUTURE."
- Isabel Allende

In the game of life, rewinding the tapes can give you a competitive edge, not just on the field, but in all aspects of your life. This idea of lookin' back at past experiences and learning from them is a crucial ingredient of personal and professional growth. Here are some practical ways you can bring this idea to life in your own journey:

1. **Climbing the Career Ladder:** Just like a coach checkin' out game tapes to step up the team's performance, studying your work history can help you pinpoint your strengths and weaknesses, and carve out a path for growth. Analyze your past work, gather feedback from colleagues and bosses, and evaluate your own performance. This self-reflection can help you gain new skills, spot opportunities for moving up, and reach your career dreams.
2. **Personal Evolution:** Reflecting on past experiences and decisions can help you gain insight into your own behavior and thought patterns. Rewind the tapes of your life, evaluate

what clicked and what didn't, and ask yourself what you would do differently if given the chance. Use this intel to make positive shifts and develop a deeper sense of self-awareness.

3. **Relationships:** Whether it's a love connection, a friendship, or a business relationship, rewinding the game tapes can help you spot patterns of behavior that might be putting a damper on your connections. Reflect on past interactions, evaluate your own communication style, and learn to understand the perspectives of others. By doin' so, you can cook up new strategies for building stronger, healthier relationships.
4. **Learning:** Learning's a never-ending ride, and hitting the rewind button on your academic or personal pursuits can help you spot areas where you need to level up and track your progress. Reviewing past experiences can help you understand what worked like a charm and what didn't, letting you make more informed decisions in the future.

By bringing the idea of rewinding the game tapes to different corners of your life, you can gain a deeper understanding of yourself and the world around you. This self-reflection can help you make better decisions, grow and evolve as a person, and achieve your goals. So, take a moment to hit rewind on the tapes of your life, and use what you learn to catapult yourself towards success.

TIP: *As you're going through your old stuff, set your intentions straight. You're in it to learn from your experiences, and the more you understand your mistakes, the less likely you are to repeat them.*

While you're at it, keep an eye out for any patterns or things you've consistently stumbled on. That's where you can zero in and make some real progress. Jot down your thoughts, lessons, and those "aha" moments in a journal. This way, you can see how far you've come and remember the wisdom you've picked up along the way.

RULE #033

LET GO OF ATTACHMENTS

As you hustle to reach your goals, do you ever feel weighed down by attachments to external factors? These attachments can lead to clinginess and dependence, fogging up your judgment and putting the brakes on your ability to take action. To break free from these chains, it's time to embrace a sense of self-reliance.

Standing on your own two feet means being independent and not relying on outside forces for your happiness and well-being. By doing so, you can escape the grip of attachment and take the wheel of your life.

Spotting the areas of attachment is the first stride in building self-reliance. Whether it's an outcome, a person, or a possession, once you've called it out, work on letting go and concentrating on what's within your control.

Growing inner strength and confidence is another piece of the self-reliance puzzle. Believing in your skills and bounce-back ability will give you the power to handle life's twists and turns. Breaking free from attachment is the secret sauce for achieving fulfillment and goals. Develop self-reliance and inner strength to liberate yourself from limitations and take control of your life. Start taking charge of your journey today.

TIP: *Identify what's weighing you down. Be real with yourself, and pinpoint those thoughts, feelings,* *or situations that are acting like anchors. Once you know what's up, you can start to work through it. Holding onto grudges and regrets only keeps you stuck in the past. Remember, we're all human, and we're all just trying to do our best. Free yourself by extending some compassion and understanding, both to yourself and to those who may have hurt you.*

It's all about focusing on the now. The past has had its time, and the future's still unwritten. But you're here in the present, and that's where the magic happens. Make the most of the moment, soak up the lessons, and let them guide you in your journey.

"LETTING GO IS NOT A SIGN OF WEAKNESS, BUT A SIGN OF STRENGTH. IT TAKES COURAGE TO RELEASE WHAT NO LONGER SERVES YOU AND EMBRACE THE UNKNOWN."

- Maya Angelou

RULE #034

SELECTIVE SUPPORT

Support and help, often seen as one and the same, are actually distinct ways of lending a hand. To make savvy decisions about how we invest our resources - whether it's time, energy, or cash - we gotta recognize this difference.

Support is all about giving emotional backup, lending a listening ear, and being a source of comfort and cheer. It's a subtle way of aiding that lets the person on the receiving end keep their independence and dignity. Help, on the flip side, is a more active form of assistance, bringing tangible aid to the table like resources, information, or hands-on support. This often means a bigger investment of time and energy and might even make the recipient feel less in control.

Since our resources ain't limitless, we gotta think hard about who we choose to support and help. By investing in those who got the chops and desire to make positive changes, we can make the most of our efforts and reach our own goals. But if we pour our resources into folks who ain't ready or able to change, we risk draining our time and energy without making a real dent.

Knowing the difference between support and help is key for making informed choices about how we invest our resources. By being mindful of who we back, we can make a real impact and hit our own targets. So, choose smart and put your resources into the people and causes that truly matter to you.

TIP: *Recognize that trust is a two-way street. You can't expect others to be open and supportive if you're not doing the same. Be genuine, authentic, and honest with the people around you. Show them your true self, and they'll be more likely to do the same.*

Communication is the key to trust and support. Be open and clear about your thoughts, feelings, and expectations, and encourage others to do the same. That way, you can build a solid foundation of understanding and respect that'll keep the good vibes flowing.

Give people the benefit of the doubt. Sometimes, you've got to take a leap of faith and trust that others have good intentions. Sure, it might not always work out, but more often than not, you'll find that people will rise to the occasion when given a chance.

Be mindful of your own boundaries, too. It's essential to strike a balance between trusting others and staying true to yourself. Know your limits, and don't be afraid to speak up if you feel uncomfortable or like your trust is being taken for granted.

"REAL STRENGTH IS NOT ABOUT HOW MUCH YOU CAN TAKE, BUT HOW MUCH YOU CAN GIVE. HELP OTHERS RISE UP, AND YOU'LL RISE WITH THEM."
- T.I.

RULE #035

DO NOT BE AFRAID TO MAKE MISTAKES

"SUCCESS IS BUILT ON A FOUNDATION OF FAILURES. EMBRACE YOUR MISTAKES AND USE THEM AS STEPPING STONES TO ACHIEVE GREATNESS."
- Cardi B

Mistakes: they're a part of life we can't avoid. Whether we're kicking off a new venture, picking up a fresh skill, or just cruising through our daily lives, setbacks and challenges are bound to pop up. But here's the thing: mistakes ain't failures; they're chances to learn and grow. In this chapter, we'll dive into the perks of embracing mistakes and learn how to face 'em with a can-do attitude.

Why Mistakes Scare Us: A lot of us shudder at the thought of messing up. We're afraid of being judged, criticized, or laughed at. This fear can stop us from taking risks, giving new things a shot, and chasing our dreams. But dodging mistakes means we're also dodging the chance to learn and grow. The fear of blunders can hold us back from reaching our full potential.

Mistakes: Opportunities for Growth: It's crucial to welcome mistakes and see 'em as chances to grow. When we slip up, we get the chance to reflect on what went haywire, pinpoint what we can tweak for next time, and make things better. This learning process is what lets us become more skilled, self-assured, and resilient over time.

Rocking a Positive Attitude Towards Mistakes: To make the most of our slip-ups, we gotta face 'em with a positive attitude. Instead of seeing mistakes as epic fails, we should view 'em as chances to learn and grow. Focus on the silver lining of your experiences, and let 'em fuel your future endeavors. Keep in mind that making mistakes is just part of the learning journey, and every blunder is an opportunity to grow and improve.

Mistakes are an essential part of life, and embracing 'em is the key to learning and growing. By tackling mistakes with a positive mindset and letting 'em inspire our future efforts, we can become more skilled, confident, and tough. So, don't stress over making mistakes – embrace 'em, learn from 'em, and let 'em push you towards success. Remember, every mistake is a chance for growth, and our best lessons often come from our stumbles.

TIP: *Fear of failure is something we all face at some point, but it's all about how we handle it that makes the difference. Remind yourself that failure is just part of the game. It ain't the end of the world, and even the most successful people have stumbled along the way. Every mistake is just another opportunity to learn, grow, and become even stronger.*

Shift your perspective and see failure as a teacher, not an enemy. When things don't go as planned, take a step back and ask yourself, "What can I learn from this?" Use those lessons to fuel your fire and come back better than ever. Success is rarely a straight line, and there'll be twists, turns, and bumps along the way. Enjoy the ride, and remember that the lessons you learn from failure are often more valuable than the wins themselves.

RULE #036

ARCHITECT YOUR BELIEFS

In his book "Outliers," Malcolm Gladwell highlights the significance of grasping the systems and infrastructure that back success. Infrastructure lays the groundwork for thriving businesses, organizations, and societies. Studying these systems and learning from the folks who've made it big, we can snatch up precious insights into what it takes to achieve and sustain success.

One of the main perks of digging into infrastructure is cranking up efficiency. By getting the hang of the systems that prop up our personal and professional lives, we can spot areas ripe for improvement to boost productivity and profitability. Plus, by building and keeping a sturdy infrastructure, we make sure our systems are reliable and trustworthy, slashing the risk of downtime and system crashes that can throw a wrench in our success.

Studying successful systems also paves the way for smarter decisions. By learning from tried-and-true strategies and methods, we can make choices that'll have a positive impact on our success. Exploring new and game-changing approaches to infrastructure and systems of success can also spur innovation and whip up fresh solutions to the challenges we face.

Studying successful folks and organizations can spark personal growth. By learning about their mindsets, habits, and strategies, we can apply these lessons to our own lives and achieve greater success in both our personal and professional pursuits. Understanding infrastructure and building our own success system is a crucial investment in our future. By doin' so, we snag the knowledge, skills, and insights needed to hit it big and unlock our full potential.

TIP: *Set SMART goals – Specific, Measurable, Achievable, Relevant, and Time-bound. Having clear and well-defined objectives will make it easier to create a system tailored to your needs and help you stay on track.*

"IT TAKES 20 YEARS TO BUILD A REPUTATION AND 5 MINUTES TO RUIN IT. IF YOU THINK ABOUT THAT, YOU'LL DO THINGS DIFFERENTLY."
- Warren Buffett, CEO of Berkshire Hathaway

RULE #037

DO NOT ALLOW EXCUSES TO BECOME REASONS

Excuses can be tempting snares that keep you from chasing your dreams. They offer a fleeting break from the sweat and toil needed to taste success. But, excuses can swiftly morph into permanent roadblocks, keeping you from ever hitting your peak potential. By not letting excuses turn into reasons, you're owning your actions and keeping your eyes on the prize, not on the hurdles that might pop up.

When you say "no" to letting excuses become reasons, you ramp up responsibility for your deeds. You become more tuned into the choices you make and the ripples they create in your life. This consciousness helps you dodge making excuses for why you ain't reached your goals, and instead, gear up to tackle the challenges head-on.

You must keep your sights locked on your goals. Excuses can yank your attention away from what you wanna achieve and shift it to the barriers blocking your way. But, when you don't let excuses take the wheel, you can stay driven and devoted to your goals, even when the path gets bumpy.

TIP: *Own your power. Remind yourself that you're in control of your life and the choices you make. Excuses might be tempting, but they don't define you. Recognize that you have the strength to push past them and create the life you want.*

Challenge those excuses head-on. When you catch yourself making an excuse, stop and ask, "Is this really true, or am I just trying to avoid something?" By questioning your excuses, you'll start to see them for what they are – roadblocks that can be overcome.

Make a commitment to yourself and your dreams. When you're truly dedicated to a goal, you'll be less likely to let excuses stand in your way. Write down your goals, share them with someone you trust, and hold yourself accountable to make them happen. Action beats excuses every time. When you feel an excuse coming on, take a small step towards your goal, no matter how tiny. Action creates momentum, and the more you do, the less power those excuses will have over you.

"DON'T MAKE EXCUSES, MAKE PROGRESS. THE ONLY THING HOLDING YOU BACK IS YOUR OWN RELUCTANCE TO TAKE ACTION."
- Langston Hughes

RULE #038

SET YOUR FORM, RELEASE, FOLLOW THROUGH

Achieving success demands a blend of grinding, focus, and stick-to-itiveness. Yet, loads of folks find themselves struggling to hit their targets, missing the right prep, hustle, and persistence to come out on top. In this rule, we'll delve deep into the importance of setting your sights, takin' action, and seeing things through to reap the rewards of success.

Laying down your objectives involves the planning and prepping stage for any venture or aim. It's all about takin' a moment to pin down your goals, sketch out a straight shot to reach 'em, and cook up a foolproof plan for success. When setting your sights, it's crucial to chew over everything that might affect your success, like time crunches, resources, and potential roadblocks.

Taking action means turning your plan into reality and moving towards your objectives. This stage is all about mustering up the grit and resolve to take the steps needed to make your dreams come true, no matter the fears or obstacles that pop up.

Seeing things through is the home stretch of the process and demands staying true to your goals and sticking it out, even when you face challenges and setbacks. This calls for bounce-back-ability, tenacity, and the skill to keep your eyes on the prize, not gettin' sidetracked by distractions or hurdles.

By setting your sights, taking action, and seeing things through, you up your odds of achieving success. This roadmap to goal-setting and accomplishment offers a clear route to success, keeping you focused on what matters. It also instills a sense of owning up to your actions and stops you from being held back by excuses or stumbles.

Setting your objectives, taking action, and following through are vital ingredients for achieving success. By takin' the time to plan, hustle, and hang in there towards your objectives, you can boost your chances of success and reach new heights in your personal and professional life. So, set your sights, take action, and see things through today to kick off your journey towards the success you've earned!

TIP: *Start with a clear vision. Know exactly what you want to achieve and why it matters to you. When your purpose is crystal clear, you'll be more motivated to push past obstacles and see your projects through to completion.*

Break it down and make a plan. Map out the steps you'll need to take to reach your goal, and set deadlines for each milestone. Having a clear path will make it easier to stay on track and committed to your projects.

"SUCCESS IS NOT JUST ABOUT STARTING SOMETHING, IT'S ABOUT FOLLOWING THROUGH WITH DETERMINATION AND PERSISTENCE UNTIL YOU REACH THE FINISH LINE."
- Denzel Washington

RULE #039

MEDIATE, MEDIATE, MEDIATE

Meditation, a seemingly unpretentious practice, packs a wallop when it comes to amplifying productivity and efficiency. By honing your attention to zoom in on thoughts, emotions, and bodily sensations, you can harvest a bounty of benefits for both your mental and physical well-being.

A standout perk of meditation is its prowess in taming stress and ramping up focus. Stress often muddles our minds, making it a struggle to concentrate and wrap up tasks efficiently. Through meditation, you can hush your mind and curb stress, letting you zero in on the task at hand. This elevated focus can lead to heightened productivity, as you can knock out tasks more swiftly and effectively.

On top of that, meditation can help you ratchet up your self-awareness, an indispensable ingredient in making things happen. By keeping a close eye on your thoughts, emotions, and physical sensations, you can better suss out what fuels your behavior and how to leap over hurdles that may hamper your progress. This heightened self-awareness lets you make savvier decisions, prioritize tasks like a pro, and hit your targets more efficiently.

Meditation can buff up your resilience – your knack for bouncing back from setbacks and challenges. When obstacles rear their heads, it's all too easy to lose motivation and focus. However, through consistent meditation, you can foster the resilience needed to stay true to your goals, even when adversity comes a-knocking.

TIP: *Find your sweet spot. Choose a space where you feel calm and comfortable, free from distractions and noise. It can be indoors or outdoors, just make sure it's a place where you can really relax and focus on your meditation practice.*

Set the mood. Create an atmosphere that helps you unwind and get into a meditative state of mind. Light some candles, play soft music, or surround yourself with soothing scents – whatever works for you.

Start by getting comfy. Find a comfortable sitting position, either on a cushion, chair, or even the floor. Keep your back straight, but not too rigid, and rest your hands gently on your lap or knees.

Now, focus on your breath. Close your eyes and take a few deep, cleansing breaths. Inhale through your nose, filling your lungs completely, and then exhale slowly through your mouth. Let your breath be your anchor as you begin your meditation practice.

Once you're settled in, bring your attention to the present moment. Let go of any thoughts about the past or future, and just be here, right now. If your mind starts to wander, gently guide it back to the present and your breath.

Remember, there's no "right" way to meditate. Be patient with yourself and let go of any expectations. It's totally normal for thoughts to pop up – just acknowledge them and let them pass by without judgment.

Start with short sessions and gradually build up. You don't need to meditate for hours to reap the benefits. Begin with just a few minutes a day and gradually work your way up to longer sessions as you become more comfortable with the practice.

Make meditation a part of your daily routine. Consistency is key, so try to carve out some time each day to practice. Even just a few minutes of meditation can have a huge impact on your overall well-being and peace of mind.

"IN MEDITATION, WE BECOME OBSERVERS OF OUR THOUGHTS, EMOTIONS, AND SENSATIONS, AND WE LEARN TO TRANSCEND THE LIMITATIONS OF THE MIND."
- Sri Sri Ravi Shankar

RULE #040

STEP UP EVERY STEP OF THE WAY!

Success ain't no one-stop shop – it's a never-ending jaunt, and to bag it, you need more than just grit and stick-to-itiveness. It demands a readiness to step up at every twist and turn, challenges or hurdles be damned. That means chipping away at your goals, no matter how teensy or trifling they might appear. Success don't come gift-wrapped; it calls for constant elbow grease and progress. By taking action, you can show your dedication to your goals and prove to yourself that you've got what it takes to make 'em real.

Stepping up every step of the way also means squaring off with and conquering obstacles. Obstacles ain't roadblocks – they're stepping stones that pave the way to resilience and grit. By stepping up and facing challenges head-on, you can grow the tenacity you need to make it. This calls for a rock-solid faith in yourself and your abilities. It means being gutsy enough to take risks and test out new things, even when you're sweating over the outcome. By believing in yourself, you can push past self-doubt and negativity that might hold you back and keep your eyes on the prize.

Sure, success ain't a slam dunk, but by staying committed and taking consistent action, you up your chances of success and score more in your personal and professional life. Take action, knock down obstacles, trust yourself, and stay the course – you can make your dreams come true and live the life you're hankering for. So, take them necessary steps toward your goals, no matter how tiny they may seem, and step up every step of the way. Start chasing your dreams today!

TIP: *Embrace your inner leader. Believe in yourself and your ability to make things happen. When you trust in your own skills and strengths, you'll be more prepared to step up and take charge of your duties with confidence.*

Get crystal clear on your responsibilities. Understand exactly what's expected of you, and make sure you're equipped with the knowledge and resources you need to fulfill those duties. The more prepared you are, the better you'll be able to step up when it counts.

"SUCCESS DOESN'T COME TO THOSE WHO WAIT, BUT TO THOSE WHO STEP UP, TAKE INITIATIVE, AND SEIZE OPPORTUNITIES WITH BOTH HANDS."
- Elon Musk

RULE #041

BE THE MAGNET

In this wild ride we call life, it often feels like we're attracting certain folks and scenarios to us. Some of us seem to pull in success and abundance with little effort, while others sweat and strain just to keep their heads above water. But what if we could learn to be the magnet ourselves, pulling in all the stuff we want and need?

Being a magnet ain't about having a lucky rabbit's foot or some special mojo. It's about cracking the code of energy and channeling it to attract what we're after. The concept's straightforward: like attracts like. When we radiate positive vibes and laser-focus on what we want, we pull more of it our way.

To be the magnet, we gotta first get clear on what we're after. This means setting laser-focused intentions and honing in on them with a positive, can-do attitude. Our thoughts and feelings are potent tools that can help us bring our desires to life. When we zero in on what we want and have faith in our ability to bag it, we send out a magnetic pulse that pulls in more of the same.

Another key piece of the magnet puzzle is self-love and self-care. When we're feeling good about ourselves and treating ourselves with kindness and respect, we radiate positive vibes that draw good stuff to us. But if we're down on ourselves and being our own worst critics, we give off negative energy that attracts more negativity and struggle.

And let's not forget about action. Just setting intentions and focusing on them ain't enough. We also gotta take strides towards making our dreams come true. This could mean signing up for classes, building connections, or pouncing on opportunities when they show up.

Being the magnet ain't a one-and-done deal – it needs consistent effort and practice. It's not just a thing, it's a lifestyle that needs daily dedication and focus. But trust me, the payoff is worth it. When we become the magnet, we pull in the people, situations, and opportunities that help us hit our goals and live the life we've been dreaming of.

Being the magnet is all about understanding the power of our thoughts and feelings and using them to attract what we want in life. It calls for self-love, self-care, clear intention-setting, and taking action towards our goals. With some elbow grease and practice, we can become the magnet, pulling in everything we desire and living the life of our dreams.

TIP: *Take inspired action towards your goals. While attracting the things you want is important, you also need to meet the universe halfway by taking action. Trust your intuition, and be ready to seize opportunities when they come your way. Stay open and receptive to change. Sometimes the things we want come to us in unexpected ways, so be willing to embrace change and let go of any preconceived notions about how your desires should manifest. Trust that the universe has your back and will bring you what's best for you. Remember, patience is a virtue. Attracting the things you want in life doesn't always happen overnight, so be patient and trust in the process. Keep your focus on your* *goals, and know that with time and persistence, you'll draw the right opportunities and experiences to you.*

Lastly, keep growing and evolving. Continuously work on improving yourself and expanding your skills, knowledge, and connections. The more you grow as a person, the more magnetic you'll become to the things you desire.

"WHEN YOU BECOME THE BEST VERSION OF YOURSELF, YOU NATURALLY BECOME A MAGNET FOR SUCCESS, HAPPINESS, AND FULFILLMENT."

- Tony Robbin

RULE #042

NAVIGATE WITH FACTS AND LOGIC

In a universe brimming with skewed info and differing viewpoints, finding a firm foothold of belief and making choices that vibe with our principles and aims can feel like threading a needle in a hurricane. But, there's a lifeline in this storm: anchoring ourselves in solid facts and leaning on our own reasoning.

Step one of this mission is to become a fact-finding machine. This means sifting through sources that are famed for their unbiased, fact-checked info and giving a wide berth to those notorious for peddling false or misleading narratives. And don't just stop there – double-check the info, cross-referencing with multiple sources, and put your critical thinking hat on to test the info's reliability.

Once you've armed yourself with a solid batch of info, it's time to crank up your reasoning skills to process it. This step is all about taking an objective look at the data, weighing up different perspectives, and tapping into logic and good old-fashioned common sense to draw your own conclusions. It's crucial here to keep emotions and personal biases on the bench, and bring an open-minded game face to the analysis.

The next phase is using your conclusions to make informed decisions. This could mean balancing the pros and cons of various options, mulling over your principles and goals, and finally making a choice that syncs with your convictions and ambitions.

Staying open to new info and being ready to revise your conclusions and decisions when new intel drops is vital. The world's a fast-spinning ball, and fresh facts and views can pop up, shifting our understanding of a situation. Embracing new information and tweaking our beliefs and decisions to accommodate these shifts is a key part of the process.

To wrap it up, anchoring yourself in facts and leaning on your reasoning is a solid strategy for decision-making and navigating the world. By gathering accurate info, flexing your reasoning muscles, and making informed decisions, you can ensure your beliefs and actions are founded on the best available intel and resonate with your values and goals.

TIP: *Develop your critical thinking skills. Practice questioning what you read, hear, and see. Dive deeper into the information presented to you and analyze it from different angles. This will help you separate facts from opinions and make more informed decisions. Seek out diverse sources of information. Don't limit yourself to a single source or viewpoint. Explore different perspectives and sources to gain a broader understanding of the world around you. This will help you form a more comprehensive and accurate view of reality.*

"THE TRUTH IS NOT ALWAYS COMFORTABLE, BUT IT IS ESSENTIAL. EMBRACE FACTS AND LET THEM GUIDE YOUR DECISIONS."

- Margaret Heffernan

RULE #043

FIND A HEALTHY BALANCE BETWEEN WORK AND PLAY

Striking the right chord between work and recreation is about discovering a harmony that syncs with your rhythm, carving out space for both the duties and delights life tosses your way. This could mean crafting specific, attainable targets for both your professional and personal world, and cultivating routines and habits that amplify these objectives. It might also mean moving self-care up the priority ladder, like making time for workouts, ensuring sound sleep, and unwinding.

What's key to understand here is that work and play aren't two ends of a tug-of-war rope; instead, they can beautifully play off each other. For instance, indulging in hobbies and passions can spark creativity and crank up productivity at work, while drawing firm boundaries in the professional sphere can help us hit the refresh button and recharge.

To nail down the sweet spot between work and recreation, it's also critical to keep a finger on the pulse of our stress levels. This could mean honing stress-busting techniques, such as mindfulness, deep breathing, or physical activity, and mastering the art of saying 'no' when needed. By keeping our stress levels in check, we can amp up our resilience and maintain a healthy work-life rhythm.

Finding a harmonious balance between work and play is a non-negotiable for our holistic well-being and success. By laying down realistic goals, making self-care non-negotiable, and keeping our stress levels in check, we can craft a life that's balanced and fulfilling, and seize the success we're worthy of.

TIP: *Get clear on your priorities. Understand what truly matters to you, both in your work and personal life. When you know what's most important, you'll be better equipped to make decisions that support a balanced lifestyle. Set boundaries and stick to them. Establish clear lines between your work and personal time, and make an effort to keep them separate. This might mean turning off work notifications during your downtime or avoiding work-related conversations during social gatherings.*

"BALANCE IS NOT SOMETHING YOU FIND, IT'S SOMETHING YOU CREATE."
- Jana Kingsford

RULE #044

STAY WITHIN YOUR CIRCLE OF COMPETENCE

"STAYING IN YOUR CIRCLE OF COMPETENCE MEANS KNOWING YOUR STRENGTHS AND WEAKNESSES, AND MAKING SMART DECISIONS BASED ON THAT KNOWLEDGE."
- Mark Zuckerberg

In this rollercoaster of life, it's alluring to step up to the plate and face challenges or seize opportunities that push us beyond our comfort zone. However, acknowledging our limitations and staying rooted within our realm of proficiency is vital.

The concept of the realm of proficiency is straightforward: it's the areas in our lives where our knowledge, skills, and experience empower us to make well-informed decisions and spring into effective action. When we anchor ourselves within this realm, we operate from a fortress of strength and confidence, minimizing the risk of fumbles or getting swept off our feet.

To map out your realm of proficiency, it's valuable to take a mental inventory of your skills, knowledge, and experience. Pinpoint the areas where you're a natural and exude confidence. Equally important is to hold up a mirror to your limitations, acknowledging areas ripe for improvement or where you might need a helping hand.

Once you've sketched out a clear picture of your realm of proficiency, make it a priority to stay true to it. This means sidestepping opportunities and challenges that sit outside your comfort zone, instead focusing on honing your skills and expanding your knowledge in areas where you shine. Be open to exploring new possibilities and challenges within your realm of proficiency that can catalyze growth and help you hit your targets.

Moreover, staying grounded in your realm of proficiency can help you distribute your time and energy more effectively. When we bite off more than we can chew, taking on too many roles or challenges that stretch beyond our realm, we risk spreading ourselves too thin and compromising our well-being and the quality of our work. By keeping our eyes on the prize - areas where we excel and can make a meaningful impact - we can ensure we're spending our time and energy wisely and efficiently.

In the final analysis, sticking to your realm of proficiency is a cornerstone of personal and professional success. By being candid about your skills, knowledge, and experience, and honing in on opportunities and challenges that sit within your realm, you can work from a position of strength, sidestep missteps, and reach your targets with greater ease and confidence.

TIP: *Get to know yourself. Take the time to understand your skills, knowledge, and passions. Reflect on your experiences and the areas where you excel. When you have a clear understanding of your own strengths, you'll be better equipped to stay within your circle of competence. Embrace your limitations. Remember, it's impossible to be an expert in everything. Accept that there are areas* *where you might not have as much expertise or knowledge, and that's okay. Embrace your limitations and focus on what you do best.*

Focus on what you can control. Invest your time and energy in areas where you have the most influence and knowledge. By concentrating on what you can control, you'll make a more significant impact and feel more confident in your decisions.

RULE #045

DO NOT GET CAUGHT UP IN THE MOMENT

In the whirlwind of our rapidly evolving world, it's too easy to get swept up in the tide, making decisions propelled by emotions and on-the-spot instincts. But to make superior decisions that serve our highest interests and future well-being, it's crucial to hit the pause button, take a deep breath, and resist getting carried away by the momentum of the moment.

Avoiding the gravitational pull of the moment starts with identifying the red flags. These might include mounting anxiety, stress, or pressure, a sense of immediacy, or an emotional response to a situation. The moment you sense you're getting swept away, it's critical to take a step back, broaden your perspective, and refocus.

An effective strategy to regain your footing is to practice mindfulness and mindfulness-rooted techniques such as deep breathing, meditation, or introspection. These tools can help you still your mind, let go of negative emotions, and gain a clearer understanding of the situation at hand.

Another helpful approach is to lean on the wisdom of a trusted friend, family member, or professional. A conversation with someone who brings a different viewpoint can gift you a fresh perspective and serve as a sounding board for your thoughts and emotions.

It's also crucial to adopt a long-term lens when making decisions. Instead of zeroing in solely on the immediate fallout, ponder the potential long-term implications of your decisions on your life and well-being. This helps you make decisions that dovetail with your values, goals, and dreams, rather than simply placating a short-term craving.

In the end, it's vital to act in a thoughtful and intentional manner, steering clear of impulsive decisions sparked by emotions or instincts. By taking a beat, mulling over your options, and making decisions grounded in the best information at your disposal and your personal values, you can ensure that your choices align with your long-term goals and overall well-being.

Dodging the trap of getting swept away by the moment is an essential ingredient in making effective decisions and navigating life's choppy waters. By spotting the red flags, taking a step back, gaining perspective, adopting a long-term view, and making deliberate decisions, you can ensure your choices harmonize with your values, goals, and aspirations.

TIP: *Stay connected to your "why." Regularly remind yourself of the deeper reasons behind your dreams and goals. This will help you stay motivated and focused on the bigger picture, rather than getting caught up in the fleeting emotions of the moment. Take breaks and practice self-care. Chasing your dreams can be exhilarating, but it's also essential to give yourself time to rest and recharge. Prioritize self-care and ensure you're taking care of your physical, mental, and emotional well-being.*

"DON'T LET THE MOMENT DEFINE YOU, DEFINE THE MOMENT."
- Jay-Z

RULE #046

REFLECT, REJOICE, AND RECLAIM YOUR WINS

In the whirlwind of our achievement-oriented, fast-forward world, it's all too easy to get wrapped up in the relentless chase for success, forgetting to pause and reflect on our journey or relish our victories. Yet, allotting time to ponder our course and laud our triumphs is vital for fostering a wholesome, upbeat perspective on life and for staying driven and spirited in the quest for our goals.

Reflection is about pressing the pause button amidst our bustling daily activities, taking a step back to examine our experiences, our thought processes, and our emotions. This introspective exercise gifts us a deeper understanding of our personal and professional evolution, offering precious insights into what's hitting the mark and what needs tweaking.

A potent way to maintain a reflection practice is to keep a journal or log capturing your experiences and contemplations. This could be as straightforward as jotting down a couple of lines each day, or as comprehensive as chronicling your thoughts and emotions on a particular project or goal. Reflection could also adopt a more structured format, like setting aside dedicated time each week or month to review your progress and pinpoint areas for refinement.

Alongside reflecting on our trajectory, it's equally crucial to celebrate our victories. This could encompass minor victories, like wrapping up a task or meeting a deadline, as well as larger milestones, like accomplishing a project or realizing a long-term ambition. Celebrating our victories serves to bolster our self-confidence and motivation and delivers a sense of gratification and fulfillment that fuels our onward journey.

There's no shortage of ways to celebrate your victories, whether it's indulging in a special meal, taking a well-deserved day off, or simply pausing to acknowledge and appreciate your tireless efforts and achievements. It's also worth sharing your victories with others, such as friends, family, or colleagues, as this can offer additional motivation and support, and contribute to a ripple effect of positivity and inspiration.

Setting aside time to reflect on our journey and applaud our victories is an essential ingredient of success and well-being. Through thoughtful reflection and heartfelt celebration of our accomplishments, we can gain a profound understanding of our personal and professional growth and maintain an optimistic and motivated outlook on life.

TIP: *Schedule regular check-ins with yourself. Set aside time in your calendar to pause, reflect, and assess your progress. This intentional practice will help you stay aware of the strides you've made and the lessons you've learned along the way. Practice gratitude for your growth. Focus on the positive changes and improvements you've made, no matter how small they may seem. By cultivating a grateful mindset, you'll be more likely to recognize and appreciate your accomplishments.*

Create a personal success journal. Document your achievements, milestones, and insights in a dedicated journal. This tangible record will serve as a powerful reminder of your progress and a source of inspiration when you need a boost of motivation.

"CELEBRATE YOUR ACHIEVEMENTS, NO MATTER HOW BIG OR SMALL. IT'S IMPORTANT TO ACKNOWLEDGE AND APPRECIATE YOUR PROGRESS."
- Oprah Winfrey

RULE #047

HUSTLE HARD, MAKE IT WORK

The timeless saying, "nothing will work if you don't," rings true in every facet of life. Regardless of the extent of our planning, dreaming, and strategizing, the real magic happens only when we leap into action. Action is the alchemist that turns our thoughts, plans, and dreams into reality, and it's the golden key that unlocks the door to our goals and the realization of our latent potential.

One of the largest hurdles many face when it comes to springing into action is the infamous procrastination. Procrastination is the art of delaying or avoiding action, often bred from a lack of motivation, a fear of failure, or a sense of overwhelm about where to begin.

To conquer procrastination and spring into action, it's crucial to start with baby steps and build momentum. This could involve taking small, achievable strides towards your goal, like jotting down a list of tasks or allocating a specific chunk of time each day to work on a project. Any form of action, however minuscule, begins to generate momentum and foster confidence in your ability to reach your goals.

Another secret ingredient to taking action is accountability. This could involve partnering with a coach or mentor who can offer support and guidance, or establishing an accountability pact with a friend or family member. Being answerable to someone else can help keep you motivated and on course, and can also stoke the fires of motivation to take action and advance.

Crucially, it's vital to adopt a growth mindset and perceive challenges and hurdles as stepping stones to learning and growth. Rather than being deflated by setbacks, view them as opportunities to learn, refine, and evolve, using them as catalysts to continue taking action towards your goals.

"Nothing will work if you don't." Taking action is the cornerstone to achieving our goals and realizing our full potential, laying the foundation for success and well-being. By taking incremental steps, holding ourselves accountable, fostering a growth mindset, and embracing challenges, we can defeat procrastination and take the necessary action to realize our dreams and goals.

TIP: *Embrace personal responsibility. Recognize that you are the driving force behind your success and happiness. By taking ownership of your actions and decisions, you'll be more motivated to put in the necessary work and make things happen. Establish a daily routine. Creating a daily routine that incorporates your goals and priorities will help you develop the discipline and consistency needed to make progress. Remember, it's the small, daily actions that eventually lead to significant results.*

"SUCCESS IS NOT A MATTER OF LUCK, BUT OF HARD WORK, DETERMINATION, AND UNWAVERING COMMITMENT."
- Emily Dickinson

RULE #048

DEVELOP HABITS THAT SHAPE YOUR DESIRED SUCCESS

Success, often, isn't a one-time event but a product of consistent actions and behaviors, accumulated over time. By crafting routines and habits that align with our goals and values, we can nurture the success we aspire to in both our personal and professional realms.

Routines serve as structured patterns of behavior we regularly undertake, adding a rhythm and predictability to our day-to-day lives. Habits, conversely, are routines that have been so thoroughly ingrained over time that they've become automatic, requiring little conscious thought.

Formulating routines and habits allows us to optimize our time, amplify our productivity, and enhance our overall well-being. For instance, designing a routine around exercise and self-care can help us sustain our physical and mental well-being, while creating a habit of dedicating time each day to a specific project can foster our progression towards our goals.

When forming routines and habits, it's vital to start small and incrementally scale up. This could mean setting a target to exercise for 10 minutes daily, gradually amplifying the duration and intensity over time. Consistency and persistence are key, so it's crucial to adhere to your routines and habits, even when the going gets tough.

One of the fundamental pillars of successful routines and habits is establishing clear, meaningful objectives. This could involve setting a specific goal like exercising for 30 minutes daily, or creating a habit of meditating each morning to kickstart the day with a clear, focused mind. Having a clear purpose and motivation for your routines and habits can fuel your motivation and keep you on course.

Another crucial aspect of successful routine and habit formation is creating a conducive environment. This could involve establishing a physical space that supports your goals, like a dedicated workspace or a serene meditation corner, or surrounding yourself with individuals who bolster and cheer on your goals and habits.

The influence of routines and habits in shaping success is potent and cannot be downplayed. By constructing routines and habits that bolster our goals and values, we can nurture the success we desire in our personal and professional spheres while maximizing our time, energy, and resources. By setting clear, meaningful goals, being consistent and persistent, and fostering a supportive environment, our routines and habits can transform into powerful instruments for success and well-being.

TIP: *Start small and build gradually. When developing new habits, it's essential to start with small, manageable changes. This will help you build momentum and confidence in your ability to make lasting change. As you gain consistency, gradually increase the challenge and complexity of your habits. Establish a morning and evening routine. Bookend your day with routines that set the tone for productivity and success. Mornings are a great time for setting intentions and priorities, while evenings* *can be used for reflection, relaxation, and preparing for the next day.*

"SUCCESS IS THE SUM OF SMALL EFFORTS REPEATED DAY IN AND DAY OUT. CREATE HEALTHY HABITS THAT SUPPORT YOUR GOALS."
- Robert Collier

RULE #049

PRACTICE DISCIPLINE & PERSEVERANCE

"THE ABILITY TO DISCIPLINE YOURSELF TO DELAY GRATIFICATION IN THE SHORT TERM IN ORDER TO ENJOY GREATER REWARDS IN THE LONG TERM IS THE INDISPENSABLE PREREQUISITE FOR SUCCESS."
- Brian Tracy

The road to success, in any walk of life, is paved with discipline and perseverance. Your level of success is truly a mirror reflection of your degree of discipline and perseverance. These traits empower us to navigate hurdles, maintain focus on our goals, and sustain a positive outlook, even when confronted with setbacks and challenges.

Discipline is our capacity to manage our actions and behaviors, sticking to our commitments and objectives, irrespective of how tough or inconvenient it becomes. It entails setting and adhering to routines, making conscious decisions, and dodging distractions and lures. By fostering discipline, we can nurture the focus and resolve required to realize our objectives.

Perseverance, contrastingly, is the resolve to continue chasing our goals, even when faced with setbacks and difficulties. It involves keeping our gaze fixed on our goals, staying motivated and hopeful, and persisting in our efforts towards our objectives, despite the hurdles and obstacles. By nurturing perseverance, we can foster the resilience and grit required to overcome challenges and succeed in our pursuits.

Discipline and perseverance are often entwined, each reinforcing and strengthening the other. For instance, fostering discipline can aid us in staying goal-focused and evading distractions, thereby enhancing our perseverance and motivation to keep advancing towards our goals.

To nurture discipline and perseverance, it's vital to commence with small steps and progressively build up. This could involve setting specific, attainable goals, and establishing routines to support these goals. It's also essential to foster a growth mindset, viewing challenges and setbacks as growth opportunities and learning experiences, rather than as reasons to capitulate.

Your level of success truly mirrors your degree of discipline and perseverance. By fostering these traits, we can nurture the focus, resolve, resilience, and grit required to achieve our goals and thrive in our pursuits. By starting small, gradually building up, and fostering a growth mindset, we can convert discipline and perseverance into potent tools for success and well-being.

TIP: *Embrace discomfort and challenge yourself. Push yourself to step outside of your comfort zone and tackle tasks that may initially seem daunting. By regularly facing challenges, you'll develop resilience and the perseverance needed to overcome obstacles. Practice patience and manage expectations.*

RULE #050

EMBRACE PURPOSE, LOVE, AND AMBITION

"YOUR PURPOSE IS NOT SOMETHING TO BE DISCOVERED, BUT RATHER SOMETHING TO BE CREATED THROUGH YOUR ACTIONS, PASSIONS, AND VALUES."
- Jay Shetty

Unraveling our life's purpose can be a daunting yet rewarding expedition. A life drenched in meaning and fulfillment typically anchors itself on three pivotal elements: seeking a cause to champion, finding a person to cherish, and pursuing a goal to conquer.

Championing a cause is about identifying a passion or purpose that fuels us, leveraging our skills and abilities to effect positive change in the world. This may encompass volunteering, aligning ourselves with a non-profit organization, or employing our talents to spark positive shifts within our communities. By championing a cause, we unearth a profound sense of meaning and purpose in our lives, and leave our mark on the world.

Cherishing a person is about cultivating profound and meaningful connections with others. This could entail finding a romantic partner, forging strong bonds with family and friends, or nurturing a supportive tribe of kindred spirits. By cherishing a person, we partake in the beauty of companionship and connection, building a support network to weather life's storms.

Conquering a goal is about setting and navigating towards aspirations that galvanize us, providing us with a sense of purpose and direction. This could involve carving a career path, launching a business, or immersing ourselves in a personal passion or hobby. By setting and navigating towards attainable goals, we cultivate a sense of purpose and accomplishment, and create a legacy that positively influences the world.

The linchpin to seeking a cause to champion, finding a person to cherish, and pursuing a goal to conquer, lies in maintaining an open mind, being receptive to exploration, and embracing novelty. This could mean venturing beyond our comfort zones, taking calculated risks, and seizing new opportunities and experiences with both hands.

Unraveling our life's purpose is a continuous journey that involves championing a cause, cherishing a person, and conquering a goal. By nurturing meaningful connections, immersing ourselves in our passions, and setting attainable goals, we foster a sense of meaning, purpose, and fulfillment in our lives, and leave a positive imprint on the world.

TIP: *Pursuing love enriches your life. When you share your life with someone you love, you create a support system that nurtures your growth and happiness. Together, you'll learn, grow, and build a life that's filled with joy, connection, and unforgettable memories. Next, love teaches you about yourself. In a loving relationship, you'll discover new aspects of yourself, uncover hidden strengths, and confront vulnerabilities. Through the* *journey of love, you'll develop a deeper understanding of who you are and what truly matters to you.*

Achieving a goal brings a sense of accomplishment and self-confidence. As you work towards your dreams and overcome challenges, you'll develop a strong belief in your abilities and the resilience to tackle even greater aspirations.

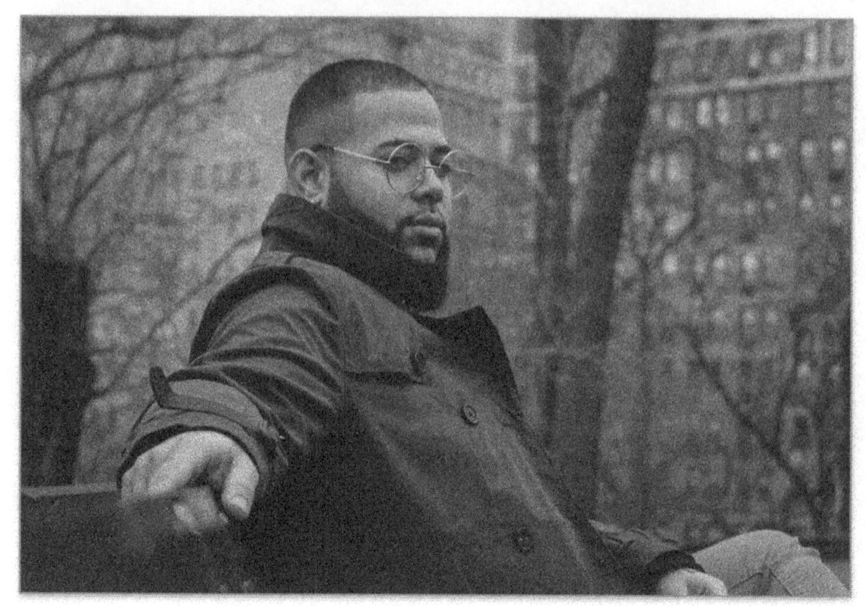

ABOUT THE AUTHOR

Steven Almeida is a entrepreneur and multi-faceted creative. He is the CEO of Autumn House Entertainment LLC, a company which produces films, music and brands for modern audiences. Steven was born in the Bronx, NY and grew up in the Harlem section of Manhattan. One of seven siblings from Dominican descent. He wears many hats--filmmaker, producer, writer, musician and brand analyst.

Ingram Content Group UK Ltd.
Milton Keynes UK
UKHW020741100723
424852UK00014B/461